COPING WITH INTERNATIONAL CONFLICT

A Systematic Approach to Influence in International Negotiation

ROGER FISHER
Harvard Law School

ANDREA KUPFER SCHNEIDER
Marquette Law School

ELIZABETH BORGWARDT
Stanford Center on Conflict and Negotiation

BRIAN GANSON

PRENTICE HALL, Upper Saddle River, NJ 07458

Library of Congress Cataloging–in–Publication Data

Coping with international conflict: a systematic approach to
   influence in international negotiation/Roger Fisher . . . [et al].
     p. cm.
    Includes bibliographical references and index.
    ISBN 0-13-591637-2
    1. Diplomatic negotiations in international disputes. 2. Conflict
management. 3. Negotiation. I. Fisher, Roger, international
negotiation advisor.
  JX4475.C595 1996
  327.1'72—dc20   96–26932
                                   CIP

Editorial director: Charlyce Jones Owen
Editor in chief: Nancy Roberts
Acquisitions editor: Michael Bickerstaff
Assistant editor: Jennie Katsaros
Editorial/production supervision and interior design: Rob DeGeorge
Copy editor: Virginia Rubens
Buyer: Bob Anderson
Editorial assistant: Anita Castro
Cartographer: Maryland CartoGraphics

This book was set in 10/12 New Century Schoolbook by ElectraGraphics, Inc.,
and was printed by RR Donnelley & Sons Company.
The cover was printed by Phoenix Color Corp.

Certain stories, examples, and charts on international conflict resolution have been drawn from the
authors' previous work, *Beyond Machiavelli: Tools for Coping with Conflict* by Roger Fisher, Elizabeth
Kopelman, and Andrea Kupfer Schneider. Copyright © 1994 by the President and Fellows of Harvard
College. Used by arrangement with Harvard University Press. All rights reserved.

 © 1997 by Prentice-Hall, Inc.
Simon & Schuster/A Viacom Company
Upper Saddle River, New Jersey 07458

Printed in the United States of America

10 9 8 7 6 5 4 3 2 1

ISBN 0-13-591637-2

Prentice-Hall International (UK) Limited, *London*
Prentice-Hall of Australia Pty. Limited, *Sydney*
Prentice-Hall Canada Inc., *Toronto*
Prentice-Hall Hispanoamericana, S.A., *Mexico*
Prentice-Hall of India Private Limited, *New Delhi*
Prentice-Hall of Japan, Inc., *Tokyo*
Simon & Schuster Asia Pte. Ltd., *Singapore*
Editora Prentice-Hall do Brasil, Ltda., *Rio de Janeiro*

Contents

WITHDRAWN

PREFACE   ix

PART I: INTRODUCTION

Chapter 1   Negotiation in the Context of International Conflict   1

The Requirement of Negotiation in International Affairs, 3
Decisions As Points of Change in the International System, 7
   Perspectives on International Relations, 8
   Choice As the Key Perspective for Change, 9
   The Benefits of Focusing on Choice, 10
Improving the Negotiation Process, 12
   An Argument for Rational Thinking, 13
   A Systematic Approach to Influence, 14

Chapter 2   Thinking Like an Activist   16

The Value of Thinking Like a Participant, 16
Tackling a Real-World Problem, 18
A Breakdown of Likely Steps along the Way, 20
Selecting a Problem for Your Action Memorandum, 24
   Generate a List of Options, 24
   Choose from among Many Options, 25

PART II: UNDERSTANDING THE PROBLEM

Chapter 3   Case Study—The Middle East   **27**

Background of Palestinian and Jewish Claims, 27
The Beginnings of a Jewish State, 29
The Creation of Israel, 31
Israeli Victory and the Refugee Situation, 33
The 1967 (Six-Day) War, 36
The Yom Kippur War, 37
The Creation of a Palestinian State, 39

Chapter 4   Understanding Partisan Perceptions   **45**

The Limits of Facts As We See Them, 46
Understanding a Conflict from Many Points of View, 47
First Position: Our Own Assumptions about a Conflict, 48
Second Position: How Other Parties Perceive a Conflict, 51
    What the Parties See: Partisan Perceptions, 51
    Why They See Things That Way: Emotions and
        Motivations, 57
    What Lies Behind What They Say: Positions and Interests, 61

Chapter 5   The Decision from the Other Side's Point of View,   **68**

Who Are We Trying to Influence? 70
What Are We Asking Them to Do? 70
When Should They Take Action? 71
Why Is Our Request Justified? 71
Analyzing Our Message, 72
Understanding the Choice As It Looks to Them, 79
    Which Decision-Maker? 80
    What Decision? 80
    Weighing the Consequences As They See Them on Each Side, 80
    Their Choice Is Our Problem, 86

Chapter 6   The View from the Bureaucracy   **87**

PART III: UNDERSTANDING THE TASK

**Chapter 7   Case Study on Arms Control—The Antiballistic
Missile Treaty**   **96**

Case Overview, 96
Background, 97

A Climate of Mistrust, 97
Negotiating "Inside Out," 99
The Talks, 101
The Role of Domestic Politics, 103
Scope for Executive Leadership, 107
Postscript: The Controversy over the Strategic Defense
Initiative, 108

Chapter 8   Understanding the Human Dimension   **113**

Getting What We Need Out of a Relationship, 113
Diagnosis of a Poor Working Relationship, 115
A Better Approach to Building a Relationship, 119
Some Features That Are Not Essential to a Good Working
Relationship, 121
An Unconditionally Constructive Strategy, 126

Chapter 9   Building a Productive Framework for Negotiation   **128**

Questioning Assumptions, 128
Focusing on Process Design, 130
Positions versus Interests, 131
Who Are the Players (and Who *Should* They Be)? 132
Changing Some Standard Moves, 135

Chapter 10   Solving the Inventing Problem   **147**

The Lack of New Ideas, 147
Bureaucratic Constraints, 148
Implicit Assumptions, 148
Status of Partcipants, 148
Lack of Experience Generating New Ideas, 149
A Lack of Creative Options Can Cause Deadlock, 149
Generating New Approaches, 151
Designing a Way Out of Constraints, 151

Chapter 11   Defining Our Purpose and Strategy   **158**

Seeing Choices through a Rear View Mirror, 158
Getting Oriented: Whose Purpose? 160
What Do They Want? 161
Why Distinguish Victory, Power, and Peace? 163
Focus on One Purpose at a Time, 166
Designing a Strategy to Realize Our Purpose, 168
What Is Our Strategy: Self-Help, Education, or
Influence? 169

PART IV: PUTTING IDEAS TO WORK

Chapter 12   Case Study—The Bombing Campaign in Vietnam   **177**

Historical Background, 177
U.S. Attempts to Strengthen the South Vietnamese
    Government, 180
Direct U.S. Involvement Begins—Bombing Campaigns, 181
President Johnson's Speech at Johns Hopkins University, 183
Breaks in the Bombing and Attempts at Negotiation, 185
Alternatives to Armed Aggression, 189
Reassessment of Bombing, 190
End of U.S. Involvement, 190

Chapter 13   Analyzing Threats and Sanctions   **194**

The Limited Effectiveness of Inflicted Pain, 195
    The Other Side Probably Anticipated Some Cost, 195
    Pain Equals Investment, 195
    Increasing the Pain Is Also Ineffective, 196
    Reversing a Decision through Pain Is Unlikely, 196
Threats Are Costly to Us, 197
    Our High Cost Gives Them Hope, 199
A Decision to Threaten Becomes a Decision to Implement, 199
Analyzing Infliction of Pain, 200
The Difference between Threats and Warnings, 207
    Considering Our Alternatives, 207

Chapter 14   Changing the Demand   **209**

Benefits of Changing the Demand, 210
    A New Question Requires a New Answer, 210
    A New Question Does Not Require Reversal of an Earlier
        Decision, 210
    A New Question Frees Us from Domestic Constraints, 210
Disadvantages to Asking a New Question, 211
Reframe the Same Demand, 211
    Improve the Offer in Their Eyes, 212
    Reduce the Disadvantages of Making the Decision, 212
    Make the Demand Procedural, 213
    Ask for a Promise to Act Rather Than an Action, 213
    Ask the Other Side *Not* to Act, 214
Divide the Problem into Smaller Components, 214
    Limit the Scope of the Dispute, 215
    Divide the Conflict into Smaller Issues, 215
    Use Small Steps to Accomplish a Larger Goal, 216

Take Advantage of Timing, 216
   Give Them the Benefits Sooner, 216
   Give Them a Fading Opportunity, 217
Make the Demand More Credible, 217
   Unless the Offer Is Credible, It Will Not Work, 218
   We Should Have a Reputation for Credibility, 218
   Credible Offers Exert More Influence, 218
   Do Not Ask for More Than Is Reasonable, 219
Make the Demand More Specific, 220
   Ambiguous Offers Have Limited Benefits, 220
   Ambiguous Offers Do Not Result in Action, 222
   Specificity Is Not Rigidity, 223
   At Least We Should Be Specific in Our Own Thinking, 223
How to Make the Offer More Credible, 224
   Increase the Probability That the Offer Will Be
     Implemented, 224
   Implementation Plans Demonstrate Commitment, 225
   Implementation Plans Demonstrate Capability, 225
Increasing Compliance Mechanisms Increases Credibility, 226
   Improving First-Order Compliance, 226
   Improving Second-Order Compliance, 228

Chapter 15   Legitimacy and International Law   231

A Legitimate Demand Exerts Influence, 232
   Playing to the Home Audience, 232
Some Ways to Formulate Legitimate Demands, 234
   Linking the Demand to Past Actions, 234
   Making the Demand Reciprocal, 235
   Involving a Third Party, 235
Confronting Moral Choice, 236
   A Workable Goal: Minimize Regrets, 237
   Sorting Out the Problem, 237
Using International Law More Effectively, 241
   Domestic Law Restrains a Government's Behavior, 242
   International Law Can Influence the Other Side, 244
   Law Acts As a Restraint, 245
   Example: The Cuban Missile Crisis, 246
Testing the Use of Legitimacy, Morality, and the Law, 249

Chapter 16   Selecting a Point of Choice   251

Ask the Person with the Power to Decide, 252
Be Sure the Decision Actually Benefits the Decision-Maker, 253
Choose a Feasible Decision-Maker, 254
Nominate Potential "Princes" on Their Side, 254
Select the Target Point of Choice, 258

Chapter 17   Finding a "Yesable" Proposition   **259**

Return to Their Currently Perceived Choice, 259
Drafting a Target Future Choice, 260
Constructing a "Yesable" Proposition, 265
Checking Our Choice, 269
Testing Our Advice, 271
Putting It All Together: Dispute Resolution As Problem-
    Solving, 277
  Analyzing a Choice, 278
  Developing Advice, 278
  Focusing on Process Design, 278
  Revisiting the "Activist Stance," 278

Index   **281**

Preface

This book captures much of what has been learned from the international work carried on under the auspices of the Harvard Negotiation Project, and by Roger Fisher and others before the Project began. The Project's purpose from its inception was to seek to apply insights from academic work to real-world problems and to use this experience to enrich and deepen academic understanding. Over the past seventeen years, associates of the Project have, for example, had the opportunity to conduct workshops on the negotiation process for the African National Congress, for members of the Inkatha Freedom Party, for most of the then all-white cabinet of the South African government, and for other groups during the period leading up to constitutional negotiations in South Africa. The Project also co-sponsored workshops conducted for the FMLN guerrillas and for government officials of El Salvador as they prepared for the negotiations that led to an agreement ending ten years of civil war. Members of the Project met and shared ideas with President Cerezo of Guatemala and President Arias of Costa Rica as they prepared for the negotiations that produced the Esquipulas II (Arias) peace plan. Additionally, ideas from the Project influenced a Reagan-Gorbachev summit, the Algerian mediation of the U.S.–Iran hostage situation of 1979–81, and the process used by the U.S. government at Camp David in mediating an agreement between Egypt and Israel in 1978.

Throughout this work, the Project's goal has been to develop and refine tools and frameworks of analysis for organized and systematic thinking about conflict and its resolution, and to share the products of this analysis with those most likely to benefit from it. This book is an effort to share this thinking process as it has developed to date. It suggests a structure for the analysis of international conflict and provides a set of tools to help bridge the gap between theory and practice, and between where parties to a conflict are today and where they would rather be. It offers diagnostic tools for looking at a complex or protracted conflict and then answering the question, "Why hasn't this conflict been resolved?" To be sure, not all conflicts can be resolved. Yet it would be difficult to name an international conflict where all parties were pursuing what might seem a wise course of action to advance their own interests.

These approaches are intended to help negotiators—whether directly involved in a conflict or acting as facilitators or advisors—to understand how others may perceive the conflict and the choices they face, and on that basis, to develop a plan for moving toward resolution of the conflict and for turning a good idea into a fresh decision that a party to the conflict might take.

The idea is not simply that people be "nice." Rather, the focus is on how to be effective. And the Project's experience indicates that these tools and the products of their application have proven useful. For example, El Salvador's ambassador to the United Nations wrote that the ideas were forceful and had been used by both the guerrillas and the government while negotiating a political solution to the conflict. From the other side of that war, Roberto Cañas, former FMLN guerrilla leader, wrote: "These ideas helped us accomplish more in one year of negotiating than in ten years of warfare."

This book presents these ideas for a university classroom. It invites you, the student or general reader, to take on the role of advisor to some real-world decision-maker in a real-world conflict. Using what you already know about a particular subject or conflict, or what you can learn from libraries, scholars, colleagues, and friends, the book offers an organized way of thinking about what one might do to improve the way people are dealing with a conflict.

You are among the people who might make a constructive difference. As you expand your knowledge about a particular conflict and as you learn to apply your experience, studies, and insights in a structured way to a decision facing a party to that conflict, you will develop your own ideas on how that conflict might be better managed or moved toward resolution. Time and again, those who have taught these materials have seen a spark of insight in a university classroom develop into a vision for change in the real world that eventually produces a step toward the resolution of a conflict by an actual decision-maker.

Not every bright idea will fly—nor should it. Yet looking at international conflict as a set of choices facing real people—choices that can be changed—is a way to understand the world as it is and a way to make it better. Trying out ideas improves the ideas, improves our understanding of international affairs, can improve the way a conflict is being handled, and certainly improves our ability to cope with future conflict.

ACKNOWLEDGMENTS

There is a constant interplay between producing ideas and producing written words. Ideas stimulate words. The writing and editing of words sharpen ideas and generate more of them. Similarly, there is a constant interaction between teaching and learning. Teachers know that in working with a group of students we are likely to learn more than the students. We come to understand some of our own ideas only through trying to explain them. At other times, we find ourselves to be students, learning from what our fellow students ask and say—from what they write and do.

The ideas and words in this book have already come a long way. They found their genesis in *International Conflict for Beginners* by Roger Fisher, now out of print. In the acknowledgments for that book, Roger wrote:

> The ideas in this book have grown over such a period of time, and have gone through such transformations, that it is impossible for me to give appropriate thanks to all those who have contributed to them. To friends, colleagues and students, I owe more than gratitude.
>
> I must, however, mention at least those who might well have appeared on the title page as co-authors. During the academic year 1964–1965 I worked with a Freshman Seminar in Harvard College on the problem of controlling the magnitude of issues in international conflict. The analytic approach used in this book was developed in that seminar and was first written up in a working draft called *What's the Message?—An Approach to International Conflict* of which the authors were the seminar members: Martha-Ann Ackelsberg, Don Berwick, Bill Blumberg, Bill Bullitt, Jackie Evans, Stuart Fuchs, Bill Kelly, Sherry Leeright, Kevin Mellyn, Peter Petri, Steve Presser, Debbie Slotkin, Tim Wilton and myself. We had a good time in the seminar and I, at least, learned a lot. In case the extent of my pleasure in their company camouflaged the extent of my indebtedness to them, let me record it here....
>
> At the London School of Economics I met George Frampton, Jr., who during the succeeding year at Harvard Law School, worked with me so closely in taking that draft apart and putting this book together that neither of us can be sure which words are whose. His contribution not only to this book but also to my enjoyment in working on it is beyond measure.

Another major burst of energy and ideas is associated with the Harvard College undergraduate course, Coping with International Conflict (CWIC), first taught by Roger in 1977. Bruce Patton, who first came to know Roger as a student in that course and who has been working and teaching with him ever since, played a major role in producing original case materials for the course (which formed the basis for some of the case studies incorporated herein) and in shaping some of these ideas and an early draft of this book. As a co-founder and Deputy Director of the Harvard Negotiation Project, and as a Lecturer on Law, he has long worked to put these ideas into practice and to enable others to do so, among them the authors of this book.

Andrea, Liz, and Brian first worked with these ideas both as teaching fellows for CWIC and in working with the Project. Liz worked with Roger and others on the Project's Central American peace initiative. Each also had the opportunity to develop these ideas further in university classrooms—Liz at Stanford University, Andrea at Stanford University and George Washington University, and Brian at Texas Southmost College. If this book proves accessible and helpful in generating better and more operational ideas for resolving international conflict, it is in large measure due to the experience and advice of our students. They have shaped our thinking and improved its teaching.

An enormous number of people have helped in the shaping and presentation of these ideas as students, associates of the Negotiation Project, and colleagues at Conflict Management Group—a nonprofit consulting firm that offers advice and training in negotiation and conflict resolution processes to governments, international organizations, and other entities. Others have provided administrative and clerical assistance. The team roster includes: Sheila Blake, Lori Britton, Richard Buchanan, Diana Chigas, Andrew Clarkson, Wayne Davis, Ivan Dubovsky, Peter Engel, Katherine Felsen, Elissa Gootman, Steven Isko, William Jackson, Debbie Katzenellenbogen, Kathaleen Kelly, Mira Kothari, Matthew Lane, Gail Lebow, Paul Mayer, Michael Moffitt, Nikos Mourkogiunnis, Evelyn Posamentier, Alan Price, Robert Ricigliano, Charles Rudnick, Peter Schlactus, William Ury, and Jeffrey Wing. Special recognition is required for Carrie Gerkey, who was instrumental in the preparation of the case studies. We are blessed to have these people as our friends and colleagues. Thank you all very much.

We would also like to thank our editors at Prentice Hall: Michael Bickerstaff, Jennie Katsaros, and Rob DeGeorge. Perhaps the highest praise could be that we all look forward to working with Michael, Jennie, and Rob, and with Prentice Hall, in the future. The following reviewers provided helpful suggestions and useful insights: Steven L. Lamy, University of Southern California; Joseph Lepgold, Georgetown University; Nikolaos A. Stavrou, Howard University; and Herbert K. Tillema, University of Missouri.

Andrea, Liz, and Brian would like to thank Roger for his insight, support, and enthusiasm for us and for our work over the years. Once in a great while one encounters a person who has an immediate and enduring impact on how one thinks, acts, and conducts one's life. You have been such a person to each of us. We thank you.

CHAPTER

—1—

Negotiation
in the Context
of International Conflict

❖   ❖   ❖

Negotiation occupies center stage in international affairs. A single day's news reports confirm this. The U.S. president appeals to both sides in Northern Ireland to put aside "old habits and hard grudges" in his attempt to turn a cease-fire into a negotiated peace. Israeli and Palestinian Liberation Organization leaders meet to discuss the Israeli withdrawal from the West Bank. North Atlantic Treaty Organization ambassadors fail to reach final agreement to deploy troops in support of the peace agreement in the former Yugoslavia. The Haitian leadership negotiates with the World Bank and the International Monetary Fund to release tens of millions of dollars in suspended loans. Delegates from seventy-five nations to the Intergovernmental Panel on Climate Change reach consensus on language concerning global warming. When war and peace are at stake, news services provide up-to-the-minute coverage, if only of the secretary of state's report that the parties have held "frank discussions on a wide range of matters of mutual concern." At the same time, perhaps in testament to the ubiquitousness of negotiation in foreign affairs, international conferences on cooperation in health, economic development, telecommunications, transportation, mail delivery, and a host of other concerns are so common as to have ceased to be newsworthy. It is impossible to conceptualize international affairs absent the bargaining table.

Critical junctures of negotiated agreement provide our enduring images of international relations. We are sometimes elated about these agreements. The never-before-heard voice of the emperor announces that Japan has accepted the Allies' terms for surrender, sparing a U.S. invasion. The short flight of President Anwar Sadat of Egypt to meet Prime Minister Begin of Israel in Jerusalem bridges a vast chasm of differences on the occupied Sinai Peninsula. President Kennedy negotiates for many days and nights with Soviet Premier Khrushchev over the withdrawal of Soviet missiles from Cuba. Former President Carter convinces Haitian dictator Raoul Cedras to step down only hours before U.S. troops are to strike. Sometimes, we recognize these choices as poor ones. Prime Minister Neville Chamberlain of Great Britain returns from Munich to announce "peace in our time." Only a few years later, we see pictures of the Allied leaders at Yalta and wonder whether Roosevelt and Churchill meant to concede to Stalin the partitioning of Europe that was denied to Hitler. Or we remain ambivalent about our leaders' choices. The Reykjavik embrace of Presidents Reagan and Gorbachev apparently reshapes the course of strategic arms negotiations. The Rose Garden handshake of Israeli Prime Minister Yitzhak Rabin and PLO leader Yasser Arafat lays out a new but yet unproven path for resolving conflict in the Middle East. Whatever our reaction to these events, we recognize them as pivotal to the course of international affairs.

So, too, we remember the follies and failures of international negotiation. The inability of the parties to negotiate the shape of the table at the Paris peace conference feeds the black humor of a generation of Vietnam movies and M*A*S*H episodes. President Carter allows himself to be held hostage in the Rose Garden by his inability to negotiate the release of American diplomats in the Ayatollah Khomeini's new Iran. A grim-faced Secretary of State Al Haig announces that the parties cannot agree on the future of some small islands off the coast of South America populated by far more sheep than people; Britain soon declares war on Argentina to keep the British Falkland Islands from becoming the Argentinean Malvinas. Greeks and Turks once again allow escalation of conflict in divided Cyprus, while India and Pakistan renew reciprocal threats and accusations. We are struck by the enduring nature of conflict between Israel and Syria, North and South Korea, the United States and Cuba. We accept that not all conflict can or should be resolved. At the same time, we cannot help but suspect that a failure to achieve peace turns more often not on some essential or intrinsic aspect of the dispute, but on the failure of the parties to pursue effectively its resolution.

We will explore in order the following basic premises of negotiation in the context of international conflict. First, international conflict is distinguished most fundamentally by the requirement of organized efforts at persuasion, or negotiation, in the resolution of conflict. Second, change in international relations in the end depends on the choices of individuals, and it is therefore the perspective of the decision-maker and the choices confronting him or her that are most critical to affecting change in the international system. Third, how key actors go about making their decisions will have a substantive impact on how or whether disputes are resolved. Unwilling merely to provide descriptions of conflicts past or present, we see our task as developing a systematic approach to improving the decisions of key actors in international conflict.

THE REQUIREMENT OF NEGOTIATION IN INTERNATIONAL AFFAIRS

National interests bring states and other international actors into constant contact. These interests include a state's paramount interest in security. A state will also pursue the accumulation of wealth, however fairly or unfairly divided within its domestic political order. States generally have an interest in an international system sufficiently pacific and stable to allow them to pursue their interests in trade, science, health, or the environment. The question of a state's interests in the international arena is not dependent on an altruistic notion of national behavior; even the schoolyard bully will have something in mind that he wants to achieve. As long as states recognize that their security depends at least in part on the actions of others outside their borders, or believe that they can accumulate more wealth or can pursue other national interests more effectively in the international arena than in isolation, they will continue to engage in what we broadly call international relations. And as long as different countries' interests are not fully congruent, they will continue to have conflicts. The necessity to negotiate the resolution of conflicts of interest between players on the international stage defines the international character of these disputes.

A typical attempt to distinguish between international and domestic legal systems relies on the lack of an enforcement mechanism in international law. In national life, police forces protect against crime and pursue criminals. Administrative agencies pursue tax cheats and polluters. One private citizen can sue another for redress of grievances in court. No analogous institutions exist, however, in the international sphere. Great powers do not dependably intervene on behalf of generally accepted legal principles. Aggrieved states and individuals are not guaranteed a hearing in front of any world tribunal. English philosopher John Austin argued that international law was not "law proper" because of the lack of an enforcer of sanctions or punishments on those who would violate the law.

Many contemporary commentators would agree. Bolstered by significant data, they view the international system as primitive and lawless. They find that functioning in the contemporary world is both dangerous and costly. Countries assemble troops on their borders to lay claim to mineral or water rights. Tens of thousands of nuclear weapons are scattered around the globe. While some are being dismantled, others are doubtlessly being built. Vast resources are spent on deadly military hardware. Threats and violence are standard ways of dealing with differences. In large parts of the world, the risk of anarchy is high. Despite their mandates, the United Nations and other international institutions such as the Organization on Security and Cooperation in Europe or the Organization of American States seem unable to deal effectively with many ongoing international conflicts. The lesson taken away from these observations may be that only troop strength, throw weights, and kill ratios determine the outcome of international events.

The international system, however, is hardly anarchistic. A letter dropped in a U.S. Postal Service mailbox in Oklahoma City will dependably arrive in practically any corner of the globe, almost without regard to the state of official relations between the countries. Telecommunications protocols concerning telephone, fax, and electronic mail put Hartford in instantaneous contact with Caracas, Harare, and Singapore. It is difficult to conceptualize the international regime that is sufficiently stable and secure to allow iron ore from Russia and nickel from Indonesia to be forged with Japanese financing into steel in South Korea, all to be exported to the United States to produce a commercial jet aircraft that will fly passengers on hundreds of thousands of personal, business, and diplomatic missions around the world. But such a system is in place. International trade and investment as well as cooperation in law enforcement, the environment, and a host of other issues continue to grow.

This is not a matter of seeing the glass of international affairs as half full or half empty, precarious or stable, depending on one's point of view. Both perspectives are true. They are reconciled by an understanding of consent as the fundamental principal of international systems, and of negotiation—including the use or threat of force—as the principal mechanism for the resolution of international disputes. Where there is negotiated understanding, the international system is fundamentally stable. Where there is not consent, the system is more precarious.

In the domestic legal order, the notion of consent is a matter of political philosophy, interesting in theory but hardly of relevance to our daily lives. Our system of laws and the mechanisms for their enforcement assume consent. One can imagine being brought before the municipal judge in night court on a charge of speeding. "Your Honor," you might say, "I never agreed that the speed limit should be sixty-five. I even lobbied against it." The judge might answer impatiently, "Yes, but democracy rules. The law was enacted by the people of this state through their duly elected representatives." "That may be true," you answer, "but I never agreed to that system. It was created—by revolution at that—well before my birth. I don't accept it as binding. I've done no person any harm and I won't accept driving slow for the rest of my life." "This is all very interesting," the judge would answer, "but if you plan on going home tonight, I suggest you either plead not guilty or pay the fine. That's the law." Implied consent is nothing more than a convenient construct in the domestic order; we do not recognize consent in any but the most abstract fashion as necessary to the functioning of the system.

The ability of the domestic legal order to operate without the need for ongoing consent of the parties is not fundamentally a function of superior firepower or force sufficient to compel compliance. Certainly the municipal judge could put the speeder in jail or order the seizure of his property to ensure the payment of a fine. But far more fundamental civil rights that put the individual in opposition to the state are protected without any apparent enforcement mechanism at all. Thurgood Marshall had no police force at his disposal as he argued *Brown v. Board of Education of Topeka;* he was representing an admittedly oppressed minority. In *Yates v. United States,* the Supreme Court in 1957 ordered the Department of Justice to release 14 men, all communists, who had been convicted under the Smith Act of teaching or advocating the overthrow of the U.S. government by force. Despite the unpopularity of his cause, and without any recourse to force of arms at all, Yates was set free by a federal government that regarded him as a danger to its very existence. No police force or higher authority could compel the Justice Department to act, and yet it did. And it is not always the state that holds the power. If everyone in the country decided not to pay federal taxes, one can hardly imagine how the IRS could compel payment by over a hundred million angry citizens. The domestic legal order in practice does not rely on compulsion or threats of enforcement actions.

By history, practice, and a fundamental preference for order, players in the domestic legal order by and large submit their competing claims to judgment and abide by the decisions, without regard to their relative power or their specific consent to the rules at play. In the international system, by contrast, the consent of sovereign states is the central organizing principle of the legal and political orders. Important disputes will be settled not by appeal to third-party institutions, but by negotiation.

A state must consent to the specific rule to which another international actor seeks to hold it. Our citizen's opposition to the sixty-five-mile-per-hour speed limit could be recognized without being taken into account in the judge's decision. A sovereign state, however, can in fact decline to reduce emissions of greenhouse gases, can maintain punitive tariffs that make international trade all but impossible, or can continue nuclear testing in the face of worldwide opposition. Even effective and broad rule-making international organizations such as the European Union, the North Atlantic Treaty Organization, and the World Health Organization rely on the consent of states for their functioning. European tariffs, for example, are set in Brussels without unanimous consent of member countries. These organizations cannot endure, however, without the specific and ongoing consent of their member nations to the rules they promulgate. France refused for decades to join the integrated military command of NATO; credible politicians in London today call for the United Kingdom's withdrawal from the EU in the face of monetary union. These are the decisions of sovereign nations. States may for a variety of self-interested reasons subject themselves to international rules, but it is the consent of states that makes those rules law.

A state must also consent to the decision-making system by which disputes about compliance with international rules are resolved. Neither Yates's attorney nor the Department of Justice could seriously contest the U.S. Supreme Court's authority to determine the constitutionality of the federal law under which Yates was convicted. There is no analogous decision-maker of last resort in the international order. It is true that a growing number of transnational commercial disputes are settled by international arbitration. The European nations have consented to the general jurisdiction of the EU court; the United States, Canada, and Mexico have created a special NAFTA tribunal. Unlike Yates or the Department of Justice presenting a case before the U.S. Supreme Court, however, the parties themselves set up the tribunal and may terminate the treaties that created their jurisdiction. States generally reserve to themselves the right to submit disputes only on an ad hoc basis to binding determinations of compliance or noncompliance with international law. In the absence of a state's agreement to allow a third party to determine whether the law has been complied with or what should happen in the event of a determination that the governing rules have not been followed, states are left to dispute these matters among themselves.

States could rely on unilateral action to resolve inevitable international disputes. A state could attempt isolation from its neighbors, or it could attempt to impose its own will, by force if necessary. The ambiguity of international law and the lack of authoritative solutions for international disputes have made unilateral action for some, at least abstractly, an attractive option. This may in part explain why the risk of violence remains a much more accepted part of international than of domestic life. Absent supervision by some supranational power, we may well come to believe that bloody noses are the predictable result of states' flexing the muscle of their competing authorities on the international playground. One might suspect that force will be used because force is available. A weapon system once developed may always find a justification for its use in the pursuit of national interest. Absent deterrence, disagreements will predictably become disagreeable. It is not surprising that many believe the projection of force is the determinative factor in the resolution of international disputes.

Unilateral action, however, is rarely sufficient to meet basic national interests in the international sphere. Rarely is a nation's goal the conquest or total control of another. Where this has been attempted, whether by the Soviet Union in Afghanistan or by Iraq in Kuwait, the cost has proven enormous. In limited circumstances force is a viable tool. Israel, for example, found no better means to slow the Iraqi nuclear program than the direct bombing of an Iraqi reactor. While military might may prove to be a deterrent to malicious action, however, it is difficult to imagine a state using force to pursue all of its international interests. Imagine a country threatening invasion in order to prevail in a dispute on telecommunications standards, or boycotting trade with a foreign nation in order to determine the proper allocation of air space to avoid commercial airline collisions. The picture painted is absurd. Unilateral action, especially involving the use of force, will by and large undermine the very interests in security, accumulation of wealth, and the sufficiently pacific and stable international system necessary to the pursuit of other national interests that prompted the state to act in the first place. Attempts to meet national interests and maximize benefits in the international

arena thus remain largely a matter of negotiation, of persuading other players to accept rules of conduct and rules for the settlement of disputes, congru-
ently with the interests of the parties.

Negotiation may take the form of explicit, face to face interaction.
Countries and other international actors regularly extend invitations to send
representatives directly to the table to discuss common interests or matters of
concern. A host of international forums, indeed the entire alphabet soup of international organizations, exist to provide encouragement of and support for
negotiation of differences among member states. While the international bureaucracy is justifiably criticized for its slow pace and wasteful methods,
these are the ways in which agreements—on fishing rights between Canada
and the United States, on international responses to infectious disease, on
mining in Antarctica and on the moon, on security and cooperation in Europe,
and on thousands of other matters—are eventually reached.

Attempts at persuasion will also often take the form of implicit negotiation. Nation-states and private actors send "messages" intended to persuade an opposing party to do something differently, whether or not their negotiators ever meet. The French government announced in 1985, for example,
that it would oppose the importation of New Zealand lamb if French agents
responsible for the Greenpeace bombing were not returned to France. France
did not stage a military operation to free its agents unilaterally, as the United
States had attempted to do to free its nationals held in Iran or the Israelis
had done to free hostages from the airport at Entebbe. France instead sent a
powerful—and ultimately successful—message intended to change the minds
of the New Zealand government officials who had to decide whether or not to
release the French agents.

Even the use of force, except when geared toward conquest, is typically intended to persuade another party to stop or start doing something.
The United States did not bomb Tripoli in 1986 because it realistically believed that Libya's capacity to support international terrorism would thereby
be diminished. The U.S. bombed Tripoli at least in part because U.S. policy-
makers believed that increasing the cost to Libya would make it decide to reduce its support of acts against U.S. interests. The Irish Republican Army
does not expect to conquer Northern Ireland, but rather intends to persuade
the British that the cost of continued resistance to IRA demands is too high to
justify not coming to the table. Unable to compel changes to the system without the cooperation or agreement, however grudging, of others, international
players will find themselves with one another—either literally or figuratively—at the negotiating table.

DECISIONS AS POINTS OF CHANGE IN THE INTERNATIONAL SYSTEM

We will look at various international conflicts through the eyes of different
decision-makers, different players in the game. These may be ranking government officials, generals, corporate executives, church leaders, or journal-

ists. They may be typical voters, guerrillas, or political opponents—anyone whose actions we believe may influence the course of a conflict or its resolution. We want to understand the kinds of decisions they make, and why they behave the way they do, so that we can understand how they might be influenced more effectively.

A focus on the choices of particular decision-makers provides this book with its organizing idea and cultivates an ability to see a given situation through the eyes of those facing a choice. It also reminds us that of all the variables in the world, choice is the only one we can affect: even the most global changes we can imagine will involve some individual deciding to do a particular thing differently tomorrow morning.

Perspectives on International Relations

Most forms of activity can be explained in a variety of ways. A dance contest, for example, would be described quite differently by an anthropologist, a psychologist, and a lawyer. If we want to know more about Boston simply for the sake of knowing something about it, any one of a large number of maps might do: a contour map, a historical map, a map of the one-way streets, of the voting districts, of the zip codes, of the high-crime areas. Each would provide us with insight about Boston.

The same is true with international relations. As we read the newspapers and watch the television reports from Turkey, China, and the West Bank, we want to know what is going on. We also want to have some explanatory structure, some bigger picture, so that we can make sense of the detailed events as part of a pattern. If we are seeking knowledge for its own sake, our aim is not narrowly confined. Any of a number of maps of the international scene may satisfy our curiosity, and the more different kinds of maps in our atlas the more comfortable we will feel about our familiarity with the terrain. The maps of history, anthropology, political science, economic development theory and other disciplines all provide frameworks into which detailed information can be placed and some kind of explanation of what is going on extrapolated.

As parties to conflicts and outside observers seek to make sense of the international system, there is a tendency to favor hard data over soft, quantifiable over qualitative information. Influenced perhaps by the physical sciences, they tend to look for accurate facts and good correlations. Our very vocabulary suggests the importance we attribute to numerical data: things "don't count" unless we can count them. As former Secretary of State Henry Kissinger observed in a famous critique of the American foreign policy establishment:

> Problems are separated into constituent elements, each of which is dealt with by experts in the special difficulty it involves. There is little emphasis or concern for their interrelationship. Technical issues enjoy more careful attention, and receive more sophisticated treatment, than political ones. Though the im-

portance of intangibles is affirmed in theory, it is difficult to obtain a consensus on which factors are significant and even harder to find a meaningful mode for dealing with them. Things are done because one knows how to do them and not because one ought to do them.[1]

Conventional wisdom suggests that the test of research lies in the extent to which it enables us to predict something that is going to happen. But the more research focuses attention on what is predictable, the more it diverts attention from what people can affect. By definition, if we know that something is going to happen, then that is something about which no one can do anything. If participants in international relations want knowledge in order to improve the world—if they want human beings by their decisions to make things better—then predictability is the wrong standard. They need to build on their interest in what is inevitable and look toward those things that actors might be able to change. This will require adding to investigations of quantifiable matters such as body counts, military hardware, and dollars. It will require consideration of purpose, perception, emotional involvement, ideology, understanding, legitimacy, and shared concerns.

Choice as the Key Perspective for Change

Our goal is not merely to describe why international conflicts have occurred and continue to occur as they do. Rather, we will attempt to understand how change could be effected in the international system. Since change in the end will depend on the choices of key decision-makers, understanding the perspective of the decision-maker and the choices confronting him or her will be critical to our efforts.

Studying international relations from a systemic perspective, looking exclusively at the big picture, omits a crucial aspect of understanding. What we attempt to understand as "international relations" is actually the cumulative effect of thousands of daily decisions. If we want to know what the process is like, we have to know how it looks from the inside. A key element of understanding why things happen is to know why foreign ministers, generals, and other actors decide as they do.

However determined and orderly international systems and institutions may look from the outside, that is not how it feels to those who are playing the game. Choices may be determined by environment and heredity, but when we get up in the morning we cannot say, "All right, heredity and environment, *you* decide which shirt I should wear today." We have to decide. Each of us has the experience of facing choices, thinking, reaching conclusions, and acting on them. To be sure, for each of us, many things have to be taken as given. But even if the world is determined in the sense that there is an antecedent cause for every event, it is determined that we must make choices. Within a substantial scope we exercise something that feels like freedom—we make choices.

---

[1]Henry A. Kissinger, *American Foreign Policy,* 3rd ed. (New York: W. W. Norton, 1977), p. 29.

The organized study of choice provides a critical perspective on international relations. It could be said that the United States organized the Bay of Pigs invasion of Cuba in 1961 because of historical forces. Considerations of the balance of power and studies of the role of international organizations will provide valuable information to us. But such systems-level perspectives leave out a startling reality. From President Kennedy's point of view, he made a decision. However convenient the shorthand, countries do not persuade or become persuaded. "Israelis" and "Arabs" as undifferentiated groups have no feelings, no perceptions, no preferences, no plans of action. Whatever the state of science and of the war in the Pacific, President Truman had to decide whether or not to drop the atom bomb. It is the actions of individuals that, in large measure, determine the course of international events.

To improve and complete an analysis of international events requires us to look at a particular choice somebody faces and to ask how things might be done better. Descriptive statements about what has happened and is happening in the world provide participants in international affairs with little knowledge about what might have been done, and more importantly, what might now be done. Analysis must sort out human mistakes from the inevitable. It must approach the question of what was possible, and what is now possible. In order to criticize a baseball manager for replacing a pitcher, it is not enough to say that it is unusual to replace a pitcher in the third inning. We need to understand the choice as it appeared to the manager: what he had to take as given, and what his options were.

The Benefits of Focusing on Choice[2]

In law school, students study choices: they look at the facts and the law as they appeared to a judge who had to make a decision at a fixed point in time. Although the international system is not as rigidly structured as the domestic legal system, one can study international relations much as one studies law, placing substantial reliance on the case method. We take the facts as given but the decision as open. We consider how a judge—any judge—in that position and faced with that choice ought to decide that case. What would be a sound way for a judge to analyze such a case? How would we, as experts, advise a judge faced with this choice to decide? Through such a process we develop our own abilities to reach wise decisions. At the same time, we seek to understand why a particular judge reached his or her particular conclusion.

Focusing on points of choice provides a way to relate the wisdom of different disciplines. It is meaningless to ask whether military or economic considerations are more important if you attempt to argue the matter without a particular choice in mind. Their relative importance depends upon the specifics of the choice facing a decision-maker: what he or she values and what he or she is trying to accomplish. Once we understand the particular decision a person is facing, then we can consider how military and economic

---

[2]Roger Fisher, Elizabeth Kopelman, and Andrea Kupfer Schneider, *Beyond Machiavelli* (Cambridge, MA: Harvard University Press, 1994), pp. 6–7, 10–12.

considerations might best be taken into account. There is no answer to the question whether law or psychiatry is more important, but if a lawyer and a psychiatrist are asked to advise a judge on the sentencing of a juvenile, we have immediately presented the different disciplines with a common question, making it possible to produce wise advice drawing on both forms of expertise.

Machiavelli's *The Prince* is a great book that is still read after almost 500 years, but not because the prince for whom Machiavelli was writing followed his advice or even read the book. Nor is it necessarily read because of the substantive content of the advice he gave, which, at least on its face, denied the relevance of morality in public affairs and justified deceit in pursuing and maintaining political power. The book is powerful because Machiavelli asked a powerful question: What advice would you give a prince? Machiavelli acknowledged international affairs as a series of choices facing key decision-makers.

Focusing on the task of producing hypothetical or real advice provides us with criteria for relevance. By hypothetically getting into the shoes of somebody facing a decision, we are likely to be reminded of the importance of nonquantifiable human factors. Taking the stance of an activist also helps us cope successfully with the question of how to deal with predictions of human behavior. We ignore deterministic predictions of how we (or our hypothetical "prince") are going to behave, but give thoughtful consideration to predictions of how others are likely to behave. We thus do not let predictions limit our scope of choice or become self-fulfilling prophecies, and we have a way of reconciling the reality of constraints with the possibility of choice.

Some have suggested that to focus on the decisions of individuals is to ignore the far greater role played by the structure of the international system. The perception is that by focusing on points of choice—junctures where particular decisions are made—we pay too much attention to the parties when the crucial issue is the structure of the system in which those parties are embedded. Under this view, diplomats are players caught up in a game, and the basic difficulty lies in the nature of the game and not in the ability of the players.

Such a structural analysis of the international situation may well be correct. No one human being may be able to make a major difference within a short period of time. That fact does not change the importance of looking at the choices facing the players. In fact, the dominating impact of the international system can be properly appreciated only when looked at through the eyes of a player.

Decision-makers in the international field are not just playing an international game; they are also playing a game about the structure and rules of that game. The underlying game is shaped by the plays that are made within it. Each move is both a move within the structure and a game-shaping move. The problem may be with the system, but the only ones who can change it are the players. Such an approach encourages clear thinking about systemic problems as well as bilateral inter-state conflicts. We will best understand the system if we look at it from the point of view of a player who wants to change it. Only then will we get a fair idea of how much might be changed in what period of time.

IMPROVING THE NEGOTIATION PROCESS

To the extent that conflicts around the world are not being managed well or are not being resolved successfully, the authors do not sense that the primary deficit is a lack of understanding of possible substantive solutions. Knowledgeable participants are able to predict with a fair degree of certainty, for example, that the broad outline of the eventual settlement between Syria and Israel over the Golan Heights will include the return of territory to Syria with security guarantees for Israel. Credible plans have been generated for nearly every persistent conflict in the world. Rather, participants lack a design for getting from here to there, a plan of action to move negotiations forward and persuade decision-makers that they can in fact reach agreement congruent with their interests.

The state of international relations today is not necessarily the way the world has to be. Who would have thought, forty years ago, that relations between France and Germany, Egypt and Israel, or the United States and Japan would look anything like the way they look now? Who could have foreseen, even a short time ago, that the political landscape in Central Europe would look as it does today? Forty years from now, or even one year from now, relations between the United States and China, between Iran and Iraq, among the Central American nations, or among the nations of the European Union may look completely different as well. If parties are to improve substantive outcomes in the international system, however, they will need to change the processes by which they seek to understand, manage, and resolve disputes.

Around the world, in military establishments, in ministries of foreign affairs, in diplomatic services, in multinational corporations, in commercial trade organizations, and in international organizations of all kinds, individuals every day are making decisions that add up to the way we conduct our international relations. Many of these people have been trained by their own experience. Others are taught at defense colleges, diplomatic academies, foreign service institutes, and universities about the conduct of foreign affairs.

To the extent that the world remains a dangerous and costly place in which to function, we believe that a critical element is missing from the professional education of actors on the international stage. Too much focus is placed on criticizing what is. Not nearly enough time is spent thinking about how international affairs could be different.

If, instead, actors are to use their knowledge to achieve positive change in the international system, they will need an approach to thinking about how much is in the realm of the possible. Not everything is possible; too many parties benefit from deadly and disruptive conflict to permit such an assumption. But some things are. This book studies the expansion of the realm of the possible in international conflict. It seeks to diagnose, through case studies and examples, the manner in which international conflict has been approached by players on the international stage. It develops a framework for improving the process of managing international conflict: for wiser decisions, more effective intervention, and less costly and more secure approaches to international disputes.

An Argument for Rational Thinking

Many think that this approach is just too rational. We have been criticized on the grounds that to calculate how other people's choices look and how they might be changed assumes that we are dealing with a rational world when in fact we are not. "That's fine," we've been told, "but what if the other side doesn't want to get to 'yes'? What if they're into 'no'? What if they're the Ayatollah or Saddam Hussein?"

It is true that reason plays a small role in the world. Government officials, like the rest of us, react emotionally. Even when people are well-meaning, there is often not enough time to produce a rational decision, and the collective decision-making of governments and other organizations often produces a decision that is a compromise reflecting no coherent design whatsoever. Our approach does not assume a world of rational actors. On the contrary, we are trying to reason about reality, with all its irrational components. That patients may be irrational is hardly a ground for doctors to be so. And even the fact that doctors get tired, emotional, or stop thinking clearly hardly means that they should. If we do well at trying to figure out what ought to be done, we may earn a larger role for reason than it now plays. The approach is to ask, "What is the best advice we could give?" The more often reason produces good answers the more likely it is to be called upon in the future.

Others point out that the approach is not that novel, it is just basic common sense. We agree! The appeal of this text is to get back to basics and to ask clear and simple questions about international affairs, such as "What are our basic purposes?" "How ought the people we are trying to influence go about formulating their goals?" "What are they trying to do?" "How might it be done better?"

Some have said that the approach is partisan—that, if applied, it promotes a Western democratic view of the world over any competing worldview. A more accurate criticism might point out that the approach is amoral and could be used by anyone for any purpose—including an evil one. The focus on process means that we lay out various techniques for dealing with international conflict; no preference is shown for people who agree with us over people with whom we may disagree on substance. The approach and all the tools provide a neutral system of analysis, and if both sides in a conflict use the approach, it does not cancel itself out. In fact, to have each adversary apply some common sense is in the interest of both, just as the simple system of dividing a cake between two children—one cuts, the other chooses—tends to promote a fair division and reduce conflict.

Our task here is to suggest a process for the management of conflict in international relations that is more likely to promote the interests of the parties. We believe it possible to develop an organized way of bringing common sense and knowledge to bear on the process of deciding what to do about an international situation. Yet there is no one set of steps, no algorithm, that will automatically lead to the best possible advice. Designing a good program of action, like designing a good house, requires a great deal of weighing of alternatives and of competing considerations. It requires cutting and fitting, and moving back and forth among various tools. And it will benefit from intuition and good judgment. This book offers a tool kit and an instruction manual. If you are the carpenter looking into the kit, you will need to decide what is useful for your particular project; if you are driving a nail, the hammer will be more useful than the dynamite. You will also be more effective with a broad repertoire of tools in your toolbox. As the saying goes, if all you have is a hammer, soon everything starts to look like a nail.

A Systematic Approach to Influence

This book is intended to provide a rational and effective presentation of the core concepts of negotiation in the context of international conflict. Because our primary objective is to look forward, its structure also provides a prescription for decision-makers and their advisors as they attempt to manage and resolve the conflicts confronting them. We base our advice on the Harvard Negotiation Project's practical experience in conflicts as disparate as the Iranian hostage crisis, the civil war in Nicaragua, and the transition of South Africa to majority government. It is our contention that the analysis presented in the balance of this book, when applied to international conflicts, can result in faster, less costly development of more effective solutions. Thus, Section I outlines our approach to conflict and the role we suggest that you take.

Section II begins with a study of international conflict as understood from the perspective of key decision-makers. Our primary case study will be the ongoing struggle between Israelis and Palestinians over the future of the territories occupied by Israel in the 1967 and 1973 wars. We explore the role of partisan perceptions in the framing of conflict, as well as the emotions and motives, positions and interests of the parties that provide an understanding both of why conflicts have not been resolved and of where the possibilities for positive change may be. We explore methods for capturing the specific choice as perceived by a specific decision-maker in a conflict as a map of future action for the conflict's ongoing management or resolution. We also explore bureaucratic restraints on the development and implementation on new approaches to international conflict.

The book proceeds in Section III to a study of individual decisions in the context of the larger international system. Our primary case study will be the history of the Antiballistic Missile Treaty negotiations between the United States and the Soviet Union. We diagnose the role of working relationships at both the national and personal level in the perpetuation and resolution of conflict and provide some prescriptive advice on how to improve relationships. We study the negotiation paradigm implicit in numerous international disputes, and explore alternatives better designed to bring parties to resolution. We explore processes by which fresh ideas and new approaches can be brought to bear on complex and persistent problems. Finally, we study the importance of the framing of purpose and basic strategy on approaches to international conflict.

The book concludes in Section IV with a study of persuasion in international conflict: how actors seek to negotiate with each other, and how they might more effectively do so. Our primary case study will be the attempt of the United States to deter, through military force and other means, North Vietnamese support of the revolutionary movement in South Vietnam. We look specifically at the use of threats and sanctions, and develop a framework for understanding their success or failure. We examine the role of legitimacy in parties' decisions, as well as strategies for increasing the role for standards, law, and norms in international conflict. We look at issues of first- and second-order compliance within the international system, designing not only strategies for becoming better players of the game, but ways of using those strategies to achieve changes in the rules of the game itself. We look finally at the framing of those new steps for the management or resolution of conflict as a new and more palatable choice for decision-makers.

At each juncture, we suggest some key questions and approaches for dealing with international problems. The tools—charts, checklists, frameworks for analysis—help organize a diagnosis and generate a prescriptive framework for thinking more precisely about what ought to happen next. Concepts are illustrated with examples and case studies. For our purposes, we may suppose that some decision-maker called us up on the telephone and said, "In a few weeks I would like to meet with you to get your advice as to what I should do about the Such and Such Problem." We are not looking for a perfect solution to that problem. Rather, we seek to generate the best advice that we as professionals can devise, bringing the lessons of history, traditional academic research and theory, fresh insight and new approaches to bear on the choice facing some real-world decision-maker. We do not assume that all conflicts can be settled peacefully, or that all negotiations will—or should—lead to agreement. We do assume that in many if not most conflicts, someone could be making wiser decisions. Not all diseases can be cured; some patients will die, just as in international relations, setbacks and wasteful violence may prove inevitable. But the concept of the best possible professional advice is a realistic objective.

CHAPTER
—2—

Thinking Like
an Activist

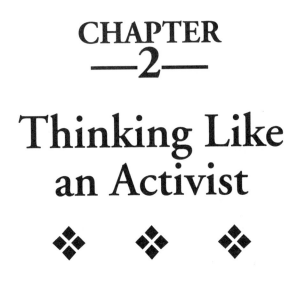

There's another famine in sub-Saharan Africa. Fighting flares up periodically in the former Soviet Union as ethnic groups try to reconfigure themselves as separate nation-states. Continuing disputes in the Middle East, Cyprus, and North Korea raise tensions, reduce opportunities for prosperity and growth, and often waste lives. In the daily paper, we see the human cost of these conflicts: a teenager with a rifle in Rwanda; a toddler in the snow next to a bombed-out house in Chechnya; a university student throwing a rock at an Israeli settlement. What would it feel like to be one of those people?

As a student of international affairs, maybe you're tired of reading accounts of international conflicts that seem remote, inaccessible, and disconnected from international relations as that subject is commonly taught in an academic environment. Your education may have provided a great deal of analytical training to help you diagnose what's gone wrong in a particular conflict situation, but this background may not have focused you on how one might devise what ought to happen next.

THE VALUE OF THINKING LIKE A PARTICIPANT

Learning by doing is good pedagogy in its own right. We expect that, by going through the exercise of examining an international conflict from the perspective of the decision-makers, generating fresh ideas and new approaches that could be presented to a decision-maker as a new and more attractive choice, and testing that advice against the realities of the international system, you will master and internalize this material more thoroughly and more easily. By actively engaging in the processes described in this book, you will emerge with a more thorough understanding of negotiation in the context of international conflict. Our experience with hundreds of students across the past two decades, however, indicates that we may expect much more from you.

The authors of this text have a bias in favor of action. We prefer to operate in the emergency room, rather than at the autopsy table. It is our goal to gather knowledge and bring it to bear in such a way that the conduct of international relations is less dangerous and less costly. To improve the conduct of international relations it is not enough to transfer knowledge of existing practices. We need to generate and spread the best and most relevant ideas that anyone can produce into the thinking of those who will be engaged in the conduct of international relations.

One purpose of this book is therefore to help you understand the conduct of international relations well enough to enjoy that knowledge for its own sake, well enough to be a constructive critic, and well enough to get actively involved to the extent that you may want to do so. We hope to realize these objectives by providing a tool kit of ideas, by encouraging experimentation, and by directing your attention to the continuing power of the question Machiavelli asks, "What advice would you give a prince?" Not all of us will be directly involved in the conduct of foreign affairs, but each of us can be a critic and an advisor, and perhaps an effective one. In the classic fable, it took only one small child to point out that the emperor was wearing no clothes.

"Thinking like an activist" means taking on some responsibility for—and making a contribution to—what the new approaches to international conflict will be. It means adopting an activist stance and participating in foreign affairs, by thinking hard about what is wrong with the world as we see it, how it might look if it were better, and what specific steps we could take to improve what we see. By "activism," we don't necessarily mean waving a picket sign at Berkeley or boycotting grapes. We ask you to target individual decision-makers and focus on developing ideas that might persuade them to make better decisions on particular issues. Marching with a picket sign or organizing a boycott are just two strategies among many for influencing someone else's decision.

We believe that formulating real advice for a real decision-maker is the best way to integrate new ideas with the lessons of history, the models of political science, and the insights of cognitive and social psychology. Accordingly, we borrow from these related fields, while making no pretense about offering a systematic overview of them. (We invite you, however, to bring your specific knowledge and expertise to bear.) Learning how to conduct international relations is like learning how to navigate. We may not be very good navigators yet, but that is the skill we are seeking to acquire, as contrasted with the activities of making navigational maps, criticizing maps, becoming a reporter for *Yacht Club News,* or otherwise talking or writing about things we have not tried to do. We are not assuming any kind of specialized knowledge or background aside from enthusiasm, sustained attention, and willingness to experiment.

Knowing enough to advise a player in the game of nations about what he or she should do not only allows one to be a good critic; it is usually enough to allow one to be an actor in one's own right, if only in a limited way. And of course, to have such knowledge is also to understand what is going on well enough to enjoy that understanding for its own sake. Every baseball fan knows the satisfaction that comes from understanding the game well enough to second-guess the decisions made by the professionals. Fans who know enough to say what advice they would have given the manager, or what advice they would now give the catcher or the runner on first, will enjoy the game more than spectators who can simply describe what is going on—and more than those who can predict what will probably happen next.

TACKLING A REAL-WORLD PROBLEM

We try to practice what we preach. If this text took a lot of trouble over *explaining* the value of an activist stance, and *analyzing* why a traditional narrative approach can limit learning, without venturing into the realm of how one might take action to improve real policies, we wouldn't be doing a very good job! The various tools and concepts introduced in this book are all means to an end: producing a real proposal for an actual decision-maker. The best use of this book—from the perspective both of pedagogy and of improving international systems—begins with your identification of a real-world problem: some conflict situation where there is suffering where there could be hope, or violence where there could be constructive development. We'll offer advice about some criteria for choosing a problem and some questions you'll want to research about the conflict you have selected. But the point of concentrating on a real problem is for you to develop a recommendation about what some identifiable person should do in the near future to help cope with that conflict—resolve it, diminish forces that are fueling it, or at least manage it with less waste and suffering to help lay the groundwork for some more gradual amelioration.

The analysis that leads to your recommendation, and the recommendation itself, are what we will call an "action memorandum," to distinguish it from the usual corporate or bureaucratic memoranda that so rarely lead to action. It is not meant to be a paper describing a conflict. No matter how much or what kind of research you do in preparation for your memorandum, only that background that is actually used by you as part of your analysis should be a part of the memo itself. It might be appropriate to include some background material in your action memo only if you have a section entitled something like, "The History of the Conflict Demonstrates that the Most Important Factors are Economic." There is no need for a section entitled simply, "History."

For example, we had one student in 1989 whose action memo was a proposal for soccer camps for children in South African townships when South Africa was governed under a regime espousing the racial separation doctrine of apartheid. In order to come up with her proposal, she had to research conditions in the black townships, which led her to conclude that a lot of young people were interrupting their educations because school boycotts had become politicized as an instrument of protest. Her objective was to encourage parents to allow their children to attend school. This was based on research she conducted about how a limited educational background in turn limited the opportunities that were available to these children when they became young adults.

She linked her soccer program to school attendance: kids couldn't participate unless they could show they had attended school that day. Her proposal had some other goals as well; for instance, she designed it so that some of the soccer coaches would be from other ethnic groups or of a different race than the soccer-playing children. This part of her proposal came from research that showed that many township kids only rarely had any exposure to someone of a different racial or ethnic group than themselves. Her research was thus a key part of her proposal. It was only through detailed knowledge about the situation in the townships that she was able to develop her proposal in the first place. But her action memo was not a research paper. Research was used in an instrumental way, to show why her proposal was worth adopting. Indeed, most of the research she conducted did not wind up in the memo at all; rather, it served to help her make better choices about the action ideas that *did* go into the memo. (Her proposal was adopted by a major funder of programs for children; she spent three years in South Africa, where she and her fellow coaches trained hundreds of children in soccer—and other—skills.)

There is no single best way to figure out who should do what in the short run about a particular international situation to bring things closer to what you want in the long run. The first part of this text is devoted to learning some skills and developing better ones that will help in that task. The process of using these tools is not linear; one must go backward and forward, working from one piece of the puzzle to another until a satisfactory recommendation is devised. Early on, your objective should be to organize your thinking and to organize an action memo that reflects that thinking.

Your memo should have two parts to it. The first part is meant to be persuasive, but not one-sided. You might think of it as a discussion paper for your colleagues on a policy-planning staff to be used in an internal debate. In an orderly and logical way, it should present the analytical steps that have led you to the conclusion that a particular recommendation should be made to a particular person.

The problem to which Part I of your memo is addressed is: "Who should do what in the near future with respect to the _____ international conflict?" The blank is filled in by the conflict on which you choose to work. Your memo presents and analyzes the problem, explaining and justifying in the process the proposal you are promoting. Note that your proposal is not "the answer" to the problematic conflict you have chosen, just as our former student's proposal about soccer camps did not "solve" the problems of racial violence and limited opportunities for blacks in South Africa under apartheid. These kinds of international conflicts have solutions only in the following very limited sense: there is somebody in a position of authority somewhere who could take constructive action, however small that step might be. If that person came to you for advice, the proposal in your action memo would be the best advice that you could give.

Part II of your action memorandum is actually a separate package to be prepared concurrently. It is in the form of one or more documents—such as a cover letter, short proposal, draft press release, and talking points—to be transmitted to a decision-maker. This transmission can happen either directly or through an entry point—someone with access who will relay your proposal to the decision-maker, ideally with a recommendation that it be adopted. (For this reason, entry points need to be persuaded that your plan is worth consideration as well.) If our hypothetical policy-planning staff agrees with your action memorandum, then your operational documents become the actual pieces of paper you would be sending out; i.e., you would actually mail the cover letter, the one-page summary of your proposal, the draft press release, and the persuasive talking points about how your proposal meets your chosen decision-maker's interests. There will probably be some overlap in Parts I and II of your action memorandum, but there is a substantial difference between presenting a full analysis that may, for example, include a discussion of why you selected this particular decision-maker and this particular entry point, and drafting the actual operational document that is meant to persuade the decision-maker to approve your proposal.

A BREAKDOWN OF LIKELY STEPS ALONG THE WAY

The hardest part of producing a usable action memo is all up-front: selecting a suitable problem and educating yourself about it. That is why the following steps are so front-loaded to favor a careful selection process. Other steps will be expanded on as you go through the text and learn more about the particular concept or tool involved. Here's an overview of the whole process before we start to break it down into manageable parts; don't worry about any new terminology you may encounter. We will be expanding on portions of this checklist throughout the book, and you will have plenty of opportunity to practice with new concepts and skills as you go along.

1. *Select a problem.* Begin by ordering a subscription to a newspaper with good international coverage; we recommend the *New York Times,* the *Washington Post,* or the *Los Angeles Times,* all of which have reasonable student discounts. The *Christian Science Monitor* and the *Economist* also make excellent supplementary reading. As you narrow your choice of a conflict for which to write a proposal, keep clippings of articles relevant to possible situations. Keep the clippings in an easily accessible notebook, and circle the names of experts or officials who are quoted in the articles on your chosen topic. Begin to compile a roster of experts, decision-makers, and other relevant players and commentators whom you might subsequently wish to contact.

2. *Explore and research the problem.* Look at the problem in the way typical partisans on both (or all) sides see it, and through the lenses of various disciplines (economist, psychologist, military strategist, and so on). This kind of partisan perceptions analysis should give you some idea of the opportunities for joint gains through fresh ideas, as well as some sense of the factors you should probably take as given. Interviewing experts and following up with reading that they recommend should also give you a feel for the important factual parameters of the conflict, of important potential actors, and some possible strategies for resolution or amelioration.

3. *Clarify your purpose.* There are many goals about which each of us cares, goals such as equality, freedom, health, education, shelter, community, possessions, and a chance to use one's full potential. Since a better world would arguably be both more just and more peaceful, and since injustice also often provokes conflict, there is a widespread tendency to confuse the pursuit of a more just society with the pursuit of peace. It is worth highlighting, however, that peace and justice are different goals. One can have a peaceful situation (no fighting, no violence) that is far from just. And it is often the pursuit of justice (or the armed resistance to perceived injustice) that generates war. Conflicts usually involve people pursuing different notions of a just outcome.

In many conflicts you will have an interest in the merits of the dispute. Here it will become necessary to sort out your objective of victory (having your way, producing the change you believe desirable) from your objective of peace (having the conflict dealt with at a minimum cost in terms of human suffering). This text is focused on the problem of alleviating international conflicts. We are concentrating our attention on the objective of peace—a world in which nations and groups pursue their own values and their own ideas of justice at minimum risk and at minimum cost in terms of bloodshed, confrontation, and stalemate. Victory as such is not our objective, except insofar as the content of a peaceful outcome determines the durability of the resulting peace. We seek to develop and to disseminate less dangerous ways of pursuing victory. If our ideas are to be accepted, they must offer a good chance of success.

A next step is thus to identify your own values, and how they play out in the particular conflict you are studying. The purpose of the advice you are developing should be either (a) to reduce the risks or costs of that conflict, or, if you prefer, (b) to move toward what you consider to be a more just situation by means that will not increase the risks or costs of the contest.

4. *Select a decision-maker as your "advisee."* This step may come at the beginning or it may come much later in the process, after you have figured out what you think needs to be done to change the conflict situation. You may want to work on some such problem as: What could a U.S. senator do about the destruction of the tropical rain forest in Brazil? Or what should a U.S. conservation organization do about the same problem? Or what could a French businessman do about the proliferation of nuclear technology? Your advisee—your "prince," if you were Machiavelli—can be a neutral in a peace-making role or a party to the conflict. For a very few conflicts, the best choice for your advisee may be the U.S. president or secretary of state, but they personally only generate a few decisions in a few conflicts. Furthermore, they have hundreds of subordinates trying to grab their attention, and whole staffs to shield them from outsiders. Finally, these actors are not at all the optimum choice for exerting influence in many situations; they carry too much political and symbolic baggage. In picking your advisee (as in every other open-ended decision you make) it is a good idea to go through a conscious, two-stage procedure: (a) create a wide range of options (here, potential advisees); and then (b) select from among them.

5. *Identify some major actors on the "other" side.* Here the task is to collect a list of potential leaders or others in positions of power involved in the conflict who will be the ultimate target of influence. In a two-party conflict where "our prince" is on one side, the target of influence or "their prince" is likely to be the leader of what is probably easiest to call "the other side," such as Castro in Cuba, Hussein in Iraq, or Kim Jong-Il in North Korea. If we were seeking to slow the destruction of the tropical rain forest in Brazil, our prince might be a U.S. senator and their prince might be somebody in the Brazilian government or in the Brazilian development and construction industry. In a three-party situation where "we" are essentially neutral and trying to produce peace between two other parties, you will want to identify significant leaders within each of the two partisan factions. You may decide to work on only one party, or you may try to produce a step (such as an invitation to a conference) that might be acceptable to both simultaneously. In either event the task you face can be represented on p. 23.

The expectation is not that on completing this book you will have become a well-trained expert eligible for immediate appointment as foreign minister. (We have, however, known students who were already prepared to do a better job than some who have held responsible positions in the conduct of international relations.) Rather, the hope is that on completing this textbook you will have learned something and, just as important, will have

I diagnose a conflict, formulate advice, and transmit that advice in the form of a suggested action program to "our prince" (decision-maker on our side) often by means of an "entry point," someone with access to the decision-maker.

[*I take my ideas on the conflict in Northern Ireland and write them up into a short, persuasive memo, an "action program."*]

Entry Point is convinced of the merit of my action program, and he or she forwards the advice on to "our prince."

[*I mail my memo, along with a cover letter, to an aide of Senator Kerry and follow up with a phone call.*]

Our Prince receives the advice, and if he or she agrees with the recommendation, decides to implement the action program. The implementation of the action program results in presenting a new choice, however small, to "their prince" (a decision-maker on the other side).

[*Senator Kerry reads my memo along with his aide's recommendation that the action plan be implemented. He now has a new suggestion to present to the representatives of the British government, or a leading Irish educator or church leader in a position to take action.*]

Their Prince considers this new proposal, which, combined with other developments independent of us, changes the choice he sees himself as facing so that he can now say "yes" to a proposal he had previously been resisting.

[*The action program for experimental history textbooks in Northern Ireland, much modified by the hands it has been through, is now transmitted to local school boards in a position to do something about implementing it.*]

A Schematic View of Activist Thinking.[1]

learned how to learn more from each day's events. Because the problem we are trying to address is how we think about and deal with conflict generally—rather than what we know about specific conflicts—this book is not primarily concerned with transmitting large amounts of factual information. Instead it seeks to develop analytical skills for systematically bringing knowledge to bear on the practical question at the heart of any action program: "Who should do what tomorrow morning?" Equally important, it seeks to develop the capacity and enthusiasm to continue using and improving those skills in

---

[1]Roger Fisher, Elizabeth Kopelman, and Andrea Kupfer Schneider, *Beyond Machiavelli* (Cambridge, MA: Harvard University Press, 1994), p. 103.

the light of future experience. We hope that you will write to us and tell us about the results of the action program you designed by working with this material; we, too, seek to keep learning from experience.

SELECTING A PROBLEM FOR YOUR ACTION MEMORANDUM

Selecting a problem to work on can be a difficult task. The task will be easier if you do it in two stages: first, generate a list of options, and second, select from among them. Failure to have a number of options on the table increases the risk that one will spend a great deal of effort working in an area of low priority, or on a problem where there is no chance that one could make a useful contribution.

Generate a List of Options

Start by looking around the world and identifying some disliked symptoms—disliked in the sense that you can readily imagine the possibility of things being better. There are plenty of these in the world today. Take a current situation where bloodshed is a reality or a significant possibility, or take some other conflict situation where resources are being wasted or tensions are multiplying. You may want to consider government-to-government situations like those involving U.S. relations with the People's Republic of China, with Cuba, with Japan, with Vietnam, with North Korea, or with states in the former Soviet Union. Or you might select a potential or actual conflict that does not, strictly speaking, cross international borders such as those in Northern Ireland, Sri Lanka, or Cyprus. Or it might be a problem that by its very nature transcends national boundaries, such as overpopulation, global warming, drug trafficking, or starvation. Define the long-term problem, as you see it, by writing in the left-hand column of a piece of paper a description of the situation today, and in the right-hand column a description of the situation you would prefer.

Go through recent newspapers and magazines, listing under the following headings items that suggest problems on which you might be interested in working (you may want to put each heading on a separate sheet of blank paper):

> ***Wars and potential wars***—places where there is ongoing violence or a risk of violence
>
> ***Machinery for dealing with conflict***—institutions, such as international organizations and courts, that are less able to deal with conflicts than they might be
>
> ***Injustice***—a situation, like hunger, poverty, or the violation of human rights, that should be changed
>
> ***Machinery for dealing with injustice***—international or national institutions that should be improved

Other undesirable international situations—other situations that may not be overtly conflictual, such as environmental pollution, overfishing, economic waste, disease, harmful education by schools and the media, and so on

Leaders who are on the wrong track—individuals in government, industry, media, or elsewhere who have apparent power to ameliorate an international problem and who are not doing so

Choose from among Many Options

When you have a wide range of options on the table on which you might work, how do you pick a single problem on which to follow through? In intellectual efforts, as in practice with artillery, accurate aim is more important than the magnitude of the charge. You are likely to spend dozens of hours on a project. If you are successful, you will come up with a suggestion that deserves the attention of someone in a position to make a difference. Choose a problem promptly but not carelessly.

Generate some criteria for selection.   Think up a list of criteria by which to choose a particular problem. Illustrative criteria are

> How much do I care about this problem?
> How much does the subject interest me?
> How much information will I be able to find out about it?
> How likely am I to be able to make a constructive contribution, however small?

Roughly rank your criteria.   Some criteria will be more important to you than others. "Will I learn a lot?" may be more important than "Do I already know a lot about it?"

Narrow your choices to a few.   Look at each problem on your lists with your criteria in mind. Select several promising candidates directly or by process of elimination.

Formulate each of the choices.   What aspect of each problem would you work on? What is the symptom you would be trying to relieve? What would be a preferred situation?

Check on the availability of information.   Before analyzing a problem and advancing an idea worth considering, you will need to have factual information and analysis with which to work. It is not necessary that you become the world's expert on a subject in order to propose a worthwhile suggestion. Busy officials rarely have an opportunity to give sustained, systematic thought over a period of weeks to one aspect of any single problem, however serious that problem may be. There is often significant scope for outsiders to contribute something, but they will still need to know the facts. Remember the example of our former student writing about South Africa: her proposal was so successful precisely because she was so well acquainted with the conditions about which she was writing. Do some preliminary research in the library and with interested organizations to establish the availability of information on each problem. Before selecting as your problem "Who might do what to reduce the Tsetse fly problem in Uganda?" make sure that some information about that problem is available to you in the *New York Times* index, in the library, from the World Health Organization, from the Uganda mission to the United Nations, at a local medical school, among Ugandan students at your college or university, or elsewhere.

   Select a problem.   If necessary, reapply your criteria. Use a point system if it helps. Or flip a coin.

   Reformulate your objective.   As you focus on a given subject, sharpen your attention to the particular aspect of it on which you want to work. If you are looking at Beirut, and trying to think of ways that city could once again become a thriving center of international commerce and culture (it was once known as "the Paris of the Middle East"), are you primarily concerned with the economic inequities between rich and poor, with the lack of political power of moderate groups, or with ways of encouraging trade and investment?

   Select the kind of objective to which you wish to give priority. Keep clearly in mind the problem on which you are working. From time to time come back and check your bearings to make sure that the symptom you are working on is the one you want to cure.

CHAPTER
—3—

Case Study—
The Middle East

The history of Arab–Israeli conflict is a classic demonstration of the role played by partisan perceptions in international negotiations. The following is intended to provide the reader with a sense of how Arab (and especially Palestinian) and Israeli conflict is viewed by many partisans on each side. It also outlines one of the specific negotiation attempts made by Secretary of State Henry Kissinger after the Yom Kippur War of 1973. The case study concludes in 1977, prior to the Camp David accords. The case provides the background material necessary to understand the application of the tools in Chapters 4–6. The materials chosen for this case and cited in the bibliography are not reflective of a broad spectrum of opinion on the Middle East. Because the case study is designed to demonstrate partisan perceptions, the quotations and interpretations in this case study often reflect strong opinions from both sides in the conflict rather than those of a neutral observer.

BACKGROUND OF PALESTINIAN AND JEWISH CLAIMS

The differing views regarding who has the most pressing claim to the land known as Palestine is best summed up, from an Israeli perspective, by Frank Gervasi: "There is no greater falsehood in history than that the Arabs are the sole legitimate heirs to the lands of an Israel that once was Palestine and before was Canaan."[1] Gervasi's book continues with his interpretation of ancient

[1]From *The Case for Israel* by Frank Gervasi, p. 7. Copyright © 1967 by Frank Gervasi. Used by permission of Viking Penguin, a division of Penguin Books USA Inc.

history and his tracing of the roots established in this land so many generations ago: "Jewish history begins some four thousand years ago. . . . Their pa-
triarch was Abraham, forefather of the Hebrews through Isaac, his son by his
wife Sarah, and of the Arabs through Ishmael, his son by Hagar, Sarah's ser-
vant. Thus Arabs and Jews descend from and venerate a common ancestor."[2]

When the Jews were dispersed from their homeland in 137 A.D., they
vowed to return, and they tried to do so for close to two thousand years. While
they were gone, Palestine never became an actual homeland (in this sense) to
any other people because it was repeatedly occupied by external forces and
ruled from elsewhere. Each conqueror (there were fourteen in thirteen centuries) left behind slaves, servants, and soldiers, whose descendants shared
no common ethnic identity. While many of the Jews were longing to return to
the homeland, there were also a handful who stayed behind in Palestine, and
whose descendants can trace their residence back to ancient times.

On the other side of the conflict lie the Arab claims to this same land:
"Jews have lived in Palestine since Moses' time, but not until about 1010 B.C.
did a central Jewish government exist there. About that year David brought
all the feuding Jewish tribes together in a single kingdom of Israel, which en-
dured for seventy years until the death of Solomon. Thereafter no Jewish government ever again controlled all of Palestine until the establishment of modern Israel in A.D. 1948. Palestine has no history as a Jewish country."[3]
Further, many Arabs view the Jews who have come to settle Israel as Europeans, whose historical origin "is immaterial to the central issue that they
are European settlers in Arab lands. Their only connection with Palestine is
that it is the birthplace of their religion."[4]

This conflict, over who has the stronger claim to the land that is
called home by two different peoples, is at the heart of much of the turmoil in
the Middle East. The bitterness felt by both sides regarding their conflicting
claims can be seen in the fact that the Jews feel that the Arabs are trying to
expel them from the region, while the Arabs view the formation of Israel as "a
program of deliberate armed aggression against a people who had lived in
Palestine for thirteen centuries. That the guns were held by conscripted
British soldiers rather than Zionist immigrants is of no consequence except
as evidence of the overwhelming force arrayed against the Palestinians."[5]

Each group views the land as its home, and therefore feels completely
justified in its battles for it. Rabbi Moshe Levinger, who led the Jewish settlement of the Israeli-occupied West Bank, declared: "To compromise on our own
home, a home that belongs not only to us but also to God, is abnormal! . . . We
were expelled from this land against our will, but we always knew that it was

---

[2]Gervasi, pp. 8–9.

[3]Eugene M. Fisher and M. Cherif Bassiouni, *Storm Over the Arab World* (Chicago: Follett, 1972),
p. 12.

[4]Fisher and Bassiouni, p. 15.

[5]Fisher and Bassiouni, p. 24.

ours."[6] The Palestinian experience seems a striking parallel of the rabbi's words, in that many of the Palestinian refugees have expressed the same sentiments.

THE BEGINNINGS OF A JEWISH STATE

Jews began to realize their ancient goal of returning to the Holy Land in the nineteenth century, with the advent of Zionism. "The first wave of immigrants went to Palestine before the turn of the century. They were for the most part young idealists, many of them students, impelled by strong ideological motives to transform themselves into farmers and builders. . . . The newcomers settled on Palestine's sand dunes and swamps, linking up with fellow Jews who had been the stewards of uninterrupted Jewish settlement in the country for nearly two thousand years."[7] By 1914, Jews constituted twelve percent of the total population of Palestine.[8]

British sympathy for the Zionist cause was expressed in the Balfour Declaration of November 2, 1917: "His Majesty's Government view with favor the establishment of a national home for the Jewish people and will use its best endeavors to facilitate achievement of this object, it being clearly understood that nothing shall be done which may prejudice the civil and religious rights of existing non-Jewish communities in Palestine." Arabs too were, at this time, sympathetic to the Jewish national movement.[9] In 1919, the King of Iraq announced his acceptance of the Balfour Declaration, as chief of the Arab delegation to the Paris Peace Conference, and Palestine was awarded as a mandate by the League of Nations to Great Britain.

However, the British were too involved with the Arab states to honor their promises to aid the Jews in the acquisition of a homeland; the Arabs had oil and the Jews did not.[10] Therefore, the Jews expanded their own territory by purchasing land from Arab and Turkish landowners. From 1918 through 1920, Arabs regularly sold their land to Jews; much was desert or swampland when purchased.

While Arabs were selling Jews their land, and their support for the Zionist cause had been made known, "suddenly, in Palestine, in the spring of 1920, the Arab welcome to Zionists turned to hostility. Murder, rape, and pillage ravaged the Jewish quarter of Jerusalem, and the social, political, and economic life of thousands of Jews living in Oriental societies was placed in jeopardy."[11] These riots followed an immigration ordinance to allow 16,500

---

[6]Walter Reich, "A Stranger in My House," *Atlantic Monthly,* June 1984, p. 58.

[7]Gervasi, p. 22.

[8]*Israel: A Country Study,* ed. Helen Chapin Metz (Washington, D.C.: Library of Congress, 1990), p. 32.

[9]Gervasi, p. 25.

[10]Gervasi, p. 34.

[11]Gervasi, p. 38.

Jews into the country during 1921, which struck fear in the Arabs about the Jews taking over the country. According to the Haycraft Commission, which was established by the British to inquire into the riots, mostly political (fear of Zionism) and economic (views of Jews as exclusive in business dealings) factors were at the root of the riots of 1920–1921. Arab fears of Zionism were inspired during that time by proclamations such as the following, which appeared in the *Jewish Chronicle* on May 21, 1921: "The real key to the Palestine situation is to be found in giving to Jews as such those rights and privileges in Palestine which shall enable Jews to make it as Jewish as England is English, or as Canada is Canadian."[12] While the Haycraft Commission determined that the Arabs exhibited no inherent anti-Semitism at this time, one of the main instigators of the riots, discussed below, was one of the first anti-Semitic Arabs.

This man, largely responsible for the riots of 1920–1921 and the killings that accompanied them, as well as for the employment of anti-Semitism for political reasons in the Middle East, was Haj Amin el-Husseini. "In a very real sense, he invented genocide before Hitler, whose aide and counselor he later became."[13] In 1920, Haj Amin had been appointed spiritual leader of the Muslims in Jerusalem (part of Palestine) by the British, but he was using his position for political ends as well.

Although Haj Amin had many followers who were actively attempting to thwart the plans for a Jewish national homeland after these riots, he had little popular appeal. Palestine's Arabs reacted to Haj Amin with relative indifference, because all of them were benefiting by their associations with the Jews—from shopkeepers to landowners to peasants. Therefore, peace reigned for about eight years, from 1920 to 1928.

The second major outbreak of violence came in 1928, when violence between Jews and Arabs at the Western Wall of Jerusalem resulted in 133 Jewish and 116 Arab fatalities.[14] A year later, Haj Amin initiated a campaign appealing to the Palestinian Arabs' religious prejudices, which led to an attack on Jerusalem on August 23, 1929 by 15,000 Arabs. The Arabs were fought off, and the Jews remained.[15]

While Haj Amin's goal—a Middle East free of Jews—paralleled Hitler's, those Jews trapped in Europe were not allowed to enter Palestine during World War II. The British rulers of Palestine closed the primary and logical escape route from Hitler, and millions of Jews were killed. According to former Israeli Prime Minister Menachem Begin, this was all a part of the British plan to reduce the number of Jews who would seek admittance to the new Jewish state.[16] While the British support for a Jewish national homeland

---

[12]W. F. Abboushi, *The Unmaking of Palestine* (Brattleboro, VT: Amana Books, 1990), p. 20.

[13]Gervasi, p. 41.

[14]T. G. Fraser, *The Arab–Israeli Conflict* (New York: St. Martin's Press, 1995), p. 11.

[15]Gervasi, p. 47.

[16]Menachem Begin, *The Revolt* (New York: Nash Publishing Co., 1977), pp. 28–29.

seemed to wane during much of World War II, as witnessed in Churchill's policy of ignoring the question of a Jewish state, the British approach changed as more information about the Holocaust emerged. Although by the end of the war Churchill had declared himself a Zionist, England still refused to address the issue of a Jewish state until after the Allies had sat down to negotiate peace.[17]

THE CREATION OF ISRAEL

On November 29, 1947, the UN General Assembly voted 33–13 to approve the proposal of the United Nations Special Committee on Palestine to divide Palestine into Jewish and Arab states. Subsequently, on May 14, 1948, the British withdrew from Palestine and the Zionists declared the existence of the state of Israel. On that day, while Israeli Prime Minister David Ben-Gurion was on the radio thanking the United States for prompt recognition of his nation, a bomb was dropped on Tel Aviv by Egyptian aircraft, beginning the Israeli War of Independence. The Egyptian action came a mere six hours after Israel had come into existence, and the next day brought an invasion of the new country by five Arab nations—Egypt, Jordan, Syria, Iraq, and Lebanon. Two more Arab countries would join the alliance against Israel before the war ended.

Arabs labeled the war as a "holy war," but Jews and most Western nations viewed it as armed insurrection against a majority decision of the UN to offer equal self-determination to Arabs and Jews in their own lands. As Gervasi notes, the war "succeeded only in killing partition and, with it, self-determination for Palestine's Arabs."[18] From the Arab view, as espoused by Haj Amin and several other leaders, the primary goal of the war was extermination and elimination of the Jewish state. While the Arabs viewed this as a religious war, the Israelis saw it as a battle for their independence.

Future Prime Minister Golda Meir looked back on the Arab decision to attack Israel: "If the Arab states had accepted the United Nations Resolution and if they had urged the Arabs of Palestine to do likewise, instead of inciting them to fight in order to undo the resolution, there would have been no bloodshed and not a single refugee. The Jewish and Arab States in Palestine would have arisen in peace and cooperation and subsequent history would have been different."[19]

---

[17]Monty Noam Penkower, *The Holocaust and Israel Reborn* (Chicago: University of Illinois Press, 1994), pp. xi and xii.

[18]Gervasi, p. 82.

[19]Golda Meir, *A Land of Our Own* (London: Weidenfeld and Nicolson, 1973), p. 142.

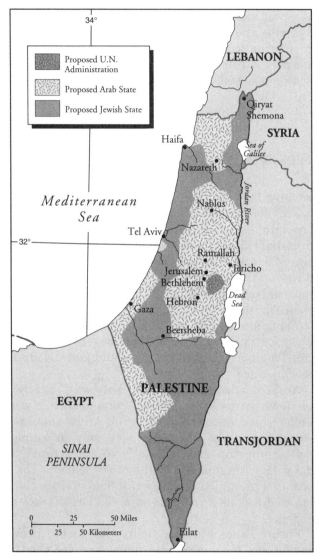

UN Partition Plan for Palestine.

On the other hand, from a Palestinian viewpoint:

The Palestinians on whose soil another national state was to be superimposed, whose destiny was consequently to undergo a devastating change,
were never consulted. In Palestine the initial response to Jewish immigration, particularly prior to the Balfour Declaration, was one of indifference; the
Arab world had in the past accepted settlement on its territory by foreign
peoples who wished to preserve their old language, culture, and traditions. . . .
However, when it became clear that the newly arrived Europeans were the
vanguard of a people that harbored intentions of being not just foreign set-

tlers, but foreign occupiers, the Zionists came face to face with spontaneous hostility from both the local population and the Arab world in general.[20]

ISRAELI VICTORY AND THE REFUGEE SITUATION

On January 7, 1949, Israel won the war, gaining 30 percent more territory. At the same time, 750,000 Arabs had fled from Israel to neighboring Arab states during the war.

There is disagreement as to the cause of this massive exodus. Many Israelis assert that "the Arab commanders had encouraged mass departures from towns and villages, promising that subsequent early victory would enable the Arab population to return and share the spoils of Jewish defeat. They were responsible for the uprooting of hundreds of thousands of their own people."[21] It has also been written that "the Arab exodus began before the State of Israel was proclaimed, and the Jewish population, the Haganah, and most particular the Jewish authorities did their utmost to prevent the mass flight."[22] Golda Meir seconds this appraisal of the situation:

> Every modern war creates a refugee problem. The responsibility, however, for the fact that Arabs became refugees must squarely lie with those who, instead of accepting the verdict of the United Nations, went to war to undo it and perpetrated the aggression of 15 May, 1948, against the state of Israel. Large numbers of the refugees left the country at the call of the Arab leaders, who told them to get out so that Arab armies could get in.[23]

In contrast, some Palestinians argue:

> The Irgun and the Hagana, two formidable and ruthless Zionist organizations, commenced a campaign of terror against isolated towns and villages. The purpose was to frighten as many Palestinians as possible into fleeing the country, thereby insuring a homogeneous Israel. In one operation alone, on April 9, 1948, a detachment of the Irgun attacked the small rural community of Deir Yassin and killed every man, woman, and child of its 254 inhabitants.[24]

Fawaz Turki also claims in his journal that it is a myth that the Arab governments urged Arabs to leave Israel; rather it was the Haganah that encouraged them to leave, as revealed later by studies of radio broadcasts. According to Turki, the Arab governments had appealed to the Palestinians "not to leave their homeland."[25]

---

[20]Fawaz Turki, *The Disinherited: The Journal of a Palestinian Exile* (New York: Monthly Review Press, 1972), p. 19. Copyright © 1972 by Fawaz Turki. Reprinted by permission of Monthly Review Foundation.

[21]Gervasi, p. 91.

[22]Gervasi, p. 91.

[23]Meir, p. 141.

[24]Turki, p. 20.

[25]Turki, p. 21.

There is even disagreement as to the situation in which the refugees have lived for the past few decades. Israelis assert:

> Every aspect of the problem has been distorted beyond recognition by the prisms of the Arabs' propaganda, which have magnified the numbers involved, exaggerated the miseries of refugee-camp life, and otherwise used the victims of their own aggression to mobilize public opinion against Israel.
>
> The Arab states have rejected every proposal by Israel—and by various international bodies—for absorption and rehabilitation of the former residents of Palestine, thereby ensuring continuance of conditions which can be exploited to advance the central objective of Arab policy—namely, destruction of Israel. Their refugees do not represent for the Arab states a human problem to be resolved at the earliest possible moment but a propaganda weapon to be preserved at all costs, regardless of the consequences to the people involved.[26]

One Arab statement, often quoted by Israelis, is that made by Mohammed Salah el Din Bin Bey in 1949, then foreign minister of Egypt: "In demanding the restoration of the refugees to Palestine, the Arabs intend that they return as masters . . . more explicitly: they intend to annihilate the state of Israel."[27] Such statements also affected the state of mind of the refugees, one of whom told an American reporter in Gaza: "We will stay here until we can fight again and take back our land."[28] Considering that such firm pronouncements were made by many refugees regarding their intentions, it was not surprising that Israel's repeated offers to absorb the refugees, or at least to negotiate directly with the Arabs about the issue, had been rejected by the Palestinians.

The first Palestinians to reenter Israel after the war of 1948–1949 were unarmed, yet "Israeli border patrols regularly killed Arabs who crossed the border, with the inevitable result that the Arabs themselves began to arm."[29] Many of these Arabs were returning to check on their properties, unaware that Israel had passed the Absentee Property Law seizing the homes and land of all Palestinians who had left their homes during the fighting of 1948. Under this law, the Israeli government gave the confiscated Palestinian property to new Jewish immigrants.

Only 12 percent of the original Palestinian population remained in Israel. They were placed under the control of the military, even though they had not taken arms against Israel or against the Arabs in 1948. "They were reduced to second-class citizenship status and discriminated against on every level. Occasional acts of violence against them did not stop with the cessation of hostilities in 1948 but continued up to 1967, when they acquired a more sinister and horrifying nature."[30]

---

[26]Gervasi, p. 110.

[27]Gervasi, p. 115.

[28]*id.*

[29]Fraser, p. 63.

[30]Turki, p. 45.

Israel 1948.

Such treatment and dislocation caused anger among many of the Palestinians. One summarized his feelings as a Palestinian as: "I hated. I hated the world and the order of reality around me. I hated being dispossessed of a nation and an identity. I hated being the victim of social and political Darwinism. I hated not being part of a culture. . . . And the world hated me because I hated."[31] Basically, "the Palestinian problem has never been to

---

[31]Turki, p. 77.

the Palestinian people a crisis, a crisis of political intent, but a tragedy, a tragedy they lived every day of their lives."[32]

THE 1967 (SIX-DAY) WAR

The refugee situation grew worse after the 1967 war. In only six days, Israel conquered East Jerusalem, the West Bank, Gaza, the Golan Heights, and the Sinai Desert, displacing many more Arabs. On May 14, 1967, two Egyptian armored divisions entered the Sinai, and were matched by an Israeli tank brigade.[33] In response to Egyptian leader Gamal Abdel Nasser's request for the removal of the UN peacekeeping forces from his country on May 19, and his simultaneous blockade of one of Israel's key shipping routes, the Israeli government ordered full mobilization on May 20.[34]

On June 5, 1967, Israel attacked Egyptian airfields at 7:45 A.M., crossing the Egyptian border on the ground approximately 30 minutes later. By that afternoon, Israeli forces had also destroyed the Jordanian air force and two thirds of Syria's air power. On June 7, Israel took the Old City of Jerusalem, and by noon of the next day, it had won most of the Gaza Strip. On June 8, a UN-sponsored cease-fire began on the Egyptian front, and Israel declared a unilateral cease-fire on the Jordanian front the following day. On June 9, Israel battled Syria for the Golan Heights and won. All fighting had ceased by June 10, and two days later, Israeli Prime Minister Levi Eshkol announced that he would not withdraw from the captured territories unless such an agreement was part of a comprehensive peace treaty negotiated in direct face-to-face talks.

After the Six-Day War, Israel maintained an occupying force in the Gaza Strip and the West Bank of the Jordan with a "policy of minimal interference in the internal civilian affairs of the area."[35] After Arabs accused the Israelis of expelling the residents of these areas, Israel announced on July 2, 1967 that it would permit former residents of the West Bank to return if they so desired and could prove previous residence. On November 22, 1967, the UN Security Council passed Resolution 242, calling for withdrawal of Israeli forces from the territories which they occupied during the Six-Day War and for a settlement of the Palestinian refugee problem, as well as recognition of Israeli sovereignty. While "the plight of the Arab refugees weighs heavily on Israeli minds, for they are a compassionate people, knowing better than most what it means to be unwanted and stateless," the Israeli forces stayed in the occupied territories.[36] From the Palestinian perspective: "If, as Zionists claim,

---

[32]Turki, p. 77.

[33]Fraser, p. 82.

[34]Fraser, p. 83.

[35]Gervasi, p. 122.

[36]Gervasi, p. 125.

Israel after the 1967 War.

the Jews of the earth nourished a dream of a reconstituted Israel in Palestine through eighteen hundred years, is it not unrealistic to believe that Palestinian Arabs would abandon hope for a return to their own land just beyond a river bank or just across an imaginary line?"[37]

THE YOM KIPPUR WAR

In early October of 1973, reports were filtering into Israel of an imminent Arab attack. However, unlike its actions during the Six-Day War, Israel decided this time not to initiate a preemptive strike, because it wanted American support and thought it needed to be seen as a victim of aggression to re-

---

[37] Fisher and Bassiouni, p. 51.

ceive it.[38] The reports of an attack proved true on October 6, when Egypt attacked across the Suez Canal. During the course of the war, Israel repelled this attack and a simultaneous one from Syria across the Golan Heights on the Jewish holy day of Yom Kippur (hence the name of the war). From October 9 through October 11, Israeli forces pushed the Syrians back to the cease-fire line throughout most of the Golan Heights. On October 14, a renewed Egyptian offensive on the Sinai front failed after twenty-four hours of fierce fighting. On October 22, the Golan Heights operation ended when Israel seized the last Syrian position (Mount Hermon), and at 6:30 that evening, cease-fires were effected on both the Golan and Sinai fronts.

After this war, U.S. Secretary of State Henry Kissinger acted as a mediator in the Middle East. On January 18, 1974, the Egyptian and Israeli chiefs of staff signed an agreement arrived at through Kissinger's shuttle diplomacy between Cairo and Jerusalem, marking the first step in Israel's withdrawal from the territories it occupied in 1967. This agreement outlined disengagement from both the Suez and Sinai, allowing for a buffer zone between the land occupied by each country, with limited-force zones bordering the buffer. Egypt also received from Israel a piece of land on the east bank of the Suez that it had not held prior to the Yom Kippur War.

This war had removed the last shred of trust Golda Meir had in the Arabs; therefore she entered the subsequent Syrian–Israeli negotiations enmeshed in complete suspicion. While Kissinger traveled back and forth between the two countries for a second round of shuttle diplomacy, Syria's demands and Israeli offers seemed to grow farther apart, rather than nearer to one another. The first Israeli offer, extended on May 3, 1974, was disengagement of its forces to a line that was actually on the Syrian side of the pre–Yom Kippur lines. President Assad viewed this offer as an insult. Two days later, Israeli officials told Kissinger that they would be willing to give Assad the eastern part of El Quneitra, a city that had been devastated during the war but had once been a vital area. The same day the Israelis were making this offer, Assad was making his demand for the whole city of El Quneitra, and the three strategic hills to the west of it as well. On May 6, the Israeli government made an official proposition, again including their retreat from the eastern part of the city. In addition, Israel proposed dividing the city into three zones, the western to be occupied by Israel, the middle by Israel and the UN, and the eastern by Syria and the UN, with a two-to-three-kilometer UN buffer zone. On May 8, Assad responded that partition of the city in such a way was out of the question, because it would prevent him from effectively repopulating the area.

A few days later, Syria increased its demands to include all of El Quneitra, the hills and three deserted villages in the south of Golan and one in the north. Assad presented these demands in the form of an ultimatum, asserting that he refused to discuss any other aspects of disengagement before

---

[38]Fraser, p. 99.

these demands were met. Therefore, Kissinger set a deadline of May 14, 1974 for agreement, after which he would return to Washington if one had not been reached. This was two weeks after discussions with the two countries had begun. On hearing that the Israelis had not accepted his ultimatum and that Kissinger was ready to go home, President Assad softened his demands, and agreement was reached on May 29, 1974. This agreement marked the first time that there had been a break in shooting on the Golan Heights since the war had broken out on October 6, 1973.

THE CREATION OF A PALESTINIAN STATE

The creation of a Palestinian state has often been viewed as the most pressing of questions in the Middle East since the 1967 war. However, from the Israeli perspective, this imposed an unfair burden. Israel first began to distrust the international community, and especially the UN, regarding this topic when the General Assembly passed Resolution 3379, declaring that Zionism is racism, on November 10, 1975. Two years later, on October 26, 1977, Israeli Chaim Herzog addressed the same body regarding the much-debated question of a Palestinian state. Jordan had control over the West Bank until 1967, he argued, "but they did not permit the establishment of a Palestinian State because then, as now, they did not want one. Jordan saw itself to be the Palestinian State, which in all honesty it is. They formed the P.L.O. in 1964. Why? They were in control of the West Bank and Gaza and could have established a P.L.O. controlled Palestinian State." He concluded by asserting that the reason they did not was because the issue was actually one of eradicating the Jews from the Arab Middle East.

"However incoherently and conditionally, leaders of the Palestine Liberation Organization and most of their followers came to accept the idea of a miniature Palestine that would be built on the Israeli-occupied West Bank of the River Jordan and the Gaza Strip."[39] An American-educated Palestinian, Rashid Khalidy, claimed that Palestinian anger could be neutralized by the Israelis if they would relinquish the West Bank, which the Israelis captured from Jordan in 1967.[40] Along these lines, the PLO, as leaders of the Palestinians, started to mobilize for independence in the 1970s.

In 1978, an Israeli Arab, Rayek Jarjoura, who was deputy mayor of Nazareth, acknowledged that the Arabs made a mistake in not accepting the 1947 UN resolution to create two states, one Arab and one Jewish. However, he continued, "I'm afraid the Jewish leadership is making the same mistake of the Arab leadership of 1948. They are refusing to recognize the right of the Palestinian Arabs to a state. This will lead to more bloodshed."[41]

---

[39]James M. Markham, "A People Scattered, Bewildered and Divided," *New York Times,* 19 February 1978, A5.

[40]Markham.

[41]Markham.

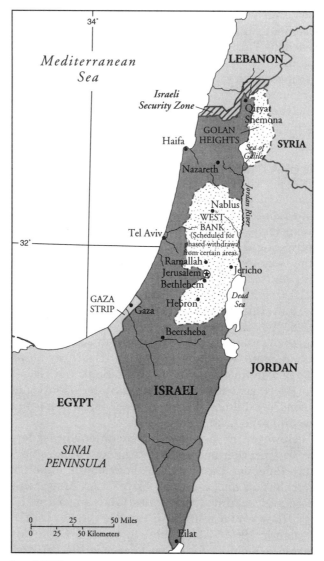

Israel 1996.

The next phase in Middle East negotiations began with the turning point in 1977 of Egyptian President Anwar Sadat's visit to Jerusalem, during which he offered "peace with justice" and called for the return of the occupied territories. This visit caused Israeli Prime Minister Menachem Begin to join Sadat in his pledge that there would be "no more war." From this initial cooperation arose the possibility of peace talks, which began the following year at Camp David with the assistance of U.S. President Jimmy Carter as mediator.

CHRONOLOGY OF MIDDLE EAST CONFLICT AND NEGOTIATIONS

1947   **November 29**—UN General Assembly votes to establish two separate states within Palestine—one Jewish, one Arab. Arab states reject the proposal.

1948   **May 14**—Great Britain withdraws from Palestine and the state of Israel is proclaimed, occupying 5,500 square miles granted to it by the UN.

May 15—Five Arab states invade Israel.

1949   **January 7**—War ends, with Israel gaining 30 percent more territory and 750,000 Arab refugees fleeing to neighboring Arab states. Jordan annexes the West Bank.

1955   **February 28**—Defense Minister Ben-Gurion initiates raid on the Gaza Strip to demonstrate Israel's military power.

1956   **July 26**—Egyptian leader Gamal Abdel Nasser nationalizes the Suez Canal, ending Israeli access, and simultaneously threatens Israel repeatedly.

October 26—Israeli armies invade the Sinai Peninsula of Egypt, not pulling out until a year later when a UN force is installed to guard the Egyptian–Israeli border.

November—Israel nominally regains access to the Suez when it agrees to a cease-fire with Egypt.

1957   **January**—UN helps clear the Suez of wrecked Egyptian ships, so that passage may resume.

1967   **May 19**—Egypt convinces the UN to withdraw its force from the Sinai and then moves troops to the Israeli border, while simultaneously blockading one of Israel's key shipping routes, the Gulf of Aqaba.

June 5–10—Israel fears attack by Egyptian forces, so decides to attack first, seizing the Sinai Peninsula, Syria's Golan Heights, and the West Bank, including East Jerusalem, within six days.

November 22—The UN Security Council passes Resolution 242, calling for the withdrawal of Israeli forces from territories occupied during the Six-Day War and a settlement of the Palestinian refugee problem, as well as recognition of Israeli sovereignty. However, Israeli troops remain in the occupied territories and no Arab nation recognizes Israel.

1973   **October 6**—Egypt attacks across the Suez Canal on Yom Kippur, while Syrian troops attack across the Golan Heights. Israeli counterattacks drive across the Suez into Egypt and within 20 miles of Damascus in Syria. Oil-producing states cut off exports to those countries supporting Israel, and oil prices quadruple.

November 11—After heavy losses on both sides, U.S. Secretary of State Henry Kissinger negotiates a cease-fire.

1974   **January 18**—Israel and Egypt sign agreement on Suez and Sinai disengagement, a product of Kissinger's "shuttle diplomacy."

May 31—More shuttle diplomacy results in the signing of a disengagement agreement by Syria and Israel regarding the Golan Heights.

September 4—Israel and Egypt sign a second Sinai disengagement agreement, after prodding by Kissinger.

November 22—The UN General Assembly passes a resolution recognizing Palestinian rights to self-determination, national independence and sovereignty.

1975   **November 10**—The UN General Assembly passes Resolution 3379, declaring that Zionism is a form of racism (the vote is 72 for, 35 against, and 32 abstentions).

1977   **November 19–21**—Egyptian President Anwar Sadat visits Jerusalem, offering "peace with justice" and calling for the return of occupied territories. Sadat and Israeli Prime Minister Menachem Begin pledge "no more war."

   December 5—Syria, Libya, Algeria, Southern Yemen, Iraq, and the PLO form an Arab bloc opposing Sadat's peace efforts. Sadat vows to negotiate with Israel alone if others will not join him.

   December 16—Begin tells U.S. President Jimmy Carter in Washington, D.C., that Israel is willing to give Egypt the Sinai Peninsula and give Palestinians control over their internal affairs in the West Bank and Gaza Strip, but the Israeli army would remain for security reasons.

   December 25–26—Begin and Sadat meet in Egypt and decide to continue negotiations through two committees. The first would be military, to deal with the Sinai, and the second political, to deal with the Palestinians.

1978   **February 3**—Presidents Carter and Sadat meet to discuss Mideast peace talks.

   March 11—Group of Palestinians based in Lebanon land on Israeli coast and kill 35 people in two buses.

   March 14—In response to increased terrorism, Israeli army begins major offensive into southern Lebanon and occupies land south of the Litani River, killing hundreds. Carter fears that Israel plans to annex the area, and he denounces the invasion as an overreaction and threatens to cut off military aid; Israel withdraws.

   August 5—U.S. Secretary of State Cyrus Vance visits the Middle East in an attempt to rejuvenate the stumbling peace talks.

   August 8—Begin and Sadat agree to meet with Carter at Camp David.

   September 5—Camp David summit begins.

   September 17—Camp David accords are signed by Sadat and Begin, allowing for normal relations between the two countries in exchange for full evacuation by Israel from the Sinai. Talks continue until a peace treaty is concluded in March 1979.

   September 20—Jordan announces that it is not bound by the Camp David accords; Syria and Saudi Arabia also condemn agreement, and Palestinians view it as an abandonment of their cause by Egypt.

   October 26—Syria and Iraq sign a National Charter for Joint Action in the fight against Israel.

   October 27—Begin and Sadat are awarded the Nobel Peace Prize; Israeli–Egyptian peace negotiations resume.

1979   **March 26**—Peace treaty is signed by Begin and Sadat, marking the first time since 1948 that Israel is at peace with one of its neighbors.

1981   **July**—Cease-fire in southern Lebanon between Israel and Lebanon arranged by U.S.

1982   **April 25**—Israel's Camp David promise to withdraw from the Sinai is fulfilled.

   June 3—Israel's ambassador to London, Shlomo Argov, is shot and seriously wounded by Palestinians.

June 6—The shooting of Argov is cited as a reason to invade Lebanon, and a full-scale invasion called "Operation Peace for Galilee" begins. Declared purpose of the operation is to create a security zone in southern Lebanon by driving the Palestinians away from the border and out of their refugee camps.

June 10—Israeli forces near Beirut, control approaches from the west and south. Assault begins on western Beirut. This becomes the first war waged by Israel in which public support within Israel wanes.

August 12—President Reagan demands that Israeli Prime Minister Begin end the "needless destruction and bloodshed"; cease-fire comes into operation later that day. Many Palestinians are evacuated from Lebanon under the protection of a multinational force that includes France, Italy, and the U.S.

September 1—President Reagan announces his peace plan, which asserts that only self-government by the Palestinians of the West Bank and Gaza could lead to a lasting peace. Prime Minister Begin rejects the plan, because of his hopes for further Jewish settlement of the West Bank.

September 14—Israeli-supported Phalangist leader in Lebanon, Bashir Gemayel, is assassinated.

September 16—Phalangist forces are allowed to "help" Israel find terrorists. However, recent civil war there left many hostilities, and the Phalangists enter two refugee camps on this evening, killing hundreds of defenseless people over the next two days. Several days later, Israeli troops leave west Beirut, and Israel is on the political and military defensive, as nations around the world target them with their outrage over the massacre.

Late September—Israeli forces replaced by Multinational Force.

1983   **May 17**—Israel and Lebanon sign an interim peace treaty, which Lebanon is pressured to renounce the following year by its fellow Arab countries.

October 23—U.S. Marine barracks in Beirut, Lebanon destroyed by car bomb. One hundred and twenty U.S. Marines killed.

1985   Israeli troops are finally withdrawn from most of Lebanon.

1987   **December 8**—Marking the twentieth anniversary of the Six-Day War in which they had been occupied, major violence breaks out in the administered territories for the first time since 1981. The *intifada* is sparked by a crash between an Israeli army vehicle and a truck filled with Palestinian workers in the Gaza Strip that caused four deaths.

1991   **October 30**—Peace conference convenes in Madrid under joint presidency of Bush and Gorbachev. Israel sits down to face-to-face negotiations with Syria and Lebanon, and accepts a joint Palestinian–Jordanian delegation.

1993   **September 9**—Arafat and Rabin exchange letters, marking the historic inception of an attempt to arrive at agreement. Arafat's letter asserts that the PLO recognizes Israel's right "to exist in peace and security," and rejects terrorism. He also writes a separate letter to Palestinian leaders in the occupied territories, calling off the *intifada*. Rabin's reply acknowledges the PLO as "the representative of the Palestinian people."

September 13—Agreement is signed by Rabin and Arafat at the White House, calling for the withdrawal of Israeli troops and administration from the West Bank and Gaza and subsequent elections for a Palestinian Council to run the areas for five years, while Israel and the PLO negotiate a final agreement.

1994   **Late March**—Israeli army and administration begins its withdrawal from Gaza.

October 26—Jordan and Israel sign a peace treaty.

BIBLIOGRAPHY

ABBOUSHI, W. F. *The Unmaking of Palestine*. Brattleboro, VT: Amana Books, 1990.

COBBAN, HELENA. *The Palestinian Liberation Organization*. New York: Cambridge University Press, 1985.

EDELHEIT, HERSHEL, AND ABRAHAM J. EDELHEIT. *Israel and the Jewish World, 1948–1993: A Chronology*. Westport, CT: Greenwood Press, 1995.

FISHER, EUGENE M., AND M. CHERIF BASSIOUNI. *Storm Over the Arab World*. Chicago: Follett, 1972.

FRASER, T. G. *The Arab–Israeli Conflict*. New York: St. Martin's Press, 1995.

GERVASI, FRANK. *The Case for Israel*. New York: Viking Press, 1967.

LANCASTER, JOHN, AND BARTON GELLMAN. "For Old Mideast Foes, Public Peace Cloaks Personal Enmity," *New York Times,* 27 February 1996: A1+.

MARKHAM, JAMES M. "A People Scattered, Bewildered and Divided," *New York Times*, 19 February 1978: A5.

MEIR, GOLDA. *A Land of Our Own*. London: Weidenfeld and Nicolson, 1973.

METZ, HELEN CHAPIN, ed. *Israel: A Country Study*. Washington, D.C.: Library of Congress, 1990.

MORRIS, BENNY. *The Birth of the Palestinian Refugee Problem, 1947–1949*. New York: Cambridge University Press, 1989.

PENKOWER, MONTY NOAM. *The Holocaust and Israel Reborn*. Chicago: University of Illinois Press, 1994.

REICH, WALTER. "A Stranger in My House," *Atlantic Monthly,* June 1984: 54–62+.

SACHAR, HOWARD M. *A History of Israel: From the Rise of Zionism to Our Time*. New York: Alfred A. Knopf, 1979.

TURKI, FAWAZ. *The Disinherited: Journal of a Palestinian Exile*. New York: Monthly Review Press, 1972.

CHAPTER
4

Understanding Partisan Perceptions

In a seminar at the State Department's Foreign Service Institute, a participating colonel seriously questioned the desirability of looking at a conflict from the point of view of one's adversary. He pointed out that to understand how our adversary saw things might cause us to question the merits of what we were doing or proposed to do. "The better we understand their concerns and their ideas," he said, "the greater the chance that we will lose confidence in the rightness of our own cause." Take an example at the moral margin: What if you were dealing with Hitler and the Nazis? As a negotiator or advisor, would you really want to understand the Nazi point of view?[1]

Yes. To "understand" does not mean to reach an understanding or accommodation with someone else. The important meaning of "understand" in this context is "to comprehend"—"comprehend" rather than "buy into"; to get a snapshot of what is inside their heads. This is like having a road map of the territory you want to invade—a clearer view of a target, a better appreciation of a mind you would like to change. This kind of understanding strengthens us, even if our ultimate goal is to overcome the other side by force of arms.

The colonel who did not want to understand the other side had a point, even if we disagree with his conclusion not to seek out others' perspectives on a conflict. The more we learn about others' concerns, the more likely we are to change our own minds and the more likely we are to revise our thinking. Opinions, after all, are based on data, and new data may have an

---

[1]Roger Fisher, Elizabeth Kopelman, and Andrea Kupfer Schneider, *Beyond Machiavelli* (Cambridge, MA: Harvard University Press, 1994), p. 19.

impact on the opinion that we formed before we learned this new information. We may in fact conclude that the cause for which we have been pressing is misconceived or that we have been misguided. While such an outcome would have been inconceivable in the case of Nazi Germany, it might have been a good outcome for U.S. decision-makers in Vietnam. Rethinking our policy may well be a benefit rather than a cost of understanding an adversary's point of view. With greater knowledge we might reduce the area of conflict and increase the chance of advancing our newly enlightened self-interest.

In any event, understanding how the parties see a conflict is invaluable when trying to influence them. In the end, the parties' perceptions—of history, the current situation, the various courses of action open to them and the relative attractiveness of those options—are the problem. If we and they saw everything the same way, there would be little to study in international relations. There would be no differences, no disputes, no conflicts, no wars. There would be little need for international agreements.

THE LIMITS OF FACTS AS WE SEE THEM

In attempts to understand or resolve a conflict, outside observers often value what they perceive as facts more than they value the understanding of those facts from the perspective of the parties to the conflict. Consider some archetypical conflicts. Neighboring countries may dispute water rights along a bordering river. An oil tanker of one country breaks loose from its mooring while in another country, causing an environmental crisis. Israel and Syria each continue to make territorial claims on the Golan Heights. Iran and Iraq contest who initiated hostilities in the Iran–Iraq war. In such circumstances third parties tend to assume that what they need to know are the facts. They study the river's watershed or establish the manufacturer of the mooring line. They study the Golan Heights or the history of religious wars between Muslim nations.

But in each situation, the key aspects of the dispute are determined by what is going on in the heads of the parties, not by some objective set of facts. Facts, even if established, may do nothing to reduce the conflict. Both parties may agree that half of a river's watershed lies in one country and half in the other, but still dispute who should have primary rights to the river's water. Both parties may agree to all the facts surrounding the ship accident, but still not agree on which party should pay for the cleanup. The detailed history and geography of the Golan Heights, no matter how carefully studied and documented, is not the stuff with which one puts to rest a territorial dispute. No study of what happened in disputes among Muslim nations will resolve issues of justification and grievance, nor put to rest the conflict between Iran and Iraq. What an outside observer experiences as objective reality is unlikely either to constitute the problem or to provide a solution.

Persuading parties to a conflict that the facts are one way rather than another becomes one more argument—perhaps a good one, perhaps not—for dealing with a difference. The difference itself exists in their heads. We as objective, outside observers may think that there is no basis for believing that an invasion of a particular country would be likely by another, or that, if it were attempted, it would be successful. However, the fears of the citizens of a threatened country, even if ill-founded, are real fears and need to be dealt with. The hopes of the leaders of a country considering military action, even if unrealistic, may cause a war.

It may even be easier to reach a peaceful settlement if the parties do not see things the same way, but rather see them differently. For example, if an owner of shares listed on the Mexican stock exchange thinks that Latin American stocks are high (and are likely to go down), and a potential buyer thinks that stocks in emerging markets are low (and are likely to go up), no broker who wants to promote a sales agreement will seek to have the two parties agree on the market forecast for Mexico. The potential for agreement lies in the parties' different perceptions of the present and their different expectations of what will happen in the future.

In the simplest terms, if we have a conflict with somebody else it is because he or she is doing, failing to do, or proposing to do something contrary to our preference. From our point of view, we would like them to change their minds. The starting point of any such effort is to find out where their minds are now. We are more likely to be able to change someone's thinking if we understand what that thinking is.

UNDERSTANDING A CONFLICT FROM MANY POINTS OF VIEW

Skilled negotiators or helpful advisors will benefit from the development of techniques that allow them to better analyze information from their own perspective. They will also need to develop the skill of being able to put themselves in the shoes of other parties to see how a situation looks from their perspectives. Looking at a conflict from our own perspective (or from the perspective of a party with whom we are aligned) we call the "First Position"; looking at it from the perspective of another party to a conflict we call the "Second Position." In a multilateral situation, negotiators will need to give separate consideration to each significant party. Furthermore, whether or not a negotiator or advisor is aligned with a particular party in a conflict, that person will generate a more useful analysis if he or she also cultivates the skill of seeing things from the perspective of a neutral third party, the "Third Position."

In this chapter, we consider what parties might want to know about other parties to a conflict and how they can think about a conflict from their multiple perspectives. We will first examine methods for a negotiator or outside party to test his or her own assumptions about a conflict (the First Position). We will then develop methods for one party, whether acting for himself or herself or in a third-party role, to put himself or herself in someone else's shoes (the Second Position). This skill can be applied in an infinite number of situations and can help find underlying interests of the parties to the conflict that might turn out to be overlapping or complementary. Second Position analysis will continue in Chapter 5, which examines the specific message that parties to a conflict may be hearing, and the specific choices that they see themselves as facing. Section III of the book, Chapters 7–11, presents the diagnoses and development of approaches to international conflict from the perspective of a third party (the Third Position). The ultimate goal is to be able more fully to understand the reasons a conflict may not be moving toward resolution, and to develop directions for action that might prove more fruitful by moving quickly and easily among all three positions.

FIRST POSITION: OUR OWN ASSUMPTIONS ABOUT A CONFLICT

It is surprisingly difficult to internalize multiple points of view of a conflict. This is especially true if the negotiator or advisor attempting the analysis is closely aligned with one or another side of a conflict. An Englishman raised on BBC broadcasts will tend to see Sinn Fein as merely the front for a terrorist organization, whether or not he thinks it is appropriate to negotiate with the political arm of the IRA in the interests of peace. He may find it hard to accept that many Irish nationalists draw a sharp distinction between the asserted right to attack British military targets during a civil war, as long defended by Sinn Fein, and the attacks on civilian targets by certain factions of the IRA, which are decried as indefensible by virtually all parties in Ireland. An Israeli active in the Peace Now movement may remember only the bold and courageous meeting of Prime Minister Begin with President Anwar Sadat of Egypt. She may not understand that many Palestinians continue to remember Begin primarily as a political operative who used terrorist means to force the British to abandon their protectorate in Palestine. In the words of a Russian proverb, we all see the world from the bell tower of our own village.

These core assumptions that negotiators and advisors bring with them limit their ability to understand the other parties to a conflict, to generate ideas that may move a conflict toward resolution, and to present persuasively ideas for action to a decision-maker on one side of the conflict or another. Our Englishman may fail to see ways in which Sinn Fein might be engaged to censure civilian bombings as violations of the laws of war; our Peace Now activist may undermine an otherwise tenable proposal for peaceful cooperation by invoking the name of Prime Minister Begin. We as analysts and potential advisors should accept that we also bring initial perceptions and assumptions to the table.

One way for a negotiator, analyst, or advisor to open his or her own mind to alternative assumptions about a conflict is by using the Assumptions/Data Tool shown in Chart 4–1.

The tool begins in the upper left quadrant by asking about a party's own assumptions. For example, an advisor aligned with the Russians who wanted to test his own assumptions about conflict with the United States might note an initial assumption that the U.S. was trying to isolate Russia

CHART 4–1
Assumptions/Data Tool

Case: _____
Date: _____

A. Assumptions	B. Base Data
What are my core assumptions about the conflict?	*On what data do I base my assumptions?*
D. Alternative Assumptions	**C. Nonconforming Data**
Taking the additional data into account, what might some alternative conclusions about the conflict be?	*What additional data might be taken into account that may be inconsistent with my core assumptions?*

and keep it economically weak. The tool then moves our advisor to the upper right quadrant to catalogue the data on which these assumptions are based. This could include, for example, the fact that NATO might permit Eastern European countries to join NATO in the future and eliminate the historic buffer zone Russia had created for itself. The more specifically one can identify the data on which the assumption is based, the more useful the tool will prove.

By moving to the lower right quadrant, the tool invites the advisor to seek out nonconforming data—that is, experiences or statements that do not necessarily support and that may even contradict the initial assumption. In negotiations and interactions with others, parties commonly filter out information that does not agree with their previously held assumptions. Thus, once a party reaches a conclusion about a situation, he or she may ignore new information that may not support that conclusion. Assumptions become even more one-sided as the party notices only information that supports the initial conclusion. By actively soliciting nonconforming data, through research and discussions with knowledgeable sources, a party forces himself or herself to look beyond prefabricated assumptions, and to question them. In this example, the Russian negotiator or advisor might recall NATO's success at maintaining peace in Europe for the last forty years or the fact that NATO has also been effective at reducing intramember conflict.

Moving to the lower left quadrant, the advisor may use the data in the right quadrants to consider assumptions different from those originally captured. Based on the totality of information, he might conclude that the United States is interested in using NATO to maintain stability among the Central and Eastern European countries. Chart 4–2 is completed using the example we have just used.

To the extent that you the student are beginning your analysis of an international conflict, it is perhaps important to note that we are asking you to challenge and broaden your initial assumptions, not to abandon them. In the example above, the conclusion that the United States wants to use NATO to maintain stability is not necessarily incongruent with the assumption that the United States may also be interested in isolating Russia. It could lead us, however, toward a more productive understanding of the conflict as a whole.

CHART 4–2
Assumptions/Data Tool

Case: _Russia–U.S. & NATO_
Date: _1996_

A. Assumptions	B. Base Data
The U.S. is trying to keep us weak and to isolate us from our neighbors.	*The U.S. has encouraged Central and Eastern European countries to join the Partnership for Peace, a precursor to joining NATO.*
D. Alternative Assumptions	**C. Nonconforming Data**
The U.S. wants NATO to expand its success at reducing conflict and maintaining stability in Europe.	*NATO has been successful at maintaining peace for the last forty years.* *NATO is good at reducing intramember conflict, i.e. Greece & Turkey.*

Just as you might advise a party to a conflict to begin by cataloguing and exploring his or her own assumptions, we invite you to challenge your own.

We should also underline that the tools presented in this book are by and large meaningless unless accompanied by honest research and serious reflection. The lessons of history, traditional academic research and theory, as well as structured discussions with advisors and colleagues—using the Assumptions/Data Tool as a jumping-off point, for example—will provide the substantive content for further analysis and generation of new ideas.

SECOND POSITION: HOW OTHER PARTIES PERCEIVE A CONFLICT

In diagnosing adversarial parties to an international conflict, as with diagnosing patients who come into a doctor's office, negotiators and their advisors will first want to know what is bothering the parties, and what those parties want to see resolved. Therefore, as you begin your efforts to understand what is on the minds of the parties to a conflict, you will want to make fairly open-ended inquiries from the Second Position:

(a) What the parties see—partisan perceptions;
(b) Why they see it that way—emotions and motives; and
(c) What underlies the parties' positions—their interests.

What the Parties See: Partisan Perceptions

When we are trying to understand the perceptions of the other side, it is often wise to start off in the Second Position—putting ourselves in the other side's shoes and coming up with our best estimate of what they would consider to be most important about the conflict, about themselves, and about us. Each party to a conflict is certain to have a different estimate of what issues are most important, and differing perceptions of the relevant history, of current facts, of their own grievances, and of the goals and intentions of all parties to the conflict. Whether a negotiator is himself or herself a party to a conflict, or whether that negotiator is dealing with a conflict between two other parties, he or she will benefit from illuminating and contrasting differing perceptions in a simple and dramatic form. Chart 4–3 illustrates a simple tool for doing this. It lists in parallel columns on a single page one party's perceptions of the issues in a conflict along with the perceptions of an opposing party. The example listed (contrasting Syrian and Israeli perceptions in early 1975) was prepared by a third party putting himself in the shoes of each side in turn and articulating his best estimate of what their voices would be. A basic structure for this approach is illustrated in Chart 4–4, where we fill in the perceptions of one side and then fill in the opposite column with the other side's perceptions on those same points. Chart 4–5 gives an example from the Cuban Missile Crisis.

CHART 4–3
PARTISAN PERCEPTION TOOL[2]

Case: _Golan Heights_
As of: _Early 1975_

SOME SYRIAN PERCEPTIONS	SOME ISRAELI PERCEPTIONS

Syria is an underdeveloped country that wants and needs peace.

The Golan is part of Syria and must be returned; if Israel wants us to respect its sovereignty, it must respect ours.

Israel's building civilian settlements on the Golan demonstrates that Israel's true goal is expansion.

Recently there has been a great change in Syrian thinking toward peace and toward acceptance of Israel.

If the United States did not give military aid to Israel, Israel would have to withdraw from Arab land and make peace with the Arabs.

Our interest in peace is demonstrated by our acceptance of the disengagement agreement, the UN resolutions, and Kissinger as mediator, and by our resuming diplomatic relations with Israel's strongest ally, the U.S. The next move toward peace is up to Israel.

In exchange for the Golan (and something for the Palestinians) we could live in peace with Israel.

Israel has no real interest in peace as demonstrated by its massive military preparations.

We will fight, if necessary, to regain the Golan, which is part of our country.

Israel is keeping the Golan, and therefore we must prepare for war.

Syria is a military dictatorship within the Soviet orbit.

The Golan is not the problem; Syria shelled Israel when Syria held the Golan before 1967.

Syria's insistence on the so-called "rights" of the Palestinians demonstrates that Syria's true goal is to destroy Israel.

Syrians did not accept Israel in 1948 and we have been fighting ever since; we know them well based on years of bitter experience.

If the Soviet Union did not give military aid to Syria, Syria would have to accept the existence of Israel and make peace with it.

Our interest in peace is well-known, and is further demonstrated by the one-sided disengagement agreement where in exchange for a few words we withdrew from substantial Syrian territory, including Kuneitra. The next move toward peace is up to Syria.

In exchange for real peace, we could return to Syria all or most of the Golan.

Syria has no real interest in peace as demonstrated by its massive military preparations.

It would be absurd for us to give up the Golan without real peace.

Syria is preparing for war, and therefore we must keep the Golan.

---

[2]Fisher, Kopelman, and Schneider, p. 26.

CHART 4–4
PARTISAN PERCEPTION TOOL
(Two-party Example)

Case: _____

Our side: _____

Their side: _____

As of: __(date)_____

Perceptions of a Typical Person on THEIR SIDE	**Perceptions of a Typical Person on OUR SIDE**
1. Five facts or points that they see as central to the conflict:	5. How we perceive the facts or points in the left-hand column:
2. How they perceive themselves:	6. How we perceive them:
3. How they perceive us:	7. How we perceive ourselves:
4. How they perceive the facts or points listed opposite in the right-hand column:	8. Facts or points not listed above that we see as central to the conflict:

CHART 4–5
PARTISAN PERCEPTION TOOL[3]

Case: _Cuban Missile Crisis_
Our side: _U.S. government_
Their side: _Soviet government_
As of: _October 4, 1962_

Perceptions of a Typical Person on the Soviet Side	**Perceptions of a Typical Person on the U.S. Side**

1. Five facts or points that they see as central to the conflict:
   A. _We have an unquestioned legal right to put nuclear missiles in Cuba._
   B. _The sovereign Cuban government invited us._
   C. _It is militarily and politically fair since the U.S. has missiles in Turkey._
   D. _The U.S. attacked Cuba at the Bay of Pigs in 1961._
   E. _We need to demonstrate that we can and will protect socialist states from imperialist invasion._

5. How we perceive the facts or points in the left-hand column:
   A. _Whatever the legal technicalities, nuclear missiles in Cuba are a gross violation of the modus vivendi._
   B. _Castro is a Soviet puppet._
   C. _We decided last summer to take our missiles out of Turkey._
   D. _The Bay of Pigs is wholly irrelevant._
   E. _The Soviet Union is not in Cuba for defensive purposes._

2. How they perceive themselves:
   - _We are the sovereign equal of the U.S._
   - _We are the defender of socialist states._
   - _Socialist revolutions are the wave of the future, and we support them._

6. How we perceive them:
   - _The U.S.S.R. is an aggressive Communist interloper in the Western Hemisphere; it promotes revolution wherever it can._
   - _With a nuclear missile base in the Caribbean, the U.S.S.R. would be a military and political threat to the whole hemisphere._

3. How they perceive us:
   - _The U.S. is arrogant and needs to be taught that we can do what they do._
   - _The U.S. is trigger-happy and quick to use illegal force._
   - _The U.S. is likely to invade Cuba and oust the Castro regime unless we defend it._

7. How we perceive ourselves:
   - _We have military force only for defensive purposes._
   - _We will never back down to Communist threats._
   - _We have no intention of invading Cuba._

---

[3]Fisher, Kopelman, and Schneider, pp. 30–31.

CHART 4–5 (Continued)
PARTISAN PERCEPTION TOOL

Perceptions of a Typical Person on the Soviet Side	Perceptions of a Typical Person on the U.S. Side
4. How they perceive the facts or points listed in the opposite column: • *The U.S.S.R. has long been vulnerable to U.S. missiles.* • *Missiles in Cuba simply accelerate the inevitable. Within a very few years our subs and ICBMs will be able to destroy the U.S. if we should ever have to.* • *It will be extremely dangerous for the U.S. to provoke a crisis.*	8. Facts or points not listed above that we see as central to the conflict: • *A Soviet missile capability in Cuba would let the U.S.S.R. destroy most of the U.S. whenever it wanted to. It would constitute a radical and conspicuous change in the balance of power.* • *The best time to deal with it is before it becomes operational.*

There are some practical questions in deciding how to use this tool. Whose perceptions is the analysis seeking to estimate? Governments and other international actors do not have monolithic perceptions. In many cases there will be a wide range of views. The most direct approach is to focus on the perceptions of those whose minds you are attempting to change. Within a government this may be the top leadership; it may be those within the leadership group who appear to be open to changing their minds. Or it may be useful to think of some particular member of a cabinet or government group, either real or hypothetical, who would have to be convinced if that government were ever going to decide the way an advisor or decision-maker would like. In order to get a decision to be made, it is often easier to target a single individual, or a small group of individuals, rather than a government. On the other hand, estimating general perceptions as we have done in Charts 4–3 and 4–5 can be helpful in understanding the general contours of a conflict. Either way, choosing whose perceptions you will concentrate on will help you focus exactly on what knowledge and insight you are seeking.

How to phrase perceptions on the work sheet is also a practical question. It appears to be most useful to present parties' perceptions in a form that they themselves would find acceptable, and that you find plausible and illuminating. It is usually best to put their perceptions in their best and most legitimate light. This does not necessarily mean writing a point the way they would express it. For example, if you were trying to ask a Brazilian developer about U.S. environmentalists trying to save the Amazon rain forest, he or she might say, "U.S. environmentalists are imperialist tree-huggers, who have no place in our country." Such a statement might not help you understand the Brazilian view empathetically. You might better appreciate Brazilian concerns if you framed the Brazilian perception as "By placing rain forests on a par with human welfare, these environmentalists, we feel, do not understand the need for our country to develop." You may or may not agree with such a statement, but it does more to illuminate Brazilian concerns than name-calling statements about environmentalists. In general, it is more useful to draft statements that describe their feelings and the impact of what others do than to draft statements that they might use to judge or describe others. Their own feelings are a more real reflection of their perceptions than a judgmental statement about others, because judgments and descriptions are themselves based on their own conclusions. They are not perceptions as such, but are made on the basis of perceptions.

How does a party or advisor learn about the perceptions of the leaders of another government? He or she first needs to gather information. This is purely a fact-finding operation. If you are the party trying to understand another party's point of view, you should not at this stage be engaging in policy judgment. You simply want to estimate, as best you can, how other people see things. What is important to them and what is not? One can uncover their perceptions in what has been written, and in what they say. You can test what you believe are their perceptions with others who may be able to offer insight. One can rarely, if ever, be exactly right about other people's perceptions, and may never know for sure how accurate one is, but the estimate is worth the effort.

Engage the Power of Role-Playing   One can use the Second Position by engaging in role-playing. If we were in their shoes, and these events had happened, how might *we* see things? Why might *we* be saying the things *they* are saying?

The chief executive officer of a company held liable for a patent infringement had called in a consultant to advise about negotiations on the dollar value of damages. Encouraged by the consultant to place himself in the shoes of the CEO of the opposing company, the executive initially resisted "playing games"; however, once he was persuaded to state the other side's case as forcefully as he could in the first person, he was so shaken by the experience that he raised his company's settlement offer one hundredfold—and fired his consultant as the bearer of bad news! Role-reversal exercises can have a powerful impact.[4]

Whether you are a direct party to a conflict, or a prospective advisor to one or more of the parties, we advocate playing a devil's advocate role, inventing the best arguments for the other side. Negotiators and advisors can talk to people familiar with the other side's point of view. They can empathize with a widow, or an orphan, or some other victim of the conflict on the other party's side, and think about how the other side might describe themselves, their concerns, and their government's purpose. Finally, they can write out a draft work sheet and ask others to go over it, including colleagues, experts, and friends from that country.

Engage the Parties to the Conflict Directly   In many circumstances it is possible to show a draft to the very people whose perceptions one is trying to understand. If access to the parties to the conflict themselves

---

[4]Fisher, Kopelman, and Schneider, p. 34.

proves difficult or impossible, one can engage surrogates for those parties: a lower-level official, a businessperson from that country, or a professor familiar with that party's point of view.

Later, in actual negotiations, showing the draft to the other side is also a useful tactic to demonstrate that one has been listening and does understand the other side's point of view. In fact, before attempting to communicate one's own view of a problem with a negotiating partner, it is often wise to go through the other side's concerns and arguments first, and to convey an appreciation of the validity of at least some of those. In 1980, a Soviet official in Afghanistan was shown a draft work sheet on Soviet concerns about the conflict there, phrased from the Soviet perspective. "This is a good list," he said, "but you did not mention the typhoid. We lose many men through typhoid." He immediately became engaged with critiquing the draft, and when it was finished to his satisfaction, he felt that he was dealing with someone who understood his concerns.[5] Such a process lays a foundation of credibility. If we can report correctly the perceptions of the other side of the conflict, the other party may be persuaded to listen more openly to our concerns and arguments.

Why They See Things That Way: Emotions and Motivations

In trying to understand the parties to a conflict, you will also want to know why they see things the way they do. In a conflict situation, particularly if it has involved violence, feelings are likely to be more important than thoughts. Participants in a conflict are more apt to be ready for battle than for cooperatively working out a joint solution to a common problem. People who are angry may not hear what the other side has to say, and are more likely to put the worst possible interpretation on actions taken by someone who is seen as an adversary.

If one wants to affect what is going on in other parties' heads, one will want to be aware of emotions and motivations that may be surging through their hearts. When one is talking with people face to face, and is sensitive to what is going on, one is more likely to become aware of any strong emotions. But when parties are dealing with each other by letter, cable, fax, e-mail, or telephone, they may be so concerned with themselves and so intrigued by the interesting ideas that they have worked up that they may ignore feelings of the other parties that are likely to drown out any rational words.

The first thing to do is to become aware of their emotions and of what may be their dominant motives. The checklist in Chart 4–6, a tool on emotions and motives, can serve to remind you or a party to a conflict to stop and think about how the other parties may be feeling. In the left-hand column are adjectives that suggest what one side may be assuming about the other. In the next column are words that warn the first party of what may in fact be the emotional condition of the other.

Using the chart as a work sheet, you can jot down your estimate of their actual emotional state, as it exists now or as it existed at the time of the events you are analyzing. Such an estimate has to be based on whatever data

[5]Fisher, Kopelman, and Schneider, p. 29.

you have, but even here it may be possible to talk with people who know how the other party feels, or, in some circumstances, with the very people whose emotional state and motivation you are considering. If you do it in a noncritical way, it is often constructive to let the other side know that you realize that they are angry and frustrated, and that you understand why.

Chart 4–7 illustrates the use of the work sheet, applied to the dispute between Argentina and the United Kingdom over the Falkland Islands in 1982. The U.S.–Mexico natural gas negotiations in 1977 are illustrated in Chart 4–8. In filling in such a work sheet it may be more illuminating to generate some hypothetical or real quotations that reveal feeling and motivation than to limit ourselves to simple adjectives. The example illustrates this approach.

CHART 4–6
EMOTIONS AND MOTIVES TOOL

Case: _____

Our side: _____

Their side: _____

As of: _*(date)*_____

A good situation (We may unconsciously be assuming they are:)	A difficult situation (They may in fact be feeling:)	Our estimate of THEIR emotions and motivations:	Our estimate of OUR OWN emotions and motivations:
rational	highly emotional		
confident	fearful		
at ease	angry		
satisfied that others are acting in good faith	distrustful		
contented	depressed		
satisfied	frustrated		
motivated by the future	motivated by the past		
motivated by hope	motivated by revenge		
motivated by realistic goals	motivated by unrealistic goals		

CHART 4–7
EMOTIONS AND MOTIVES TOOL

Case: _U.K. vs. Argentina_

Our side: _British leadership_

Their side: _Argentine leadership_

As of: _1982_

A good situation (We may unconsciously be assuming they are:)	A difficult situation (They may in fact be feeling:)	Our estimate of THEIR emotions and motivations:	Our estimate of OUR OWN emotions and motivations:
rational	highly emotional	_fairly emotional_	_fairly rational_
confident	fearful	_overconfident_	_confident_
at ease	angry	_angry_	_highly irritated_
satisfied that others are acting in good faith	distrustful	_distrustful_	_British good faith_
contented	depressed	_angered by British high-handedness_	_annoyed_
satisfied	frustrated	_vengeful_	
motivated by the future	motivated by the past	_"our legitimate claim has been ignored for too long"_	_teaching them a lesson_
motivated by hope	motivated by revenge	_"more negotiations will not help us— we need force to be heard"_	_we can't abandon the British inhabitants of the islands_
motivated by realistic goals	motivated by unrealistic goals	_returning the Malvinas to Argentina_	_a show of force will humiliate them and solve all our problems_

CHART 4–8
EMOTIONS AND MOTIVES TOOL

Case: _U.K.–Mexico Natural Gas Negotiations_
Our side: _Mexican leadership_
Their side: _American leadership_
As of: _1977_

A good situation (We may unconsciously be assuming they are:)	A difficult situation (They may in fact be feeling:)	Our estimate of THEIR emotions and motivations:	Our estimate of OUR OWN emotions and motivations:
rational	highly emotional	_emotional_	_want to be treated fairly_
confident	fearful	_overconfident— U.S. is arrogant_	_confident that we can supply the U.S._
at ease	angry	_confident that they can control us_	_upset that they think they can manipulate us_
satisfied that others are acting in good faith	distrustful	_they are trying to manipulate us_	_trying to reach an agreement that benefits both sides_
contented	depressed	_contented_	_feel picked upon, insulted_
satisfied	frustrated	_tired of Mexican nitpicking_	_frustrated with U.S. arrogance_
motivated by the future	motivated by the past	_remember the Alamo_	_want U.S. economic ties and market_
motivated by hope	motivated by revenge	_motivated by control_	_motivated by building a new relationship with the U.S._
motivated by realistic goals	motivated by unrealistic goals	_think we are a puppet_	_want to be treated fairly, as equals_

Having diagnosed the emotional component within the leadership, one may wish to look also at emotions that exist among constituents and supporters, in whom emotions often play a more dominant role.

This is not the time to be formulating advice about how to deal with the parties' emotions, but you should expect to find clues as to what kind of actions by one side or the other might be most constructive. Might it help for some party to discuss the problem with them? Would a session for "letting off steam" be desirable? Might frustration and alienation be reduced by finding some manageable tasks that the parties could tackle jointly? Just as office outings can offset the frustration of coping with unmanageable problems at work, so modest, joint undertakings may be able to reduce some of the frustration produced by a protracted conflict.

For example, an advisor to a Canadian Parliament member could suggest the formation of a number of lower-level, technically oriented joint "working groups" of Quebecois and Anglo-Canadian civil engineers, city planners, or school administrators to brainstorm some ideas about what the details of an independently administered but affiliated Quebec might look like. How would the sewage systems work? Or preschool education? The advantages of such small, constructive steps in highly charged situations include symbolic gestures of acceptance or good feeling; establishing some common bonds on a personal basis, thus tending to separate the substance of the conflict from issues of personal relations; and spending time working on options for the future, thus reducing the prominence of past grievances.

What Lies Behind What They Say: Positions and Interests

A third way of gaining understanding about parties to a conflict is to look behind their statements for concerns that may not be expressed. Typically, one party makes statements of its position, describing what it will and will not do. The other side makes comparable statements about what it will do, what it will never do, and what it insists upon. Listen carefully to what they say but do not take their words as the last word. If we take these words seriously, as establishing fixed positions that will not change, then there is rarely the possibility of agreement. In a conflict, the positions of opposing parties often appear not only inconsistent but fixed and impossible to change.

Agreement is promoted, in part, by discovering shared interests. Negotiators will need to engender some flexibility in the other party's positions and, in order to serve their own interests and to maximize the chance of a peaceful accommodation, will wish to find some flexibility in their own position as well.

Fortunately, the problem is not to reconcile the words of the parties, but to reconcile their underlying interests. There is a natural tendency to concentrate on stated positions, since it is the conflicting positions that constitute the outward symptoms of a dispute. But to concentrate on another party's position is likely to cause that position to harden. The more that position is worked out in detail and the more often it is repeated, the more committed to it that party will be.

Further, to focus on their position, with our objective being to persuade them to retreat, suggests to them that the contest is one of will in which their objective is not to budge. This method is much like playing chicken. Such a contest rewards the party who is more irrational and stubborn than the other. Where stubbornness is seen as the key to success, agreement becomes difficult as both parties lock in. One thing we know is that we will want their position to change. The less that position becomes worked out in detail, the less it is talked about, and the less committed to it they become, the better off a negotiator will typically be.

Furthermore, a wise solution is not determined by a compromise on positions, but rather by the degree to which a solution takes care of the underlying interests of the parties. Many people become so locked into a position that they forget the very interests that led them to take that position—and overlook the fact that those interests may be met in other ways. Illustrative is the story of two students quarreling in a library. One wanted the window open; the other wanted it shut. A compromise between their positions, leaving the window half open, provided too little fresh air for the first and too much draft for the second, blowing his papers about. By looking behind their opposing positions to their underlying interests, the librarian was able to resolve the conflict by reconciling their interests instead of their positions. She opened a window in the next room that provided fresh air without a draft.

In looking behind the positions of the other side, we will first be seeking interests that we and they may share. Both passengers in a lifeboat want to get to shore and may subordinate their differences in pursuit of that common purpose. But we will also be looking for areas where their interests differ from ours. Upon examining their respective interests, passengers in a lifeboat may discover that one prefers bread and one prefers cheese, leading to a prompt and amicable division of the rations.

There is a common tendency to assume that an adversary's interests and ours are directly opposed. If we are concerned with security, we tend to assume that they want to harm us. If we want a low price for oil, we tend to assume that their primary concern must be a high price. In the U.S.–Mexico natural gas negotiations of 1977, for example, the United States wanted a low price for Mexican natural gas. It may well be, however, that a major interest of the Mexicans was not necessarily in the price of natural gas but in being treated equally and with the dignity befitting a sovereign nation. From their perspective, after more than a century of being ignored or looked down upon by the North American government, the Mexican negotiators wanted their government and their natural resources to be treated with respect. By looking behind the Mexican position that the price should be high, the United States might have been able to address separately issues of respect on their merits—by method or tone of communications, for example—and issues of price on their merits—through third-party assessments of a fair price, for example. The parties might then have discovered interests that could have been better reconciled to the satisfaction of both.

Another common tendency of parties is to treat as unimportant those concerns of an opposing party that are seen as not standing in the way of an agreement. At the Law of the Sea Conference, many developing countries were keenly interested in the issue of technology exchange so that they would be able to acquire from countries that were highly industrialized the advanced technical knowledge and equipment they wanted for deep-seabed mining. The United States and other industrialized countries saw no difficulty in meeting this desire, and therefore saw the issue of technology transfer as unimportant. But by devoting more substantial time to working out practical arrangements for transferring technology, they could have made their offer to transfer technology far more credible and far more attractive to the developing countries. By dismissing the issue as an unimportant detail to be dealt with later, the industrialized states gave up an opportunity to provide (at low cost to themselves) developing countries with an impressive achievement and a real incentive to reach agreement.[6]

Parties to a conflict frequently are interested in different subjects, have different values and different priorities. One party to a conflict is likely to be more concerned than the other with getting public credit for achieving agreement; one may be more interested in playing the domestic political game than the international game, and so forth. Chart 4–9, a brief checklist, suggests some common variations in interest that are worth looking for.

A way to contrast these different positions and interests is to write out in parallel columns statements of position that identify the dispute. These phrases record what each party to the negotiation is saying. Then, looking first at one side and then at the other, jot down phrases that suggest underlying reasons for those positions. If they were asked to explain why they took their position, what might they say? How would they justify it in terms of their needs or concerns?

In particular, a negotiator should look for aspects of the situation where the parties have shared interests and those where the parties' interests are not in opposition, but differ. There are bound to be some shared interests on which it may be possible to build. But there are also bound to be features of the conflict where one party can satisfy the other without sacrificing its own interests.

Chart 4–10 suggests one way of organizing our thinking about looking behind positions for interests. The suggested subheadings of substantive interests, symbolic interests, and domestic political interests are simply three of many possible categories. It might also be useful to have a category of "shared interests." For some conflicts, reconcilable interests might best be illuminated by listing separately long-term interests and short-term interests. The checklist in Chart 4–9 suggests other possible categories for varying and improving the tool.

In Chart 4–11 the tool has been filled in with Syrian and Israeli positions and interests with respect to the Golan Heights as of 1975. The positions of the two countries were in direct conflict. Yet by studying their underlying interests one could begin to see possible ways of reconciling them.

---

[6]Fisher, Kopelman, and Schneider, pp. 38–39.

CHART 4–9
CHECKLIST
of some frequent differences of interest

One party is more concerned with	The other party is more concerned with
form	substance
economic considerations	political considerations
internal	international
symbolic	practical
immediate future	more distant future
ad hoc results	the relationship
hardware	ideology
progress	respect for tradition
precedent	this case
prestige, reputation	results
political points	national welfare

CHART 4–10
POSITIONS AND INTERESTS TOOL
(Looking behind opposing positions for interests that may be reconcilable)

Case: _____
Our side: _____
Their side: _____
As of: __(date)_____

THEIR SIDE   **OUR SIDE**

Positions

Interests

Substantive interests   Substantive interests

Symbolic interests, and   Symbolic interests, and
interests in precedent   interests in precedent

Domestic political interests   Domestic political interests

CHART 4–11
POSITIONS AND INTERESTS TOOL
(Looking behind opposing positions for interests that may be reconcilable)

Case: _Golan Heights_

Our side: _Israel_

Their side: _Syria_

As of: _Early 1975_

THEIR SIDE	OUR SIDE

Positions

Syria must get back the Golan Heights.	We Israelis must keep the Golan Heights.
Israeli troops must withdraw from the Golan.	Our Israeli troops must remain in the Golan.

Interests

Substantive interests	Substantive interests
Syrian farmers should be free to farm on the Golan Heights.	Avoid the kind of shelling that took place from 1948 to 1967. Reduce the likelihood of war. Be in a strong military position if there is to be a war. Avoid hostile Syrian forces' being in a strong offensive position.
Symbolic interests, and interests in precedent	Symbolic interests, and interests in precedent
The principle of no territorial expansion should be respected. Syria's foreign territory should be respected. Syria's sovereign equality should be respected.	Avoid setting a precedent of returning land won in a defensive war.
Domestic political interests	Domestic political interests
The Syrian public should be confident in their government.	The Israeli public should be confident in their security.

Understanding how the parties view the conflict can help in your efforts to gain knowledge about a conflict, to criticize a party's actions, or to influence a party to do something you want. How they view the conflict comes from how they feel about the conflict. By examining their emotions and motivations leading up to a conflict, we can begin to create our own perceptions and understanding for where their perceptions come from. The result of emotions and perceptions leads to positions and judgments. It is the interests that lie behind these positions that can truly give us insight into where there is room for accord and where agreement may be reached, and can help us focus our actions on meeting those interests. These tools can be applied not only to understanding the Second Position, or understanding another party to the conflict, but are also useful in evaluating and assessing our own interests. What are our perceptions of the conflict? What are our emotions? How should our purposes and strategies best accomplish our interests?

CHAPTER
—5—

The Decision from the Other Side's Point of View

We have suggested that governments frequently try to bring about a decision they want by increasing the cost to another government of not making that decision, and that this method of influence is both ineffective and costly. The attractiveness of the choice we want an adversary to make is affected not simply by the pain we threaten to inflict if they do not make the choice, but rather by the total combination of many elements. The set of consequences of doing what we want (including both the benefits and the disadvantages) must be more appealing to them in sum than the set of consequences that will ensue if they do not do what we want. The choice we present to them must be palatable.

The set of questions we ought to be asking about each of these elements—the demand, the offer, and the threat—will enable us to analyze how the choice we are presenting looks to the party we are trying to influence and what we can do to alter the scheme so as to be more effective in getting them to make a decision. Who is it we are asking? On whom will the consequences fall if they do not make the desired decision? Will they fall on the same "who" as the group we are asking to make the decision? What is the decision we are asking them to make? What is it that we are saying will happen if they do or do not make it? When will these consequences occur? And why are we asking for this decision—is it a legitimate request, a reasonable demand? Are there reasons that they ought to make that choice? If they do not do what we want why would implementing the threat be legitimate?

The object of our policy is to cause someone else to make a decision.

To do so we must alter the decision or the consequences of making it and of not making it so that they will now see the total choice in a favorable light. It is *their* perception of the demand, threat, and offer that is crucial, not ours. Our task is to change their perception by arranging the desired consequences so that, on the basis of the total attractiveness of the combination of the demand, threat, and offer, they will want to make that decision.

Changing the threat by increasing the threatened pain—military deterrence, damage infliction, weapons development, threats of sanctions—encompasses only a small part of influence. These are the undesirable consequences to the adversary of not making the decision we want. Herman Kahn's book *On Escalation* is essentially a description of forty-two ways to change the way this one factor looks to an adversary. He suggests how to make the consequences of being "bad" look less attractive, more immediate, or more probable. His entire book is about escalating a threat for the purpose of exerting influence. We need equally detailed books dealing with the problems of whom we are trying to influence, what we want them to do, and how to make that look attractive. Successful influence depends on a consideration of all parts of this decision, not just one, and on a consideration of how the various parts ought to be coordinated.

An element that is unimportant to us may be important to an adversary. One of the sticking points of international conflict is that each party thinks that because it regards some issue as unimportant it will be easy for the other party to back down on it. But it is the adversary's perception of what is important that controls their decision, not our perception or some objective standard. No matter how incomprehensible their preferences at first seem to us, if we want to influence them, we should deal with them on their own ground. If they prefer prestige to economic welfare, an effective policy will offer them prestige. They may be more influenced by the name attached to a million-dollar aid program than by the fact that it is being offered. The fact that we may find an adversary's choices baffling does not make the decision irrelevant; it makes all the more important our consciously considering how the various elements may look to them. What do they think we are asking them to decide, what do they think the consequences will be, and how do they value those consequences?

Our premise is that most international objectives can be achieved only by something more than our own actions: by having other governments make decisions. If this is so, both we and our adversaries must prefer the decision we want them to make over its alternatives. If only we prefer it, they will not make it; if only they prefer it and want to make it, then it would not be a goal of our policy. Unless there is some common ground there is no hope for influence. We seek to make it appear to them that the sum of the consequences of going along is profitable enough for them to make the decision—that is, it is better than the sum of the consequences of not going along. In game-theory terms this is simply saying that international conflicts are not zero-sum games.

WHO ARE WE TRYING TO INFLUENCE?

The first question is "Who?" Who is it we would like to have make a decision? After Rhodesian independence in 1965 the British government did not articulate clearly the target of their sanctions, nor was there public discussion of the effect of their policy on the people they claimed to be influencing. Sanctions were intended to make it hard on "Rhodesia." Recognizing that Rhodesia was simply a piece of geography, the British government said that it was the politically responsible community leaders within Rhodesia who were the precise target of influence. The sanctions were presumably aimed at a typical businessman in Salisbury—perhaps a banker with political experience.

Suppose that this banker is the "who" we are trying to influence. It is then the consequences to him that are crucial. What is his choice? He gets up in the morning, reads the newspaper, and says to his wife, "I see that Harold Wilson wants us to return to constitutional government, and I suppose he is talking to me. Perhaps I had better go down to Government House and tell them that I am prepared to return to constitutional government. But if I do, what will happen? I will go in and the British governor will ask, 'You and who else? Do you have the support of the army? Did you bring others along?' And I will have to say, 'No.' Then he will say, 'When there are enough of you, let me know.' I will walk out and quite likely be picked up and put under house arrest like others of whom the government is suspicious." The consequences to such a man of making the decision Britain was asking him to make were considerably worse than the consequences of not making it. Britain was not offering him any benefits for making the decision.

Making effective policy requires the coordination of all elements—the demand, the offer, and the threat—to make an adversary's choice easy and desirable in his eyes. Once we know whom we are trying to influence, we should see whether we are making the offer and the threat to the same person or group. In Rhodesia, the first effects of economic sanctions fell on the blacks, who had no voice in any government or private decision making and about whom those with responsibility for changing the course of independence cared little. On the other hand, in 1963 the government of Ceylon (now Sri Lanka) was successfully influenced by an offer of the United States to resume economic aid if the government worked out with a U.S. oil company a satisfactory arrangement for compensation. Although the offer was directed at the people of the country, the government was deeply interested in the aid. The critical point is the nature of the influence exerted by the offer and by the threat on that group to which we are presenting a choice.

WHAT ARE WE ASKING THEM TO DO?

The second question is "What?" What is it we want them to decide? What do they perceive will be the consequences of making that decision (the offer), and what do they perceive will be the consequences of not making it (the threat)? If it is their decision that counts, they must know of the decision we are trying to get them to make. The more mechanically easy it is to make that decision the more "yesable" the proposition with which we confront them—the more likely they are to make it.

What is the offer? What do they see as the advantages (and disadvantages) of the situation they would be in if they went along with us and made the desired decision? In Vietnam, for example, the United States offered fair elections, economic aid programs, various levels of U.S. disengagement, and withdrawal. There are two questions to be asked about the benefits we are promising to extend to them if they make a desired decision. First, are these benefits things that are really attractive to them? Second, will these benefits actually occur? Another way to improve an offer is make the disadvantages of going along appear less costly. In making the decision we want, they will suffer domestic and international costs. We can exert more influence by acting to minimize these costs.

WHEN SHOULD THEY TAKE ACTION?

The third question is "When?" The decision we are asking them to make will be more palatable if the threat and the offer are well correlated to the time at which the decision is required. When U.S. bombing of North Vietnam began in 1965, there were spokesmen for the U.S. government who said, "We do not want their promises, nor do we expect North Vietnam to stop its support for the Vietcong immediately. The decision we want them to make is to taper off over the next three months." If that was true, the message was demonstrably wrong in its timing. It was, "Slow down your support over the next three months or we will bomb you tomorrow." But any child would laugh if a parent said, "No television tonight unless you are good next week." The child knows that the parent has to decide before she does.

WHY IS OUR REQUEST JUSTIFIED?

The last question is "Why?" The word is used here in the sense of seeking justification. Is our demand justifiable? How legitimate is it in our adversary's eyes? In terms of morality and humanity, international law, and past actions by ourselves and our adversaries, how justifiable does our demand appear to them?

Legitimacy is usually considered to be icing on the cake. But the legitimacy of our demand as perceived by an adversary is important. They will be more likely to make a decision if it appears legitimate to them. This is true not only because an adversary will see that we can win third-party support for a legitimate demand. Every government must also consider its internal situation. An adversary government must justify its decisions to its own people; it is constrained at least in part by what its own citizens will say about the decision. Also, governments and government officials are influenced by what they themselves think is right.

Most government officials want to do the right thing by their own standards. No matter how wrong we think our adversary is, we can best see how to influence them by realizing that they think they are on the side of right. Part of exerting influence is convincing them that to make the decision we want them to make would be the right thing to do in terms of the values accepted by them. This is another aspect of the proposition that solving a conflict involves an attempt to get them to make a decision that both is favorable to us and appeals to them.

Similarly, a threat can be legitimate if its implementation would be morally or legally justified. Such a threat is more likely to exert influence than one that appears to be rank blackmail.

ANALYZING OUR MESSAGE

Our starting point should be clear: what we have been saying and doing so far has not worked, at least not in the sense of producing the result we want. One approach is to ask ourselves: What is the message? What have we been saying? What is the message they have been hearing? Is the message they have been hearing different from the one we have been sending? There is always an implicit "message" from us to the other party that suggests, with varying degrees of clarity, ambiguity, or omission that there is something they ought to be doing. The message is implied by threatening or warning of possible consequences if they do not do it, and offering or predicting different consequences if the desired action is taken. Look over Chart 5–1 at this point. A useful way of organizing the relevant information about an existing international situation in which we are involved is to examine key elements of the "message" that our words and deeds may have been communicating to another party. As of a fixed point in time, what is the net effect on them of everything that we have said and done in terms of three basic elements: what we are asking for, what we are threatening, and what we are offering? Examine with care the message that we are currently communicating, both those aspects that have been clearly expressed and those that have been left unsaid.

Elements the Other Side Needs to Hear		Narrative
DEMAND	Address	*A way of getting the attention*
	Addressee	*of a particular party*
	Tone	*with a particular tone of request or demand*
	Party or Actor	*to have the same or another party*
	Action	*take a desired action*
	Time	*by a particular time*
	Legitimation	*for a valid reason.*
THREAT OR WARNING	Minimum Required	*If at least a certain action is not taken*
	Deadline	*by a particular time,*
	Actor	*then some party*
	Degree of Probability	*with some lesser or greater degree of certainty*
	Consequences	*will take unfavorable action*
	Time	*by a particular time*
	Legitimation	*for a valid reason.*
OFFER OR PROMISE	Minimum Required	*If at least a certain action has been taken*
	Deadline	*by a particular time,*
	Actor	*then some party*
	Degree of Probability	*with some lesser or greater degree of certainty*
	Consequences	*will take some favorable action*
	Time	*by a particular time*
	Legitimation	*for a valid reason.*

[1]Roger Fisher, Elizabeth Kopelman, and Andrea Kupfer Schneider, *Beyond Machiavelli* (Cambridge, MA: Harvard University Press, 1994), p. 45.

What we are asking for (the "demand") is what we want them to do in the future. Often we spend our time complaining about the past, leaving it highly uncertain just who it is we want to do something and just what it is they are supposed to do. Our request for action (often unstated) also involves elements of timing (when is it supposed to be done?) and legitimacy (what makes our request legitimate?).

The consequences of not doing as we would like may be communicated by a threat or perhaps by a warning of events beyond our control that could result from their failure to take appropriate action. The effectiveness of this part of the message not only depends on its content (what are the consequences? when will they occur? who will impose them? and what makes them legitimate?) but on the clarity with which those elements are communicated, their credibility, and their probability.

Similar considerations apply to the third basic aspect of our message: the offer. The impact of the "good" consequences that we are saying will follow if they do take the desired action depends on answers to the same set of subsidiary questions: who? when? what? and why are those consequences legitimate?

The same technique of message analysis can illuminate a historical event by helping us to understand what one party to a conflict was "hearing" from another.

A good starting point for considering the message we ought to send in the future is to write out the (ineffective) message that we are sending now. Chart 5–1 provides a checklist for constructing the message that we are now sending. Not all elements will be significant in every case. But the fact that on some points nothing has been said may often be more important than things that were said.

There are actually two versions of such a message: what we think we are saying and what they are actually hearing. This is demonstrated by the Message Tool in Chart 5–2. The more important of the two versions for us to think about is the message as they hear it. During the bombing of North Vietnam by the United States, the U.S. government was sending a message to the government in Hanoi. Some of the things that made the bombing policy wholly ineffective in influencing the actions of the government of North Vietnam become apparent when one contrasts the message that the United States thought it was sending with the message the way it was apparently being received in Hanoi.

Analyzing conflict as communication highlights two central problems that are involved whenever one government tries to influence another. The first is the formulation of the message; the second is its transmission. The message the United States was sending to North Vietnam at the time of the bombing operations was poorly formulated in some basic respects. It was never clear to North Vietnam exactly what they had to do in order to have the bombing stop. Of course, they knew that if they unconditionally surrendered, stopped all support to antigovernment forces in South Vietnam, withdrew all their forces, cut off supplies, apologized, and offered to pay compensation for damage done, then the United States would stop the bombing. But they also knew that was more than the situation required. How *much* more was not clear to them. In addition, the purely mechanical question of the timing of the desired performance and the consequences of the threat was such as to make the threat likely to be ineffective. In substance the message was: "We will bomb you again tomorrow unless you slow down your supplies next week." Since each day they knew they would in any event be bombed the next day, there was no great incentive to stop what they were doing.

Another example will illustrate the importance of formulating a message so it confronts the other side with a clear choice such that the consequences of deciding as we would like will look more attractive to them than the consequences of not doing so. This analysis, Chart 5–3, looks at what the British government was saying to Catholic activists in Northern Ireland when it tightened controls over press coverage in 1988. Again, one can see that the content of what was being said was not likely to influence the recipient to do what the sender wanted done. In Chart 5–4, we look at the content of the message sent from President Bush to General Noriega before the U.S. invasion of Panama. If that message even remotely reflects the situation as Noriega perceived it, it is easy to understand why he did not accede to American demands.

CHART 5–2
MESSAGE TOOL
What's the Message: As Sent? As Received?

Case: _____

Our side: _____

Their side: _____

As of: ___*(date)*_____

As Sent

What we (   ) have
apparently been saying

_____

As Received

What they (   ) have
apparently been hearing

_____

(demand)

(threat)

(offer)

CHART 5–3
MESSAGE TOOL
What's the Message: As Sent? As Received?

Case: _Northern Ireland_
Our side: _Great Britain_
Their side: _Northern Irish Catholics_
As of: _1988_

## As Sent	## As Received

What we *(British Government)* have apparently been saying

What they *(Northern Irish Catholic activists)* have apparently been hearing

Hey, loyal British subjects

Hey, trouble-making Catholics

(demand)

Support the law, the British government, and your queen.

Indicate that you are ready to betray friends and neighbors by ceasing to tolerate violent protest by the IRA because loyalty to the crown is important and violence is wrong.

(threat)

If not, you will be tolerating the use of violence for illegal ends, and we will make every effort to reduce media coverage of your struggle.

If you fail to do as we ask, you can wait, keep your options open, and continue to garner financial support and sympathy from the U.S.

(offer)

If enough of you are loyal to the Crown, we will permit closer relations with the Republic of Ireland to the South.

If you do what we ask, you will probably accomplish nothing, be shunned by your community, continue to suffer religious discrimination, and risk both your career and any chance to exert future influence.

And we can then negotiate away any discrimination against the Catholic population in the North.

CHART 5–4
MESSAGE TOOL
What's the Message: As Sent? As Received?

Case: _Noriega in Panama_
Our side: _U.S._
Their side: _Noriega_
As of: _December 1989_

<table>
<tr><th>As Sent</th><th>As Received</th></tr>
<tr><td>What we (U.S. Government) have apparently been saying</td><td>What they (Gen. Noriega) have apparently been hearing</td></tr>
<tr><td>Hey, you law-abiding loyal ally</td><td>Hey, former friend turned public enemy</td></tr>
</table>

(demand)

Stop smuggling drugs because it is illegal and harms our country.	_Stop doing what we have previously allowed and condoned for years. Publicly admit that you backed down to U.S. pressure and appear to be a U.S. puppet._

(threat)

If you don't do that immediately, then we will have to take drastic action to stop the flow of drugs from Panama into the U.S.	_If you don't, we say we may invade._

(offer)

If you do make a public announcement agreeing to start discussions with us and stop the drug flow immediately, then we will be appreciative.	_If you do as we ask, you won't get anything, and all further options are closed._

When parties are adversaries, caught up in a conflict, living in different countries, speaking different languages, having their words and deeds edited by the media, transmitted around the world, and summarized in brief headlines, the chance that the message received is the same as the message transmitted approaches zero. Even when parties are face to face in the same room, misunderstanding is likely. The difficult mechanical process of communication is exacerbated by putting the worst interpretation on what one's adversary says or does. That tendency is made worse by the belief that that is the conservative thing to do; by the common desire to convince spectators how evil one's adversary is; and by the fact that the worst interpretation often seems consistent with one's own perception.

The results of such practice, however, are far from constructive. Subtle overtures for settlement are snubbed, opportunities for peace lost, and the vicious circle of reenforcing hostility accelerated. When we assume, for instance, that the only way to get Saddam Hussein to leave Kuwait is by military force, we have created a self-fulfilling prophecy. After years of supporting General Noriega, we decided unilaterally that he should no longer run the country, rather than using our influence to change the situation.

There are many reasons why governments do not follow a "rational" strategy to exert influence on a foreign government. During the war in Vietnam, the United States government failed to offer North Vietnam the specific terms of a cease-fire, in part because some officials in the U.S. government had already concluded that a cease-fire would probably not be accepted, and in part to avoid exacerbating internal divisions within the U.S. government and between the U.S. government and the government of South Vietnam in Saigon. In the light of this diagnosis and others, we may formulate the kind of international relations advice that we think should have been given to the decision-makers in each case. As Graham Allison has pointed out in *Essence of Decision* (1971), those decision-makers are involved in more games than just that of the rational international actor. They may ignore our advice, just as a judge may be too tired or too busy and may ignore the brilliant advice of a law clerk. Those facts do not alter the desirability of our knowing what the content of good advice would be.

UNDERSTANDING THE CHOICE AS IT LOOKS TO THEM

The Message Tool helps clarify our picture of the whole conflict situation. But before we can make a plan about what we should do next, or how we might usefully change what we are now doing in order to be more persuasive to the other side, we need to be more precise about what we mean by "the other side." We will be most effective if we target an individual decision-maker who is in a position to make a difference. Focusing on one decision-maker is what we mean by a "prince"—not necessarily the head of state, or royalty, or a man, but someone placed to make a difference.

We want to use what we know and what we can guess to construct an analysis of the existing situation as it appears to their prince—to the particular person our side has been trying to influence. What is the primary decision that person sees himself as facing? Taking into account not only the message that we have been sending but all other factors as well, how do the pros and cons of making that decision appear to him? What is his currently perceived choice?

Which Decision-Maker?

As in the Message Tool, the first task is to identify the person we have been trying to influence. This is usually the "adversary," the "enemy," the head person "on the other side" or some obvious leader in a conflict situation. We may later decide to give up on that person and try to influence somebody else, but for present purposes we will want to select the person whom people on our side have to date been trying to influence. We may call this target of influence "their prince."

What Decision?

The second task is to identify the decision that their prince thinks he or she is being asked to make with respect to the subject at hand. Consider Prime Minister Margaret Thatcher at the time of the Falkland/Malvinas crisis. What did she think she was being asked to say "yes" to? At various times in the past, she might have perceived herself as being asked to abandon self-determination for the Falkland Islanders and turn the islands over to Argentinian rule, or to turn the country over to a military junta. Usually the person being pressed will describe what he or she is being asked to do in extreme terms: "They are asking me to give up everything." "They want us to surrender."

Weighing the Consequences as They See Them

Having identified the presumptive target of influence and the question the person or organization faces at that point, the remaining task is to construct a chart listing consequences important to that person that he or she would probably anticipate as following a decision one way, and consequences that would follow a decision the other way. It is most unlikely that the person faced with a choice has in fact written out such a list. Nonetheless, we can better understand the difficulties we will have in exerting influence if we make explicit those considerations that are probably important to the person whose mind we hope to change.

This list is intended as a way of organizing and presenting our estimate of our "adversary's" existing state of mind. It is a form of analysis of the current situation. It is a way of presenting our best estimate of what is, not what ought to be—it helps us answer the question, "Why are things dead-locked now?" Although we are trying to estimate a current reality, the con-struction of such a list is not so much a mechanical act as a creative one. Per-haps the best way to start is to put ourselves in that person's shoes and try to feel and think what that might be like. As we discussed in the previous chap-ter, we need to think of *their* partisan perceptions, their emotions and motiva-tions. If he were to say "yes" to the choice that he believes he is now being asked to make, what unfavorable consequences might he expect? What, if any, favorable ones might he expect? On the other hand, what favorable con-sequences does he now believe would be likely to follow his saying "no"? What unfavorable consequences might he anticipate in that event? This process should generate a number of key points. Charts 5–5 and 5–6 outline and give a general example of a Currently Perceived Choice Tool.

CHART 5–5
CURRENTLY PERCEIVED CHOICE TOOL

Case: _____

As of: ___(date)_____

The Currently Perceived Choice of _____

Question faced: "Shall I _____

_____ ?"

Consequences If I Say "Yes"	Consequences If I Say "No"
− [negative consequences listed in order of importance]	+ [positive consequences listed in order of the subjects on the left]
−	+
−	+
BUT:	**BUT:**
+ [positive consequences in some logical order]	− [negative consequences, listed to match, if possible, those on the left]

CHART 5–6
CURRENTLY PERCEIVED CHOICE TOOL[2]
(General Example)

Case: _____

As of: _(date)_____

The Currently Perceived Choice of: _A leader_____

Question faced: _"Shall I now abandon a position that we have heretofore taken and_
_make a concession to the other side?"_____

Consequences If I Say "Yes"	**Consequences If I Say "No"**
− _I may lose power, be criticized_	+ _I keep power and support_
− _Our side backs down_	+ _We stand firm_
− _We will have to figure out what concession to make_	+ _There is no bureaucratic hassle_
− _Any concession will reduce our bargaining position_	+ _We maintain our bargaining leverage_
− _We give up the opportunity of getting anything better_	+ _We can always make some concession later if we have to_
BUT:	**BUT:**
+ _We may improve the chances of obtaining an agreement_	− _We may postpone reaching an agreement_

> This chart shows why the person is, from his or her perspective, reasonably saying "no" to the question.

---

[2]Fisher, Kopelman, and Schneider, p. 51.

The task of constructing this sort of list, which we call a Currently Perceived Choice (CPC) chart, can be seen as involving four types of activity:

1. Coming up with a way of phrasing the choice as the decision-maker herself sees it;
2. Generating possible consequences that may be perceived as important by the person at the point of choice;
3. Drafting these consequences in simple, clear phrases;
4. Selecting the half-dozen or so most important of these on each side of the choice and placing them in a meaningful order.

A second way of generating consequences of possible importance to the decision-maker or "prince" you have targeted is to create and then run through a checklist of considerations that might well be important to any leader who is being asked to make an important decision. A comprehensive checklist would be too cumbersome to be useful; one could generate a shorter list that might include the following points, phrased from the leader's point of view:

CATEGORIES OF CONSEQUENCES FOR A DECISION-MAKER[3]

For me personally:
- will I lose office? power?
- will people criticize me? praise me?

For my country domestically (e.g., party, government, people):
- short-term consequences? long-term consequences?
- consequences by categories:
  economic? military? legal? political?
- opportunity costs—will it prevent something better?

For my country internationally:
- international political support? what will be the effect on our friends and allies?
- will the precedent be a good one or a bad one?
- is the action consistent with our principles?
  is it the "right" thing to do?
- can I always do it later if I want?

Running through such a checklist can help generate ideas that we can assess by trying to put ourselves in the shoes of the decision-maker.

After generating a range of points, we can formulate the more impor-

---

[3]Fisher, Kopelman, and Schneider, p. 53.

tant ones in short, suggestive sentences written from the point of view of the person faced with the choice. Each of these can be prefaced with a "+" or "–" sign indicating how that point appears to the decision-maker. With this tool, there is great freedom for judgment as to whether a given item is considered as a positive consequence on one side of the ledger, as a negative consequence on the other side of the ledger, or whether it is best to have it appear on both sides.

After drafting brief phrases that will suggest the important consequences, these can be listed in some order that helps illuminate the situation. Experience suggests that the order used in the tool in Chart 5–5 is one that works well in many cases. First, you figure out who your decision-maker is. Second, you frame the question he or she is facing. Third, you list the consequences to the decision-maker from the *decision-maker's point of view* if he or she says "yes." Finally, you list the consequences if the decision-maker answers "no" to the question presented.

Chart 5–6 presented a general example illustrating considerations that are likely to be affecting a person who sees his side as being asked to make a concession. It helps explain why negotiations often become stalemated; neither side sees good enough reasons for making concessions; it is easier to wait.

Chart 5–7 is an example suggesting how Prime Minister Yitzhak Shamir might have perceived his choice regarding the West Bank in 1989.

CHART 5–7
CURRENTLY PERCEIVED CHOICE TOOL

Case: _Israel / West Bank_

As of: _1989_

The Currently Perceived Choice of _Israeli Prime Minister Yitzhak Shamir_

Question faced: "Shall I _agree that the principle of withdrawal from occupied territories applies to the West Bank_ ?"

Consequences If I Say "Yes"	Consequences If I Say "No"
– _I will lose support from my strongest political base, the Likud bloc_	+ _I maintain the heart of my political support, the Likud bloc_
– _We weaken our moral claim to the West Bank whether or not an agreement is reached_	+ _We maintain our moral claim to Judea and Samaria if the talks fail_
– _We give up our chief bargaining point in exchange for nothing_	+ _We reserve our full bargaining position_
– _We increase the chance of a PLO-dominated state on the West Bank_	+ _We reduce the risk of a Palestinian state_
– _I back down to Egyptian and U.S. pressure_	+ _We stand up to U.S. pressure_
– _I make commitments about the West Bank when there is no Arab who can make any commitment to us about it_	+ _We avoid negotiating over the West Bank until we face Arabs willing and able to make commitments about it_
– _We weaken our ability to negotiate strong provisions on security and settlements_	+ _We maximize our chance of obtaining favorable terms on security and settlements_
	+ _We can always back down later if we have to_

BUT:	**BUT:**
+ _George Bush will be happy_	– _The U.S. government will be unhappy and may drag its feet on more arms_
+ _There is a good chance for resuming peace negotiations_	– _I will get some political criticism at home from the Labor Party_

Like the telescoped perspective of a city that a subway map provides in order to be useful, the Currently Perceived Choice Tool has limitations. By focusing on the specific choice of one individual it may obscure differences of opinion within a government and the complex interplay that takes place within a bureaucracy. Sometimes a two-step process is helpful, in which we first list the consequences to the individual of suggesting to his colleagues that their government decide as we would like them to, and then below that list the consequences to the government or to the decision-makers as a group. The example in Chart 5–7 looking at Prime Minister Shamir's choice tries to deal with this problem by listing some consequences as ones that he might think of as personal ("I will lose support . . .") and others as affecting the government ("We give up our chief bargaining point . . ."). There may be better ways to illuminate these different kinds of anticipated consequences. On the other hand, it is important to realize that decision-makers themselves rarely sort out their thoughts as precisely as we are trying to do, and we are seeking an appreciation of their very human choice, not some mathematical calculation.

Their Choice Is Our Problem

A Currently Perceived Choice chart usually explains why someone has not made a decision. The other side's perceptions, their emotions, their interests, and what they hear us as saying have not only provided the material with which we are able to construct their currently perceived choice. Looking separately at each of those subjects has given us some clues on how to proceed. We may want to correct misperceptions, reduce emotions, respond to their interests, and transmit a more effective or more easily understood message than the one they have been receiving. In looking forward as in looking back, all these considerations impinge upon the choice of someone we are trying to influence. A good approximation of our problem is to change that choice from the one that has been seen to one that will be seen at some date in the near future. At the moment of time we are considering (either the present or some date in the past) the person we would like to make a decision has not made the decision we want. Our problem is to change the choice faced by someone on the other side so that that person is likely to decide as we would like.

CHAPTER
—6—

The View
from the Bureaucracy

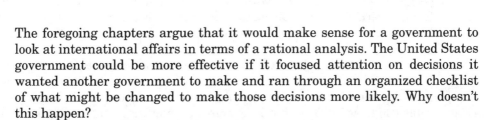

The foregoing chapters argue that it would make sense for a government to look at international affairs in terms of a rational analysis. The United States government could be more effective if it focused attention on decisions it wanted another government to make and ran through an organized checklist of what might be changed to make those decisions more likely. Why doesn't this happen?

People in government usually have two answers: "These ideas are entirely too theoretical," and "We go through that kind of analysis already." In a sense, both statements are true. The limited role that reasoned analysis of a problem can play becomes explicable when we step inside the government and look at what goes on. Machiavelli was advising a single prince, a man who could make a governmental decision all by himself. Today a governmental decision is the product of a vast bureaucracy which, in turn, is democratically responsible to a large constituency. If we do not like the decisions that come out, we must look at the machinery that produces them.

A hypothetical account of a single decision will put a little flesh, if only make-believe, onto the organizational skeleton that determines how a foreign policy decision is formulated. Let us assume that a deputy assistant secretary in the Office of International Security Affairs in the Department of Defense has just received a copy of a cable from Moscow reporting that fighting has broken out in Uzbekistan, that Russia is sending in reinforcements, and that some Islamic countries are talking about intervening in Uzbekistan to help end Russian occupation.

One course of action would be for him to sit down and carefully formulate possible decisions that the United States might seek from Russia, from the rebel leaders in Uzbekistan, and from the various Islamic states. He might work out as best he could how the pros and cons of each of those decisions probably look to the people concerned at the moment, and then consider how those pros and cons might be altered to make more likely those decisions we would like the various parties to make. He could then work out proposed actions by the United States that would appropriately structure the choices open to the governments concerned and convincingly communicate those choices to them. He could prepare the operational documents required to produce these actions by the U.S. government. Finally, he could prepare his written analysis of the alternatives and of their comparative costs, risks, and benefits to the United States.

It would take a great deal of effort for this official to work up such papers. But it is not laziness that causes him to avoid such theoretical analysis. If he were to start on this task, others in the U.S. government would have reacted to the incoming news long before he came up with his results. His study would be bypassed by events. His work would probably have no impact on the action taken. Furthermore, it is not his job to consider all aspects of U.S. foreign policy relating to the Uzbek crisis: he is to focus on military matters. Others are to be concerned with former Soviet states, with U.S. relations with Russia, with the U.S. information program, with U.S. actions in the United Nations, and so forth. Those problems are not the task of the deputy assistant secretary.

So, the official starts at the other end and begins to work on a cable to Moscow. He knows that the first person who works on a draft has an advantage. As he writes the draft a number of considerations are in his mind: If the cable can be worded so that it is simply an application of a prior decision or a prior statement by the president or another high official, the cable will be more difficult for others to object to, it can be cleared at a low level, and it can be dispatched more quickly. He looks through his loose-leaf notebook of presidential and other quotations relating to armed intervention and wars of independence. At the same time, he is thinking about what his immediate superior, the assistant secretary, would want him to come up with. After all, a deputy is supposed to produce a draft his boss would want to recommend to the secretary, or be able to justify if it should go out without the secretary's clearance.

A deputy assistant secretary knows that there will be a meeting on this cable among those in the different offices and departments involved. He does not want this meeting to become bogged down in big and unanswerable questions. If his cable involves anything that is new or controversial, it is likely to meet opposition. Experience has taught him that a short cable that is covered by prior policy statements wins more support than a cable that breaks new ground. A bright idea is, almost by definition, inconsistent with prior government policy. It is likely to get shot down by consensus of those present at the meeting. Worse than that, the deputy's reputation and effectiveness within the government will be weakened if he advances an idea that is rejected. Too many failures and he will become known as someone who is unrealistic—as someone to whose views one need not pay much attention.

While this deputy is working on a draft cable, half a dozen other people in the government are thinking about the Uzbek problem and are also thinking about what it is that they should suggest. They are reviewing past governmental statements on former Soviet states, intervention, and the role of the United Nations in such uprisings. Each of them is also thinking about the kind of proposal that could be cleared throughout the government with the least difficulty and delay.

At the meeting on the situation in Uzbekistan the discussion will be practical. The immediate question will be what the United States should do or say in response. It is not surprising that agreement tends to settle on the lowest common denominator. There is no need to reach agreement on reasons if those present can reach agreement on the immediate action to be taken.

The outcome of the meeting could likely be a cable to the U.S. embassy in Moscow, with copies to other embassies, asking that the respective governments be reminded that the United States has always been in favor of self-determination but is opposed to the settlement of such questions by bloodshed and violence, that the United States is willing to work with others in bringing about a peaceful resolution of the problem, and believes that this should be accomplished within the framework of the United Nations. United States ambassadors will also be asked to make sure that the governments concerned appreciate the dangers of intervention and the risks inherent in the situation. There will also be no objection from other departments to the State Department's proposed release stating that the United States government is concerned over developments in Uzbekistan, that officers have been instructed to follow the situation closely, and that the president is being kept fully informed.

Such a decision may not be the wisest one for the United States government to make. It tends to be the easiest and hence the most probable. It does not focus on the task of influencing what other countries do or on their decisional problems. Such a cable is the product of domestic institutions and it reflects the concerns of the people who staff these institutions. The case of the deputy assistant secretary suggests some of these concerns. Three general features of the way governments work help to explain why good people usually produce inadequate decisions:

1. Subordinate officers act as deputy judges, not advocates.

If the government is to act wisely, it should consider not only the most probable decisions, but also some that at the outset appear unpromising. In looking for what to do, the net should be cast widely and the cases in favor of a number of quite different suggestions developed. In a court of law the adversary process is used to make sure that positions that may not at first appear to have much merit are fully explored. The lawyer who is defending an accused person is not asked to make the argument he thinks has a high chance of being adopted, but rather to advance his client's point of view. He is presenting considerations that ought to be taken into account—and weighed against others—in reaching a decision. The arguments in favor of one course of action are fully explored and clearly articulated before becoming watered down by offsetting considerations. This adversary process tends to ensure that the judge gives full consideration to a wide range possibilities in making his choice.

The role of a government officer who suggests a course of action to his or her superior is quite different. To be sure, there is within the government a great deal of controversy and a great deal of advocacy. By and large, however, it is like an argument among judges, not among counsel, because each official is supposed to take all factors into account. The junior staff officer in the State Department or in the Defense Department in recommending action with respect to the bombing of North Vietnam was expected to make a "realistic" recommendation that takes into account the political costs on the Hill that the president may incur in making one decision or another. Domestic political considerations are considered at every level. The president is rarely given the chance to hear what someone thinks "ought" to be done if only domestic considerations would permit. The person who advises the president about what ought to be done and the person who advises the advisor are expected themselves to take into account the domestic considerations and to make a realistic proposal.

The State Department officer was not expected to recommend an end to the bombing of North Vietnam unless he or she believed that such a decision was politically feasible. The president, finding that even his foreign policy advisors did not recommend an end to the bombing, was reluctant to end the bombing. Each person from the bottom up adjusts his or her expert view to take adequate account of political realities. It is no wonder that the domestic political climate weighs heavily in the final decision.

2. The premium placed on success tends to minimize effectiveness.

There are substantial personal costs to a government official in pushing ideas that are rejected. It might occur to a State Department official that the United States ought unilaterally to drop some of its restrictions on travel and trade with Cuba. She might think that this would increase the strength of U.S. influence within Cuba or that it would demonstrate U.S. flexibility. What would happen if that idea were to be advanced but not adopted? One possible treatment of this outcome by her superiors would be favorable commendation. They might thank her for raising the point, assure her that the government could not know that they were pursuing the wisest possible course except by comparing it with alternative policies, explain their reasons for rejecting the idea, and urge her to continue to reexamine policies and suggest new ideas no matter how unlikely their adoption seemed.

Such comments are possible, but experience suggests that they are not common. The officer is more likely to be told that her suggestion is contrary to the existing policy, and she may be made to feel that making the suggestion showed poor judgment. Perhaps a public statement would be issued to deny that the government was giving any consideration to removing restrictions on trade or travel with Cuba. This might be accompanied by a further statement that all responsible officials of the government were in support of the government's policy.

The White House issued such a statement following publication in December, 1962 in the *Saturday Evening Post* of the "charge" that Adlai Stevenson had suggested during the Cuban Missile Crisis that the United States might withdraw its missiles from Turkey in exchange for the withdrawal of Soviet missiles from Cuba. In fact, the president had decided several months before that our nuclear missiles should be withdrawn from Turkey. If the Soviet missiles could be withdrawn from Cuba in exchange for something we had decided to do anyway, the risks of war might be reduced at no practical cost to the United States. It would have been grossly irresponsible of our officials if that idea had not been advanced within the government and thoroughly canvassed. But in this case, Mr. Stevenson felt compelled to deny that he had ever made the suggestion, and the White House issued a statement that Mr. Stevenson "strongly supported" the president's decision.

Such statements bring home to a government officer that it is poor strategy to make suggestions that are not adopted. In rare cases an officer may be asked to play devil's advocate, but otherwise he had better be on the side of the angels; it is in his interest to be identified after the event as having been on the side that favored the policy that was adopted. As of any one day, an existing policy is more likely to be continued than changed.

The safest bet is to be opposed to change and reject new ideas. This method of achieving a high degree of success is widespread (but not universal) within the government. It produces a general reduction in the effectiveness of government officers. An officer may start off with a high expectation of getting things done—but it is almost always more difficult to get decisions through the governmental bureaucracy than the inexperienced person believes. A number of projects fail. The officer becomes more realistic. He is able to reduce his failure rate:

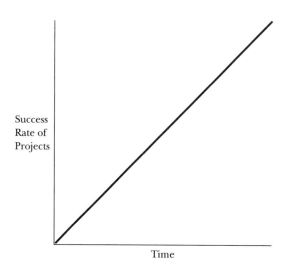

He reduces the number of his ideas that are shot down, however, by reducing the number proposed. So "improvement" is accomplished by reducing the number of things he tries to do—by reducing the amount of change he seeks to bring about. The less he tries to do, the less he gets done. A schematic graph of what a person actually gets done in the first two years in government might look something like this:

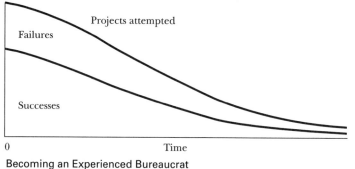

Becoming an Experienced Bureaucrat

This chart summarizes the bureaucratic life of a New Dealer, a Kennedy appointee, or almost any idealistic young person who joins the foreign service. With the passage of time, she becomes more realistic, more practical. She stops advancing "half-baked" ideas. She becomes more careful in the ideas she advances. Most of those she now advances are adopted. But she is getting less than half as much done as when she started.

3. Decisions expand with time.

A third institutional feature that causes a government to act irrationally is the undue weight that governments often give to prior decisions.

It is impossible at the time a decision is made to distinguish precisely between what has been decided and what has not. Governments often *try* to define the scope of what has been decided. Sometimes there is an attempt to make the decision big—a decision of "policy." In 1932, for example, Secretary of State Stimson declared that the United States "does not intend to recognize any situation, treaty, or agreement which may be brought about by means contrary to the covenants and obligations of the Pact of Paris of August 27, 1928. . . . "[1] The decision was defined to apply to a large category of cases and for a long period of time. On other occasions the attempt is to define the scope of the decision narrowly. The decision of the United States in 1955 to provide compensation to the Japanese fishermen who were injured by fallout from nuclear tests in the Pacific in 1954 was intended to be a "one-shot" decision applying only to that particular situation. The statement accompanying the compensation said it was being tendered *ex gratia,* without reference to the question of legal liability.

Despite what may be said at the time a decision is made, however, the effective scope of what has been decided cannot be defined at that time. That scope is determined by subsequent actions of the government. Situations will necessarily arise that involve facts not thought of or not fully appreciated at the time the first decision was made. People will then have to decide whether or not the first decision affects what should be done now. Even the explicit statement that a decision shall not be a precedent cannot eliminate its effect as a precedent. At the least, it has set a precedent for accompanying future decisions with the statement that they are not a precedent.

There is a degree to which a decision ought, as a rational matter, to govern future conduct. As long as the facts and the perceived choices are substantially the same, then a decision by the same or a higher level of government ought, presumptively, to be followed. As a general rule, there is no reason to expect that a fresh decision in such a case will be any wiser than the first. There are positive costs in diverting intellectual resources from other problems to the reconsideration of a solution already devised in a similar situation. Further, there are administrative advantages in consistency. The task for the person faced with a subsequent choice in such a case is to determine whether the facts and choices are so similar to those considered at the time of the first decision that the differences do not justify reexamining the problem.

However, governments tend to give prior decisions either greater or less scope than they deserve. Conclusions reached on one set of facts are applied to different facts. Conclusions reached on limited information continue to be followed even after much more information is available—information that could be expected to lead to a different decision. Conclusions reached in haste are followed even though there is now time to think through the matter more carefully.

---

[1]Hodgson, Godfrey, *The Colonel: The Life and Wars of Henry Stimson, 1867–1950* (New York: Knopf, 1990), p. 158.

There are a number of reasons for this harmful practice. Although consistency is a virtue, it is deemed by officials to be even more of a virtue than it is. This is a result of a government's concentrating its attention in foreign affairs on its own decisions rather than on the decisions of other governments. If we think of actions in the field of foreign affairs as announcements of our policy and the making of our decisions, then changes in policy or the reversal of decisions suggests that mistakes have been made. If we recognize, however, that in foreign affairs the important decisions are those of other governments and that our actions are best considered as attempts to influence them, consistency becomes less of a virtue. Persistence in pursuing an unsuccessful means of exerting influence is certainly not presumptively the wisest course of action.

Another reason inducing governments to treat a past decision as a currently valid one is the administrative ease of doing so. It is far simpler to treat a matter as one governed by a prior decision than to treat it as a new problem. Every day new matters come up. The preliminary question confronting an official is to decide whether or not the matter is governed by the prior decision. One might guess that of all the situations in which this preliminary question is raised, about half would be found to be covered by the prior decision and half would not. The incentive for the official to resolve the preliminary question one way rather than the other, however, is strong. If he decides that this matter is governed by the prior decision, his work is done. Time is saved, the problem is dealt with, and he can go on to other things. If, however, the official decides that the problem is essentially a new one, he has taken on a lot of work, not only for himself but for others as well. They must develop the alternatives, examine the pros and cons, and reach bureaucratic agreement on what should be done. Faced with such disparate consequences it is not surprising that, unconsciously if not consciously, the preliminary question is usually resolved in favor of treating the matter as governed by prior decision.

The limited authority of each official further operates to cause past decisions to grow with time. A presidential decision not to trade with Castro's Cuba was reached under certain factual conditions. The decision was presumably not to trade with Cuba for the time being. Without further authority, lower officials of the government can apply that decision to factual circumstances different from those considered by the president. They can also extend indefinitely the period of time for which trade shall be cut off. They can probably even tighten the implementation of the decision so that it applies to trade through third states. Lower officials do not, however, have authority to change the original decision to block trade. Even if they believe that the factual situation has so changed that the reasons underlying the prior decision are no longer applicable, they cannot on their own authority say that the decision is no longer controlling. They cannot say that a reasonable time has now passed and that trade can be resumed. Only the president can cut off the continuing effect of his prior decision.

It is not surprising that, with this one-way authority, decisions tend to grow with time and to be applied to facts and circumstances radically different from those originally taken into account. Although the president is free to say that his prior decision is no longer applicable, he is unlikely to do so unless that question is put on the agenda and brought to his attention with staff recommendations. It is usually an uphill fight for any staff person to try to do so.

The following of a prior decision has a cumulative effect. Precedent builds upon precedent. Each time a prior decision is treated as applying to somewhat different facts, there is now a precedent that itself will be applied to facts still further removed from those originally considered. This is particularly true in the case of policies designed to extend into the future. The decision not to trade with Cuba is extended one day after the next. The gradual change in hats from yesterday to today will rarely seem sufficient to justify drawing an end to the original decision and reexamining the matter afresh. In government decisions as in the law, the dead hand of the past thus governs more than it should. A decision to take a step in a particular direction becomes a decision to pursue that course indefinitely until major and obvious considerations require some shift.

CHAPTER
—7—

Case Study on Arms Control— The Antiballistic Missile Treaty

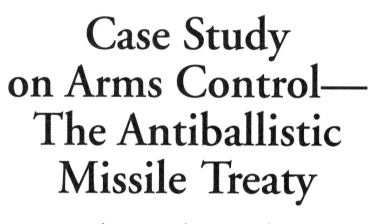

CASE OVERVIEW

Say you are a U.S. president who aspires to negotiate a reduction of nuclear weapons with another nuclear-armed state. In order to realize an arms control agreement that will garner the constitutionally required two-thirds approval by the Senate, you will need to orchestrate five levels of negotiations: one within the executive branch; one with key players in Congress; one with affected allies; one with the American public; and, of course, the actual negotiations with delegates of the other nuclear-armed nation itself.

Examining a set of successful arms control negotiations that subsequently became swept up in the American political process is a way of understanding some of the constraints and opportunities of such multilayered diplomacy. This case study of the Antiballistic Missile Treaty of 1972, negotiated between the United States and the then-Soviet Union, shows one way in which substance and process influence each other. Issues of substance, for example, are always embedded in a bureaucratic process. An understanding of the limits imposed by bureaucracy can also define the scope for individual action and initiative.

This case study provides background material useful for understanding the application of the tools in Chapters 8–11. The materials chosen for this case and the bibliography are, accordingly, designed to demonstrate how structural constraints on the negotiation can impact the parties and the outcome. The case study should not be considered a comprehensive review of arms control negotiation but rather an illustrative example.

BACKGROUND

A Climate of Mistrust

In the early 1960s, the United States and the Soviet Union shared a competitive relationship fraught with conflict that was a legacy of the early cold war. Given the climate of intense mutual distrust, each superpower had "a strong preference for relying on its own effort to secure its security rather than depend[ing] on cooperative arrangements with a powerful, distrusted ally for this purpose."[1] Seeking stability through dominance rather than cooperation—through unilateral actions such as weapons programs rather than through joint projects such as weapons freezes or reductions—animated the powerful "peace-through-strength" faction in the U.S. Senate, headed by Senator Henry M. Jackson.

By contrast, adherents to what has been called the "interdependence" school of thought believed that it was in the best interests of the leaders of the Soviet Union and the United States to cooperate, because both countries stood to lose so much in any nuclear exchange. Interdependence analysts and decision-makers, headed by Senator Edward Brooke, believed that arms control negotiations were an expanding-sum game that both sides could win.[2]

The Antiballistic Missile (ABM) Treaty signed in 1972 was one part of the Strategic Arms Limitation Talks, or SALT I negotiations, as they came to be known. The SALT negotiation process began in 1969, but its origins were in the mid-1960s. President Johnson and Secretary of Defense Robert McNamara were concerned that the U.S. Congress might feel pressured to replicate a Soviet ABM system that was being developed to protect Moscow. The White House made secret overtures to the Soviets at the end of 1965 to explore interest in limiting ABM systems. In early 1966, after the Soviets had somewhat reluctantly approved a request for private talks, Johnson wrote to Soviet Premier Kosygin:

> I think you must realize that following the deployment by you of an antiballistic missile system, I face great pressures from members of Congress and from public opinion not only to deploy defensive systems in this country, but also to increase greatly our capabilities to penetrate any defensive system which you might establish. If we should feel compelled to make such major

---

[1]Alexander L. George, Philip J. Farley, and Alexander Dallin, *U.S.–Soviet Security Cooperation* (NY: Oxford University Press, 1988), p. 4.

[2]The "interdependence" label is used by former arms control negotiator George Bunn in his masterful analysis *Arms Control by Committee: Managing Negotiations with the Russians* (Stanford, CA: Stanford University Press, 1992). This case study draws heavily on his insider knowledge and research for his chapter "SALT I: The ABM Treaty and an Opportunity Lost to Ban MIRVs," pp. 106–131.

increases in our strategic weapons capabilities, I have no doubt that you
would in turn feel under compulsion to do likewise. We would thus have incurred on both sides colossal costs without substantially enhancing the security of our own peoples.[3]

At the June 1967 summit meeting in Glassboro, New Jersey, McNamara attempted to change Kosygin's perception that Soviet plans for an ABM system
were potentially preventing casualties and deaths, and induce him instead to
see ABM systems generally as a factor fueling the arms race. Unable to get a
firm commitment from Kosygin to proceed with talks that might limit ABMs,
McNamara countered with a plan for a "thin" ABM shield to defend the
United States. The announcement identified the threat to be shielded against
as a possible Chinese attack—which would presumably be much smaller than
a possible Soviet attack. But military experts noted that such a system could
be extended, perhaps ultimately to protect American missiles from Soviet attack. As former arms control negotiator George Bunn has explained, this
phase of McNamara's diplomacy probably lacked urgency because McNamara
doubted whether any conceivable technology could ever really protect the
American population against a Soviet first strike.

The Glassboro summit and the Johnson–Kosygin letters at least
hinted to each side the other's interest in curbing defensive and offensive
missiles. But in the meantime, the arms race had escalated significantly. Mc-
Namara's deputy for research and engineering announced in late 1967 that
the United States was developing multiple independently targeted reentry
vehicles (MIRVs), which would multiply the force of long-range missiles
enough to overwhelm a Soviet ABM system, as well as acting as a deterrent
to the deployment of Soviet offensive systems.

Some officials in the Johnson administration wanted to propose a ban
on MIRVs in initial arms limitation talks, but Johnson himself did not wish
to expend the political capital with the Joint Chiefs of Staff and the Senate
necessary to offer a proposal to ban MIRVs, at least until he could determine
whether negotiations with the Soviets would be productive. So MIRV tests
went forward in the summer of 1968. Meanwhile, the Soviet Union and its allies invaded Czechoslovakia on August 20, 1968. Now American outrage made
it impossible to announce arms talks, even though a U.S.–Soviet announcement of a summit conference to launch the talks had been set for the next
day. Johnson canceled a scheduled press release.

Events seemed to be conspiring to postpone the talks into the new
Nixon administration. The incoming Nixon team objected to any attempt to
reschedule the summit conference after the 1968 election but before Johnson
left office. Negotiations did not begin for another year, and by then the Soviets had more ICBMs and SLBMs (submarine-launched ballistic missiles)

---

[3]Quoted in Glen T. Seaborg, *Stemming the Tide: Arms Control in the Johnson Years* (Lexington,
MA: Lexington Books, 1987), p. 415. See also Farley, "Strategic Arms Limitations: SALT I," in
Coit D. Blacker and Gloria Duffy, eds., *International Arms Control*, pp. 220–21.

than the United States, counting those under construction as well as those deployed.[4]

During the presidential campaign of 1968, Richard Nixon had painted himself as a hard-nosed exponent of the peace-through-strength school. Nixon had derided his opponent, Hubert Humphrey, a strong supporter of the 1968 Nuclear Nonproliferation Treaty (NPT), as being too conciliatory. Yet Nixon's inaugural address proclaimed an "era of negotiations." Nixon and his national security adviser, Henry Kissinger, believed that the Soviet Union's stake in more cooperation and less confrontation with the United States would grow if the Nixon administration could forge links among different U.S.–Soviet issues. They hoped that joint interests, such as reducing the risks of nuclear war and curbing military budgets, would be strong enough to induce the Soviets to be more forthcoming over other disputes in regional trouble spots like Vietnam and the Middle East. Nixon and Kissinger also hoped that, over time, the Soviet Union's interest in joint gains would ultimately act as a check on other, more traditional methods for expanding Soviet influence, such as invasion, subversion, and arms shipments to Third World countries.

Military planners and arms control experts in the Nixon administration were skeptical of a strategy that relied too heavily on notions of increased cooperation. These experts sought limits on the continuing growth of Soviet missile stockpiles and on its new ABM system. They wanted to protect the U.S. retaliatory force—not the U.S. population—from a Soviet missile attack, to close off what later came to be called the "window of vulnerability" for American intercontinental ballistic missiles (ICBMs), and to reduce any incentives for the Soviets to launch a first strike. They concluded that meaningful strategic superiority over the Soviets could not be maintained, and that "strategic equivalence" was a more realistic goal.

Soviet leaders, too, disagreed with the Nixonian notion of linking arms control to broader questions of their foreign policy. They balked at the approach of using arms control negotiations to check what Americans saw as issues of Soviet misbehavior. Soviet leaders shared a common interest, however, with the United States in improving bilateral relations.

Negotiating "Inside Out"

Internal negotiations that are multiphase and multiparty are notoriously difficult to plan and execute. Nixon walked a fine line between appearing tough enough as a commander-in-chief to bring the "peace-through-strength" senators on board, while also appearing flexible enough as a negotiator to get some members of the more conciliatory "interdependence school" to support the administration's defense budgets. Herbert York, one of President Jimmy Carter's test ban negotiators, pointed out that, because of the need to placate

---

[4]See Bunn, p. 109, note 10.

the peace-through-strength senators, "the negotiation instructions to our delegations overseas have always been characterized by extreme caution and conservatism."[5]

The internal dynamics of how a negotiating proposal is hammered out have consequences, in turn, for the shape of the "external" proposal as it is presented to the other side. Developing a rigid or one-sided internal position from which concessions are extracted through painful bilateral negotiations is a recipe for what we discuss in Chapter 9 as a "positional bargaining" approach—a process with built-in incentives for delay, stalemate, or less-than-optimal agreement. It also presents a dilemma for the negotiators by setting up a stark dichotomy between tough and flexible, or "hard" and "soft" approaches to negotiations:

> If our position is close to what we want as an outcome, the Soviets will start negotiating from there and we are likely to end up being pressed to accept an unsatisfactory outcome. If, however, our position is padded with a great deal of room for negotiation, the Soviets may not negotiate seriously but, instead, use the asserted one-sidedness of our proposals as propaganda in the arena of international public opinion . . . With regard to domestic and allied politics, if we open with a "hard" offer and later retreat from that position, we may appear "weak." This could harm prospects for ratification of the agreement. But to open with a "soft" offer and hold firm is to run the risk of being seen as "uncompromising."[6]

Nixon and Kissinger shared a creed of establishing tight secrecy and vigilant central control over the conduct of international relations, at the level of both policy planning and day-to-day conduct of business. To facilitate control of the foreign policy bureaucracy, Nixon chose his old friend William Rogers as secretary of state, even though Rogers had little foreign policy experience. Kissinger or his staff chaired a variety of interagency committees under the National Security Council (NSC), rather than using the secretary of state or his staff, as had been the case in prior administrations.

Options for SALT were usually developed by an interagency committee, chaired by Kissinger, that came to be called the Verification Panel. These options were later presented to the NSC with Nixon presiding, but by then many of the decisions had been made. After NSC meetings, the final decision was often circulated in a White House memorandum to the other agencies.

> Nixon and I [Kissinger] could use the interdepartmental machinery to educate ourselves . . . these [interdepartmental] studies showed us the range of options and what could find support within the government. We were then able to put departmental ideas into practice outside of formal channels."[7]

---

[5]Herbert York, "Bilateral Negotiations and the Arms Race," *Scientific American* 249, vol. 4 (Oct. 1983): 149–56, at 149.

[6]Leon Sloss, "Lessons Learned in Negotiating with the Soviet Union: Introduction and Findings," in Leon Sloss and M. Scott Davis, eds., *A Game for High Stakes: Lessons Learned in Negotiating with the Soviet Union* (Cambridge, MA: Ballinger, 1986), p. 5.

[7]From *The White House Years* by Henry A. Kissinger, pp. 147–48. By permission of Little, Brown and Company.

The Nixon-Kissinger system gave the two leaders effective control over the range of options that could be presented to the Soviets, as well as giving them needed information about the views of the Arms Control and Disarmament Agency (ACDA), for example, on such options. This information, together with effective liaison with America's allies, repeated briefings for key congressional leaders and committees, and informal explorations with the Soviets, enabled Nixon and Kissinger more effectively to appraise what was possible, both internally and externally.

Given the Nixon-Kissinger objective of total White House control over U.S–Soviet negotiations, their system certainly offered an ingenious organizational design. But Kissinger also sought to control the day-to-day conduct of key negotiations. As George Bunn observed, "He carried Nixon's penchant for secrecy so far as to deny information about these negotiations even to the secretary of state and the negotiating delegation itself, an approach that led to confusion, delay and mistake."[8]

THE TALKS

Kissinger began meeting secretly with Soviet Ambassador Anatoly Dobrynin immediately upon taking office in early 1969. Kissinger recounted that

> Dobrynin and I began to conduct preliminary negotiations on almost all major issues, he on behalf of the Politburo, I as confidant to Nixon. We would, informally, clarify the basic purposes of our governments and when our talks gave hope of specific agreements, the subject was moved to conventional diplomatic channels.[9]

In these preliminary meetings, Kissinger began with explorations of interests and options for agreement before any statements of position were called for. He saw this approach as useful in dealing with differing factions within the American and Soviet governments:

> They run a bureaucracy that is even more complex than our own . . . So I have always felt . . . that a dialogue with the Soviets should begin on the philosophical level. You tell the Soviets what it is you are trying to accomplish and why and that enables their leader to go to the Politburo and say, "This is what the Americans say they are trying to achieve. Why don't we at least examine it?" The other way [of beginning with a statement of our position], numbers of nuclear weapons are strained, first through our bureaucracy, and then through theirs. What starts out as an American bureaucratic compromise goes over to their side, where all their sharpshooters get a crack at it.[10]

---

[8]Bunn, p. 112. See also, for example, the accounts in Tom Wicker, *One of Us: Richard Nixon and the American Dream* (NY: Random House, 1991), pp. 463–64, 468–72, 476–79.

[9]Kissinger, p. 139.

[10]Kissinger, "Henry Kissinger interview," quoted in Bunn, p. 112.

Based on this analysis, Kissinger decided that the first round of talks should be "exploratory," with a high-level (but not head of state) exploration of possible formulas for agreement. As a result, SALT began in November 1969 with a five-week exploration of interests and options before any formal position was taken by either side. Keeping the talks secret also minimized loss of face or other damage to the negotiations if an idea were not approved at the highest levels. Nixon and Kissinger could learn about the range of possibilities without appearing to make concessions to the Soviets that might alienate the peace-through-strength faction in the Senate.

From the American perspective, a highlight of this opening round of SALT was Soviet Ambassador Vladimir Semenov's statement that "mutually acceptable solutions should be sought that would insure the security of each side equally rather than through efforts to obtain unilateral military advantages."[11] According to Gerard Smith's and George Bunn's summaries, written statements such as Semenov's were read out by each side at the negotiating table, despite Smith's urging a less formal process. However, authorities in Moscow and Washington were initially more comfortable with preapproved formal statements and "a large amount of 'negotiation' by speeches."[12] Smith and Semenov were able to speak together after the speechmaking sessions. Each negotiator would speak to a counterpart on the other side, away from the table, to explain the formal statements and to ask questions about them. Both sides also floated hypothetical "what if" questions, such as "If our delegation were instructed to propose X, what do you think your delegation would be instructed to reply?"[13]

During this round, the Soviet side also presented options rather than positions. As with the Americans, the Soviets stipulated that the ideas they were presenting were not to be considered formal proposals. For example, Semenov outlined three different approaches to limiting ABMs: a total ban; a limited deployment (presumably including the existing Moscow system); or a full shield for an extensive area (though according to George Bunn, he clearly opposed the last possibility). Bunn observed, "Indeed, it quickly became evident that the Soviets had changed their minds about ABM systems. Their comments about the U.S. program gave a clear indication that their primary aim was to limit ABMs—probably to a local system such as their own around Moscow."[14]

The negotiators of the exploratory round also addressed the perennially thorny issue of verification. The Soviets adamantly resisted on-site inspections, a recurring issue from the Nonproliferation Talks of the 1960s. The SALT agreements, which were ultimately signed in 1972, therefore focused

---

[11]Gerard Smith, *Double Talk: The Story of SALT I* (Lanham, MD: University Press of America, 1980), p. 83.
[12]Smith, p. 81.
[13]Smith, p. 81.
[14]Bunn, p. 115.

on technology such as strategic missile launchers and ABM systems, where deployment could be verified without on-site inspection. While many seemingly intractable issues regarding numbers of MIRVs, overseas aircraft bases, and submarine-launched missiles were not resolved until Kissinger's trip to Moscow in April 1972, Smith's assessment was that the exploratory approach to the first round "had proven well designed to ferret out the coincident and conflicting interests of the United States and the Soviet Union.[15]

The Role of Domestic Politics

Negotiations, of course, can be carried out for a variety of purposes other than reaching agreement. Getting credit from a domestic constituency (for being tough or for continuing a dialogue); impressing or reassuring allies; discrediting internal opponents; and retaining White House control over the process are all purposes discernible in the ABM negotiation process that may have had little to do with achieving a shared vision with the Soviets.

Arguably the most important outcome of the initial exploratory round was the decision by the Politburo and Central Committee of the Soviet Union to continue the talks. While what some negotiators call a "turning point of seriousness" had been passed by the time the first round ended in December 1969, a detailed formula for combining limits on both ABMs and offensive missiles took another year and a half.[16] Former arms control negotiator George Bunn offered the critique that

> while the decisionmaking process set up by Nixon and Kissinger proved useful in producing alternatives, it was unable to provide a clear presidential goal or a consensus within the government that could serve as a guide to those writing instructions for the negotiators. Just as in prior administrations, major differences remained within the negotiating committees of the two branches of government. As always, compromise solutions resulted.[17]

Bunn also identified the following dilemma: If the negotiations within each of the U.S. government committees are conducted one after the other before any U.S. proposal is ever made to the Soviet Union, a president may expend political capital before knowing what might be negotiable with the Soviets. Moreover, the resulting proposal may be hard to change and so one-sided that the Soviets think the United States is not interested in serious negotiations, and use this "lack of seriousness" about arms control in order to score public-relations points with allies and critics.

The Americans debated several approaches to linking offensive missile limits to ABM limits, and which options rose to the surface was largely a function of internal bureaucratic dynamics. For example, Nixon had proposed

---

[15]Smith, p. 99.
[16]See Bunn, p. 116.
[17]Bunn, p. 116.

an expanded version of the Johnson-McNamara ABM plan (the "thin" system for shielding against possible Chinese or accidental attack), to include protection of four missile fields from a possible Soviet attack. Nixon felt that favorable Senate votes on such an approach in 1968 and 1969 had increased pressure on the Soviet Union to negotiate an ABM agreement. According to Bunn, the proposed ABM system thus came to be referred to as a "bargaining chip."

As early as 1968, the Arms Control and Disarmament Agency (ACDA) and the State Department had been worried about a perceived "window of vulnerability," and had urged negotiation with the Soviets to try to ban MIRVs. But by the early 1970s, the Americans were ahead in developing MIRVs, even though field testing was not complete. If the Soviets were to catch up in MIRV development, however, the larger Soviet missiles would be able to carry more MIRVs. The fear was that if there were limits on launchers but not on warheads, the Soviets could ultimately have access to many more warheads than the Americans, and could plausibly threaten to destroy most American ICBMs in a first strike. Further, the Soviets seemed ahead in ABM deployment. While the Americans had developed what many thought was a superior system, they had not deployed anything yet.

Yet the possibility of limiting or banning MIRVs was increasingly hard to keep open as negotiating positions took shape, because American MIRV testing and Soviet deployment of single-warhead missiles was proceeding so quickly. Indeed, Kissinger had decided early on that a serious attempt to control MIRVs was not worthwhile because of opposition from the Joint Chiefs of Staff and the peace-through-strength lobby in the Senate. Nevertheless, Kissinger designed an ingenious two-part strategy: the United States would first offer two completely different alternatives to the Soviets, one banning MIRVs and one cutting missiles capable of carrying many of them at one time. If, as he anticipated, these were both turned down by the Soviets because of the conditions attached, Kissinger would then proceed with a formula that did not restrict MIRVs but controlled ABM systems and froze ICBM launcher levels.

Thus, each of the Americans' two MIRV alternatives under discussion was designed in large part to appease a particular constituency in the Senate. Senator Edward Brooke of Massachusetts led the "interdependence" faction, which sought to ban MIRVs. This group was the driving force behind a 72–6 majority in favor of a resolution describing the MIRV threat in terms of mutual vulnerability and calling for a prompt freeze on all further deployments of both offensive and defensive strategic weapons. Meanwhile, the peace-through-strength faction sought to curtail the number of large, MIRV-capable Soviet missiles while continuing with the American MIRV program. The strong majority for the Brooke resolution notwithstanding, Kissinger believed that the peace-through-strength faction could block a two-thirds vote on a treaty banning MIRVs. Kissinger's "alternatives" were something of a setup, offering the illusion of choice not just to the Soviets, but to contentious domestic constituencies in the Senate. The scheme was designed to present the Soviets with an option favored by each of the two factions, but then to move forward with something Kissinger thought was more realistic.

Nixon authorized chief negotiator Gerard Smith to present these two options to the Soviets. Without advising Smith, however, Kissinger had already told Dobrynin about the two approaches before they were ever offered, noting that if "the Soviets decided they were interested in a more limited agreement in the interim, we were prepared to explore that as well."[18] So the Soviets knew going in that they could always turn these options down and wait for something better.

By late 1970, an ABM-only agreement appeared to be the most likely outcome, as opposed to a comprehensive treaty limiting both ABMs and MIRVs. This was consistent with Kissinger's presentation to Dobrynin, suggesting that the two comprehensive approaches could be set aside in favor of a more limited option. Beginning in early 1971, Kissinger and Dobrynin negotiated a joint press release that, along with its attendant secret elaborations and understandings, became a formula for future negotiations.[19] Two important points were announced in the press release: first, both sides had abandoned the search for jointly agreed limits on the number of MIRVs on each missile. Second, the linkage between limits on ABMs and limits on offensive missiles was all but severed. Kissinger's analysis was that the press release provided the formula for SALT I, known as the Interim Agreement, which he described as an agreement that "arrest[ed] a continuing Soviet program that was deploying over two hundred ICBMs and SLBMs a year. In exchange for this we accepted a limit on ABM, our bargaining chip, which our Congress was on the verge of killing anyway."[20]

Negotiations became increasingly informal as the May 1972 date for a Nixon–Brezhnev summit approached. Raymond Garthoff, an American delegate, often engaged in "ad referendum" negotiations—so called because any potential consensus needed to be referred to a principal player before becoming official. Garthoff's opposite number on the Soviet side was Nicolai Kishilov, and the two negotiators were collectively referred to as "the wizards" by Semenov. Garthoff reports that the wizards' informal meetings became a principal channel for negotiating many of the most difficult provisions.[21] Outstanding ABM issues—number and location of sites slated for coverage; distance between permitted sites; radar monitoring of sites—were also addressed by delegation-to-delegation negotiations. Nixon sometimes modified proposals himself, relaying his wishes to Gerard Smith. Smith believed that Nixon feared internal disagreement from the "hawks": the De-

---

[18]Kissinger, pp. 525, 544–45.

[19]See Bunn, p. 120 for excerpts from the press release and a more detailed analysis of this stage of the talks.

[20]Kissinger, pp. 820–21.

[21]See the account in Bunn, p. 123.

fense Department, the Joint Chiefs, and the peace-through-strength Senate faction.

Congress and its shifting coalitions of voting majorities had a great deal of influence on the SALT agreements, in a variety of ways. First, the fact that a Senate majority had authorized an ABM system as early as 1968 seems to have convinced the Soviets that the United States might actually deploy such a system. Yet that majority was so slim by 1969—one vote—that it seems to have convinced Nixon and Kissinger that they could not count on Senate support over the long term. Nixon and Kissinger then seem to have concluded that any plan for a truly extensive ABM system might best be used as a bargaining chip, to be ultimately bargained away.

Secondly, congressional unwillingness to authorize funds for an ABM system providing coverage only for the nation's capital influenced the American delegation's move away from a tentative agreement with the Soviets to permit ABMs only around Washington and Moscow. The decision not to push for a total ABM ban was influenced by peace-through-strength conservatives who supported an ABM system to protect missile fields, not populations. Given the support for some kind of ABM system in the Senate and in the Pentagon, gaining a two-thirds Senate majority for a treaty prohibiting all ABMs on both sides would likely have been impossible.

Broadly, the ABM Treaty that was signed as part of the Interim (or SALT I) Agreement in May 1972 limited the United States and the Soviet Union to one ABM deployment area each. This area must be restricted, and could not be expanded to provide a nationwide ABM defense. Each side was also limited to 100 interceptor missiles and 100 launchers. In a provision that would later be the focus of an internal American interpretation battle, the scope for technological improvements was also limited, prohibiting, for example, the development of launchers that could send more than one interceptor at a time. The treaty, which is of unlimited duration, also included a built-in dispute-resolution system. The Standing Consultative Commission (SCC) is an ongoing, bilateral U.S.–Soviet review panel established to implement the ABM Treaty's provisions. The SCC is a forum for the private negotiation of differences where possible treaty violations can be discussed and possibly resolved with minimal risk of embarrassment to the two sides.

The Senate passed the ABM Treaty by an 88 to 2 majority. The Interim Agreement, restricting offensive weapons, received a comparable vote in both houses. These favorable votes were not foregone conclusions during the negotiations, however. Bipartisan support for cautious arms control was combined with a "public perception of Nixon as a tough anti-communist who would not be likely to let the Soviets get the better of him."[22] In 1972, Nixon also began to publicize his ongoing peace overtures to North Vietnam, and traveled to China to make peace with Beijing. His public approval ratings rose dramatically, and according to reporter and Kissinger biographer Sey-

---

[22]Bunn, p. 126.

mour Hersh, Nixon "came home from the May summit in Moscow with re-election in hand and his reputation as a peacemaker assured."[23]

Scope for Executive Leadership

As a student of diplomacy and the art of leadership, National Security Adviser Henry Kissinger had studied decision making in previous U.S. administrations. He reported unfavorably:

> If key decisions are made informally at unprepared meetings, the tendency to be obliging to the President and cooperative with one's colleagues may vitiate the articulation of choices. This seemed to me a problem of decision-making in the Kennedy and Johnson administrations. On the other hand, if the procedures grow too formal, if the President is humble enough to subordinate his judgment to a bureaucratic consensus—as happened in the Eisenhower administration—the danger is that he will in practice be given only the choice between approving or disapproving a single recommended course. Since he is not told alternatives, or the consequences of disapproval, such a system develops a bias towards the lowest common denominator.[24]

A report by a New York City lawyers group led by two former arms control negotiators advocated strong presidential initiative, and concluded:

> It is essential that the President take personal charge of the arms control enterprise. There is simply no substitute for his authority. Assuming that he is seeking an agreement on realistic terms, that means there will be dissent in some quarters. In this situation, only the President can impose and maintain discipline on the bureaucracy. Only he can insist on the prompt formulation of positions that are not merely the least common denominator between governmental agencies.[25]

The notion of the "least common denominator" as a fate to be avoided in bureaucratic negotiations recurs in these quotations by diplomats and other insiders in the arms control field. Nixon's strategy for marshaling support for the SALT agreements was an extremely proactive one: straight off the plane from Moscow, Nixon went directly to a joint session of Congress to advocate the ratification of the agreements. He also spearheaded the effort to convince the American public of the value of the agreements, and used his many public addresses to that end.

Nixon's approach to Congress was to "hold the hawks by continuing adequate defense [and to] hold [the] doves by pointing out that without SALT,

---

[23]Seymour Hersh, *The Price of Power: Kissinger in the Nixon White House* (NY: Summit, 1983), p. 481.

[24]Kissinger, pp. 40–41.

[25]Report of the Committee on International Arms Control and Security Affairs of the Association of the Bar of the City of New York, p. 134. Stanley R. Resor was the chair and Alan F. Neidle was the project director for the study. According to Bunn (see n. 4 at 272), both had long experience as arms control negotiators and participants in the process of preparing instructions for negotiators.

the arms budget would be much larger because of an all-out [arms] race and no hope for permanent offensive arms limitations."[26] Nixon stage-managed his administration's testimony to Congress in support of the SALT agreements, while Kissinger gave detailed White House briefings to over a hundred senators and representatives. Further, Nixon facilitated a purge of key ACDA officials regarded by congressional hawks as "too liberal" in order to assure the support of the defense conservatives. Finally, in order to maintain the support of the Pentagon for the agreements, Nixon authorized "safeguards" in the form of expensive development and modernization programs for high-technology weaponry. As George Bunn has noted, "The B-1 bomber, MX missile, cruise missile, and Trident submarine all owe some of their initial budgetary push to the Nixon administration's campaign to sell the SALT I agreements."[27]

POSTSCRIPT: THE CONTROVERSY OVER THE STRATEGIC DEFENSE INITIATIVE

In 1983, the tenth year of the ABM Treaty, President Ronald Reagan made a nationally televised speech that stunned the arms control community. He introduced the Strategic Defensive Initiative (SDI) program, which quickly became known as "Star Wars." "What if free people could live secure in the knowledge that their security did not rest upon the threat of instant U.S. retaliation to deter a Soviet attack, that we could intercept and destroy strategic ballistic missiles before they reached our own soil or that of our allies?" Reagan asked rhetorically.[28]

Reagan's question was illustrated with a child's drawing of families playing happily under a protective umbrella. The illustration suggested that such an SDI umbrella would protect people—presumably the "free people" Reagan mentioned in his text, perhaps an entire population—and would thus involve ABM systems far beyond the scope of the 1972 treaty and its 1974 protocol, which contemplated only a single, land-based system to protect a limited area, such as a site for retaliatory weapons. By 1985, National Security Adviser Robert C. McFarlane offered a fully articulated interpretation purporting to reconcile SDI with the ABM Treaty. This new interpretation authorized the United States to develop and test the latest advanced technology, such as space-based weapons systems using lasers and particle beams, with no restrictions short of actual deployment.

Yet Article 5 of the ABM Treaty included a commitment not to de-

---

[26]Quoted in Bunn, p. 126, from President's Office Files, White House Special Files, Nixon Presidential Materials.

[27]Bunn, p. 127.

[28]President Ronald Reagan, "Address to the Nation on Defense and National Security," *Weekly Comp. Pres. Docs.* 19 (28 March 1983): 442.

velop, test, or deploy mobile land-based ABM systems and their components, and that provision had been interpreted by the treaty's dispute resolution forum as prohibiting the deployment of ABM launchers and radars that were not of permanent, fixed types. This article of the ABM Treaty was often read in conjunction with a formal, "Agreed Statement" of interpretation, known as Agreed Statement D, which specified that "in the event ABM systems based on other physical principles and including components capable of substituting for ABM interceptor missiles, ABM launchers, or ABM radars are created in the future," any limitations on these futuristic systems would have to be negotiated in light of the preexisting provisions of the treaty.[29]

The Reagan administration did not challenge the clear language of the ABM Treaty authorizing each side to deploy only one fixed, land-based ABM system. Rather, the dispute with Congress, in the press, and in the research departments of universities centered around whether it was permissible to develop and test space-based advanced technologies, short of actually deploying them. Gerard Smith, chief U.S. negotiator for the ABM Treaty, had testified before the Senate Armed Services Committee in 1972 that the restrictions on development in the ABM Treaty "would start at that part of the development process where field testing is initiated on either a prototype or breadboard model."[30] Smith also indicated that concerns about lasers and other futuristic technologies were "considered and both sides have agreed that they will not deploy future type ABM technology unless the treaty is amended."[31]

By contrast, Richard N. Perle, Reagan's assistant secretary of defense for international security policy and one of the main developers of the Reagan administration's interpretation, offered a different take on the treaty language. He asserted that the relevant ABM treaty provisions merely suggested that any limitations would be subject to future bilateral negotiations.

The debate about the most legitimate interpretation of the ABM Treaty raised important constitutional questions about dispute resolution among the different branches of the U.S. government. SDI demanded, at a minimum, a permissive interpretation of the ABM Treaty. Many arms control experts and international lawyers denounced such a loose reading as an unwarranted reinterpretation by the executive branch, and therefore a usurpa-

---

[29]Several negotiated clarifications to particular treaty articles were appended to the treaty. They were known variously as Agreed Statements and Common Understandings. Chief U.S. negotiator Gerard Smith asserted that such provisions were "as binding as the text of the ABM Treaty." See Gerard Smith, p. 344. See also "Agreed Statements, Common Understandings, and Unilateral Statements Regarding the Treaty between the United States of America and the Union of Soviet Socialist Republics on the Limitation of Anti-Ballistic Missiles," May 26, 1972, *United States Treaties* 23: 3456.

[30]Military Implications of the Treaty on Anti-Ballistic Missile Systems and the Interim Agreement on Limitation of Strategic Offensive Arms: Hearings before the Senate Comm. on Armed Services, quoted in Kevin C. Kennedy, Treaty Interpretation by the Executive Branch: The ABM Treaty and 'Star Wars' Testing and Development, *American Journal of International Law*, vol. 80, 1986, p. 860. A breadboard model is an experimental deployment to test feasibility.

[31]Ibid., p. 20.

tion of the Senate's authority to ratify treaties after informed advice and consent.

Specifically, the two most important questions were: When the Senate gave its advice and consent to the ratification of the ABM Treaty, did it see itself as consenting to this "permissive" interpretation? And if not, could the U.S. judiciary—or some other deliberative body, such as the World Court—somehow invalidate the administration's new interpretation, or demand that the latest interpretation be resubmitted to the Senate?

International lawyers, current and former diplomats, pundits, and academics debated these questions through the late 1980s. Political realities suggested that a domestic controversy such as the SDI/ABM debate would never be submitted to an international body such as the World Court. U.S. Supreme Court precedent also indicated that the high court would likely reject consideration of SDI/ABM issues as a "political question," over which the courts had no proper jurisdiction. Deliberative bodies with little authority to actually impose their will on the U.S. administration—the Senate itself, political action groups, the ABM Treaty's own dispute-resolution committee—took up the dispute and sometimes involved the American public in their debates. As a postscript to the negotiation of the ABM Treaty, the SDI debate illustrates how negotiations continue in the domestic arena even after international diplomatic questions seem to be "settled" with a signed and formally executed treaty.

In 1989 the Soviet Union collapsed and fragmented into constituent republics, and the SDI debate took on a new political cast. Had the program's exorbitant expense of over $25 billion dollars hastened the Soviet collapse? And wasn't this the ultimate purpose of a successful bargaining chip—to bankrupt the competition without actually having to be deployed? In a post–cold war world where the current U.S. administration perceives multiple, potentially destabilizing threats, SDI programs have a continuing appeal to some factions in the Senate and the defense establishment. Michael Lind of the *New Republic* explained why an SDI "umbrella" still seems so desirable: its appeal lies in its "promise of replacing politics with mechanics . . . an expert at the Heritage Foundation informed me when I was working there that, 'if we have SDI, then we won't need allies.' "[32]

Yet technology is rarely a panacea relieving officials of the hard work of negotiating. For the foreseeable future, we will need political scientists as well as rocket scientists to address problems of international security and arms control.

---

[32]Michael Lind, "TRB from Washington," *New Republic* vol. 214, no. 11 (March 11, 1996): 4.

CHRONOLOGY

August 1963	Limited Test Ban Treaty is signed banning nuclear weapons tests in the atmosphere, in outer space, and underwater.
Late 1965	Secret White House overtures to explore Soviet interest in limiting ABM systems.
January 1967	Outer Space Treaty governing the activities of nations in exploring and using outer space, including the moon.
June 1967	U.S.–Soviet Summit Meeting in Glassboro, N.J.
1968	U.S.–Soviet Nuclear Nonproliferation Treaty is signed.
Mid-1968	First American MIRVs are tested.
August 20, 1968	Soviets invade Czechoslovakia.
November 1968	Richard Nixon elected U.S. president.
Early 1968	Henry Kissinger begins meeting secretly with Soviet Ambassador Anatoly Dobrynin to conduct "preliminary negotiations."
1968 & 1969	U.S. Senate votes to approve Johnson–McNamara "thin" ABM system.
November 1969	Opening round of SALT negotiations in Helsinki, Finland.
February 1971	Seabed Treaty banning the emplacement of nuclear weapons on the seabed floor.
May 1971	Joint Kissinger–Dobrynin press release published, containing their "formula for agreement."
September 1971	Nuclear Accidents Agreement to reduce the risk of accidental outbreak of nuclear war between the U.S. and the U.S.S.R. is signed.
September 1971	"Hot Line" Modernization Agreement to improve the U.S./U.S.S.R. communications link is signed.
April 1972	Kissinger's secret trip to Moscow to prepare for summit at which SALT I is signed.
May 1972	SALT Interim Agreement (SALT I) signed by Nixon and Brezhnev at Moscow summit, limiting strategic offensive arms.
May 1972	SALT ABM Treaty limiting antiballistic missile systems is signed.
August 1972	Ratification of the ABM treaty is advised by the U.S. Senate.
July 1974	ABM Protocol: the ABM Agreement is modified to permit coverage of just one site on each side, for protection of either the capital or a missile field.
March 1983	President Ronald Reagan's televised "Star Wars" speech, proposing a protective shield for an entire population.

BIBLIOGRAPHY

ADELMAN, KENNETH L. "Arms Control with and without Agreements," *Foreign Affairs* 63, no. 2 (Winter 1984–85): 240–63.

ARMS CONTROL ASSOCIATION. *Arms Control and National Security: An Introduction.* Washington, D.C.: ACA, 1989.

BARNHART, MICHAEL, ed. *Congress and U.S. Foreign Policy: Controlling the Use of Force in the Nuclear Age.* Albany, NY: Suny Press, 1987.

BLACKER, COIT D., AND GLORIA DUFFY, eds. *International Arms Control: Issues and Agreements.* Stanford, CA: Stanford University Press, 1984.

BUNN, GEORGE. *Arms Control by Committee: Managing Negotiations with the Russians.* Stanford, CA: Stanford University Press, 1992.

CARTER, APRIL. *Success and Failure in Arms Control Negotiations.* Oxford: Oxford University Press, 1989.

FISHER, ROGER. "Negotiation Inside-Out: What Are the Best Ways to Relate Internal Negotiations with External Ones?" *American Behavioral Scientist* 27, no. 2 (Nov.–Dec. 1983). 149–66.

GARTHOFF, RAYMOND L. "Negotiating with the Russians: Some Lessons from SALT," *International Security,* vol. 1, no. 4 (Spring 1977): 3–24.

GARTHOFF, RAYMOND L. "Negotiating SALT," *Wilson Quarterly,* vol. 1, no. 5 (Autumn 1977): 81–85.

GEORGE, ALEXANDER L., PHILIP J. FARLEY, AND ALEXANDER DALLIN, *U.S.–Soviet Security Cooperation: Achievements, Failures, Lessons* (Oxford: Oxford University Press, 1988)

KISSINGER, HENRY, *The White House Years.* Boston: Little, Brown, 1979.

SEABORG, GLEN T. *Stemming the Tide: Arms Control in the Johnson Years.* Lexington, MA: Lexington Books, 1987.

SLOSS, LEON, AND M. SCOTT DAVIS, eds. *A Game for High Stakes: Lessons Learned in Negotiating with the Soviet Union.* Cambridge, MA: Ballinger, 1986.

SMITH, GERARD. *Double Talk: The Story of SALT I.* Lanham, MD:University Press of America, 1980.

YORK, HERBERT, "Bilateral Negotiations and the Arms Race," *Scientific American* 249, vol. 4 (Oct. 1983): 149–56.

CHAPTER
—8—

Understanding
the Human Dimension

A "working relationship" is one that works—one that deals well with differences. Understanding the problems with the working relationships among the parties to an international conflict can increase our understanding of why that conflict has not been resolved. Generating ideas for improving a working relationship can prove an important element in any plan for managing conflict.

We are concerned not only with the one-on-one relationship between two decision-makers or between an advisor and a decision-maker, although many examples draw on the one-on-one dynamic for the sake of clarity. We also want guidelines that will help build and maintain institutional relationships among different sectors of the foreign policy community (the State Department, Pentagon, Joint Chiefs of Staff, National Security Council) as well as relationships among nations. "International conflict," the topic of this book at the broadest level, is, after all, largely about what happens when working relationships cease to work effectively.

GETTING WHAT WE NEED OUT OF A RELATIONSHIP

In every relationship, we are likely to want immediate substantive results, such as money, comfort, economic well-being, profit, property, or security (in sum, "victory"). We want the kind of relationship that will best help achieve such purposes.

In addition to good substantive results, we also want to know that we have been listened to with respect. After an encounter, we may have an emotional reaction that may overshadow the substantive outcome. After a meeting with one person, we may feel competent, confident, and content—the sort of feelings we echo when we say, "It is always a pleasure to deal with you." After a meeting with someone else, we may feel uneasy, tense, or angry. Whether we are negotiating with our spouse over where to go on vacation, with a client over fees, or with the People's Republic of China over protection of intellectual property, we want "power" in the sense of having a relationship that leaves us feeling affirmed and empowered in our ability to get things done. We want to be able to say: "I can work things out with those people." If we don't feel positive after the last transaction, we may dread the next and have more difficulty dealing with it.

President Clinton's deputy U.S. trade representative, Charlene Barshefsky, recounts her first encounter with Wu Yi, China's trade minister, known as the Iron Lady. According to a profile of Barshefsky in the *New Yorker* magazine, Wu had peremptorily ordered Barshefsky to "sit," and a startled Barshefsky complied. "Barshefsky had gone through this routine before," noted the profile, "sitting in her hotel room for hours waiting for appointments. Making someone feel uncertain and isolated is common Chinese strategy, like isolating the opponent in the Asian board game Go. . . . The Chinese make this an endurance strategy."[1] Barshefsky later indicated that she found dealings with Wu difficult and unproductive, and seemed to prefer dealing with the Chinese minister's staff.

One signal that Barshefsky's persistent, patient, businesslike strategy was yielding results came two years later, at a negotiation where Minister Wu started to signal acceptance of a tough position paper drafted by Barshefsky. "Wu had sometimes been combative, but on that day she appeared to be taking a different tack, laughing and making humorous observations." She gave Barshefsky's delegation more time than they had been scheduled for, acknowledged the software piracy problem with personal anecdotes about her own experiences as an engineer, and "gave Barshefsky three bearhugs goodbye. . . . Barshefsky thought she had come close to achieving her goals."[2] While a smooth and comfortable working relationship is not a reliable proxy for substantive achievements, it can make substantive progress easier to realize.

In addition, we also want the ability to create an environment conducive to dealing with differences, and specific skills to help us with that task. We know that the other party to any relationship also has interests—interests that may differ from ours. And as we try to deal with our differing interests, we will discover that we have differing perceptions and values. As time passes and as we learn more, the interests, perceptions, and values of

---

[1] Elsa Walsh, "Profile: The Negotiator," *New Yorker* (March 18, 1996), p. 89.
[2] Walsh, p. 96.

both sides are likely to change. These differing wants, perceptions, and values, and the changes in them that take place over time, provide the endless grist for every relationship. We want to know that we can work through such differences without one party kicking over the table or walking away, because in international relations "walking away" is never really an option.

Suppose I am seeking a big investment from a relative who thinks it is a mistake to mix family and business. Or suppose one country is looking forward to a live-and-let-live relationship based primarily on trade and investment, whereas its neighbor would like to use its resources to influence the politics of an entire region. A good relationship should deal successfully with such differences, including differences about the kind of relationship the parties should have. It is this problem-solving aspect of a relationship that we call a "working" relationship.

Competing and changing interests create problems. The working relationship we need is one that produces solutions that satisfy the competing interests as well as possible, with little waste, in a way that appears legitimate in the eyes of each of the parties. The solutions should also be durable and efficiently reached.

A robust relationship should be able to produce such outcomes in the face of differing values, perceptions, and interests. It should be able to cope successfully with times when we disapprove of something the other side did and when both sides feel anger rather than satisfaction. It should be strong enough to keep the problem-solving process going even if we develop conflicting views about the relationship itself.

DIAGNOSIS OF A POOR WORKING RELATIONSHIP

A working relationship may be diagnosed as poor when the following factors are present.

What we want and what we need in a working relationship are unclear.

We all find some relationships easier to deal with than others. In this sense, we may know a good relationship when we see one, but may fail to understand the qualities that make it good. Our assumptions about relationships are often inconsistent with the kind of relationship we need in order to get what we want. These inconsistencies lead to confusion about our objective of building a good working relationship.

We use the word "relations" and "relationship" in many ways. In one sense, "relations" are those to whom we are related by blood or marriage. In another sense, "relations" refers to the state of affairs between two countries. When a couple speaks of "having a relationship" they may mean that they are living together. The United States is often held to have "a special relationship" with the United Kingdom, yet even U.S. diplomats will have widely divergent views of just what that means. When people describe relations between individuals or among nations in such vague terms as "cold," "formal," or "friendly," they often have no practical definition of a good relationship.

It is easy to confuse good relations with approval. One way of expressing strong disapproval of another's conduct is to terminate the relationship: "After what he did, I will never speak to him again!" Such "banishment" is common to personal, business, and diplomatic relations. A government may recall its ambassador and "break diplomatic relations" to express disapproval of another government's behavior. It is therefore not surprising that people frequently assume the reverse, that establishing or maintaining a relationship demonstrates approval of the other's conduct.

But expressing disapproval by disrupting a relationship is often a shortsighted approach. Refusing to deal with someone will rarely solve an immediate problem and it will almost certainly impair our ability to solve future problems. If we know that circumstances will require our ongoing interaction with another person or institution—whether in the family, in the office, or internationally—then we should continue to deal with them now even if we disapprove of their conduct.

If two nations are caught up in an escalating conflict that may lead to warfare, the last thing they should do is break off relations, even if one believes the other's behavior to be egregious. In the late 1980s, President Bush felt he was demonstrating this proposition when he refused to curtail U.S. diplomatic relations with the People's Republic of China in the wake of China's suppression of student demonstrations in Beijing's Tiananmen Square. "How can we influence them to give up these misguided policies unless we talk to them?" Bush often asked during this time. But at the same time, in the summer and autumn of 1989, he was refusing to respond to overtures from Nicaragua's then-President Ortega to reestablish diplomatic communication between Nicaragua and the United States. His justification was that the United States did not approve of Nicaragua's government. Arguably, he should have considered that the same principle he was applying to China was equally applicable to Nicaragua, on the theory that the United States is more likely to be persuasive as an active presence.

We are confused by the role of shared values.

In general, the greater the extent to which we and the other side share values and perceptions, the fewer differences we will have and the more easily we will find a basis for dealing with them that both of us will consider fair. We may thus tend to equate a good relationship with shared values.

But it would be a mistake to define a good relationship as one in which we agree easily, just as it would be a mistake to define a good road as one that is easy to build. While it is easier to build a good road across a prairie than through mountains, a good road through mountains may be more valuable. Similarly, a good relationship among parties with sharp differences, such as between the United States and China, may be more valuable than one among parties who find it easy to agree.

We see our goal as avoiding disagreement.

Many of us are taught as children that it is "naughty" to quarrel. We are led to believe that the "right" kind of relationship is one in which there is no apparent disagreement. Serious as well as small differences are swept under the rug. Partly as a result of such an upbringing, many people feel uncomfortable with conflict of any kind.

A particular vision of this kind of relationship is one in which others do what we want. A father might say, "I have an excellent relationship with my son; he does everything I ask and he never talks back." Many authoritarian governments, from Nigeria to South Korea, have believed that a good relationship—with allies or constituents—is one without dissent. In the United States, some people apparently believe that our relationship with Honduras, for example, is better than that with France because Honduras follows U.S. policy more often. No matter how well we think we know what is best for someone else, absence of conflict or overt dissent is an unreliable litmus test for measuring the quality of a working relationship.

Who "we" are is treated as fixed.

Once we find ourselves in an adversarial relationship, we tend to think of "them" as someone on "the other side." We exclude the possibility of developing a relationship so effective that there are no longer two opposing sides, but two partners facing the future, side by side.

Looking forward to a change of roles goes beyond the professor's advice: "Be nice to your students—someday one may be your boss." It means keeping open the possibility of so changing a relationship that adversaries become partners. Such changes are common in the history of U.S. foreign relations. With each of several foreign enemies—Great Britain, Canada, Mexico, Spain, Germany, Japan, and China—the United States has now developed a constructive working relationship. The same is true of the former Soviet Union and many of the Eastern bloc countries. While our immediate goal may be improving the way our side deals with their side, our long-term goal may be bringing our sides together.

We ignore the impact of partisan perceptions.

Each of us needs the kind of relationship with someone else that will enable us to cope successfully with whatever problems come along. As we seek such a working relationship with the other side, there is a great risk that we will fail to appreciate how differently the other side views the world.

If our disagreements are significant, we will almost certainly have strikingly dissimilar perceptions of ourselves, of each other, of what is important, of what our relationship is today, and of what it might become. Unless we understand these differences, they will interfere with our ability to solve problems. This kind of understanding means not only making a rigorous attempt to step into their shoes and see what their partisan perceptions are, but also accepting that our vision of the world is in part a product of our own partisan perceptions.

A successful strategy for building a working relationship has to recognize that partisans will perceive their differences differently. In this respect, the U.S.–Soviet relationship was particularly difficult. Officials of the two countries, living in different cultures, observing some facts at close range and others at a distance, and approaching those facts with different ideologies, values, and interests, could not possibly have the same perceptions.

The fact that perceptions are going to differ, and with a strong partisan bias in favor of the side holding them, is a serious obstacle in building a relationship that can deal well with differences. Partisan perceptions about substantive matters create some differences and make others more difficult to solve.

Partisan perceptions about the way the two sides interact can be even more damaging. If we value cooperation, understanding, and honesty, we are almost certain to see our conduct as more cooperative, more understanding, and more honest than the other side sees it. Likewise, if we have serious differences with the other side, we are likely to see their behavior as lacking those qualities. As a result, we are likely to blame the other side for problems in a deteriorating relationship and to justify our own behavior as better than theirs: "They never listen to us, so it's not worth talking to them."

We rely on reciprocity.

The principle of reciprocity is familiar in substantive negotiations, where a favor or concession by one side is exchanged for a similar favor or concession by the other. Two people will deal more skillfully with their differences if both behave rationally, both fully understand each other's perceptions, both communicate effectively, both are reliable, neither tries to coerce the other, and each accepts the other as someone whose interests and views deserve to be taken into account; in other words, the good relationship that we seek is reciprocal. Former arms control negotiator George Bunn, in his analysis of the SALT I negotiations, noted that "reciprocity in concessions" was an important factor in the progress of the talks. He elaborated:

> Neither side seemed to follow a precise tit-for-tat strategy for concessions and retractions. There was, however, reciprocity. A detailed study of SALT I bargaining moves suggest that a series or group of concessions on one side

seemed to be followed by a concession on the other. The practice seemed more like tit-for-two-tats or tit-for-three-tats.[3]

We may disagree about exactly what is reciprocal. (Should the standard be what proportion of the whole is cut, or whether the numbers on both sides are equalized?) But the principle of reciprocity is a generally accepted external standard of fairness in substantive negotiations.

However, the consequences of partisan perceptions can be particularly acute if either side uses reciprocity as a guide for behavior. Since a reciprocal relationship is our goal, and since reciprocity is a sound basis for substantive agreements, there is a natural tendency to rely on some form of reciprocity as the key to building an effective working relationship. This tendency, however, is dangerous. In one form, a reciprocal strategy looks like an application of the Golden Rule: "Do unto others as you would have them do unto you." In another form, it constitutes a hostile policy of "an eye for an eye": we will treat the other side as badly as they have been treating us. Either policy is risky, insofar as it dictates behavior in response to others, rather than independent of them.

A BETTER APPROACH TO BUILDING A RELATIONSHIP

Knowing the goal is not enough. This chapter has identified the ability to deal well with differences as a goal for every relationship. To achieve our substantive goals, we need effective working relationships, relationships that have a high degree of rationality, understanding, communication, reliability, noncoercive means of influence, and acceptance. Each of these elements is part of the *process* of interaction between two people and is independent of their substantive interests.

It helps if we balance reason and emotion.

Many aspects of a relationship are not rational. We often react emotionally, not logically, in pursuit of some purpose. Emotions such as fear, anger, frustration, or even love may disrupt otherwise thoughtful actions. Emotions are normal, necessary, and often essential to problem-solving. They can convey important information, help us marshal our resources, and inspire us to action. Wisdom is seldom found without them. Nonetheless, the ability of two parties to deal well with their differences will be greater to the extent that reason and emotion are in some kind of balance.

We cannot work well with another person when emotions overwhelm

---

[3]George Bunn, *Arms Control by Committee: Managing Negotiations with the Russians* (Stanford, CA: Stanford University Press, 1992), p. 123.

our reason: we cannot make wise decisions in the middle of a temper tantrum. But neither is logic alone sufficient for solving problems and building a relationship. Rather, we need both reason informed by emotion and emotion guided and tempered by reason. This balance between logic and emotion is a practical definition of working rationally.

Understanding helps.

If we are going to achieve an outcome that will satisfy the interests of both sides at least acceptably, and leave both sides feeling fairly treated, we will need to understand each other's interests, perceptions, and notions of fairness. Unless we have a good idea of what those on the other side think the problem is, what they want, why they want it, and what they think might be fair, we will be groping in the dark to find an outcome that will meet their interests as well as ours. The other side, too, will be seriously handicapped unless they understand how we see things. Whether both sides agree or not, the better we understand each other, the better our chance of creating a solution we can both accept.

Good communication helps.

Understanding requires effective communication. And even though in general we may understand each other, the quality of a particular outcome and the efficiency with which it is reached are likely to depend on communication about that particular issue. The more effectively we communicate about our differences, the better we will understand each other's concerns and the better our chances for reaching a mutually acceptable agreement. But the manner and extent of our communication do more than improve understanding. The more openly we communicate, the less basis there is for suspicion. The United States' distrust of the Soviet Union began to diminish as soon as it began opening its doors to the West. And the more we believe the other side has heard and understood our views, and we theirs, the more likely we will feel that an agreement is fair and balanced. Within reasonable limits, the more communication, the better the working relationship.

Being reliable helps.

Our communicating with the other side is not worth much if the other side does not believe us. And commitments that are entered into lightly or disregarded easily are often worse than none. Blind trust will not help us work with others, since misplaced trust will damage a relationship more than healthy skepticism. But well-founded trust, based on honest and reliable conduct over a period of time, can greatly enhance our ability to cope with conflict. The more honest and reliable we are with respect to each other, the better our chance of producing good outcomes.

Persuasion is usually more helpful than coercion.

In a particular transaction, both sides may be more interested in the immediate outcome than in their long-term relationship. Each will try to affect the other's decisions, and the way in which they do so will have a profound effect on the quality of the relationship. At one extreme, we can try to inspire their voluntary cooperation through education, logical argument, moral persuasion, and our own example. At the other extreme, we can try to coerce the other side by worsening their alternatives and by warnings, threats, extortion, and physical force. The more coercive the means of influence, the less likely it is that the outcome will reflect the concerns of both sides, and the less legitimate it is likely to be in the eyes of at least one of us. The less coercive the modes of influence, the better our ability to work with each other.

Mutual acceptance helps.

If we are to deal well with our differences, we need to accept each other as someone worth dealing with. Feeling accepted, worthy, and valued is a basic human psychological need. Unless the other side listens to our views, accepts our right to have views that differ from theirs, and takes our interests into account, we are unlikely to want to deal with them. And if we do not deal with each other, we will not even begin to resolve our differences.

Acceptance is not an either/or phenomenon but a matter of degree. The higher the degree of acceptance, the better the chances of working out our differences and producing good outcomes. Indeed, generally speaking, the more a relationship partakes of each of the qualities outlined above, the greater the ability of the people in that relationship to solve their problems wisely and effectively.

SOME FEATURES THAT ARE NOT ESSENTIAL TO A GOOD WORKING RELATIONSHIP

We can further separate issues of process from issues of substance by noting some of the qualities that are *not* required in a relationship that deals well with differences. Such a relationship is not dependent on the following elements:

Disagreement or approval.

In no way should our guidelines require substantive agreement. While agreement makes relationships more comfortable, the more serious our disagreements the more we need a good working relationship to cope with them. A good working relationship does not require approval. It should survive situations in which each side seriously disapproves of the other's values, positions, aspirations, or conduct. When someone wants to "break" relations with those of whose conduct he disapproves, he usually does so to send a message and exert pressure toward changing that conduct. We can influence the behavior of others more effectively, however, if we continue to deal with them so that we may understand their interests, make sure they understand ours, and bring to bear on them our full persuasive powers.

We can convey disapproval by means other than terminating a relationship. At the height of the notoriety of Senator Joseph McCarthy, he was brought as a guest to the Metropolitan Club in Washington, D.C. and introduced to the distinguished lawyer John Lord O'Brian. It is reported that when the senator held out his hand, Mr. O'Brian said, "Senator, as a symbol of my strong disapproval of what you are doing, I would rather not shake your hand. If you would like, I would be happy to come to your office at some time convenient to you and we could discuss our differences."[4]

Lawyers routinely—and rightly—represent clients of whose conduct they disapprove. The better the working relationship between lawyer and client, the better job the lawyer is able to do. And the better the working relationship that the lawyer has with *opposing* counsel, the better the client is served.

In the past, the United States wisely continued to maintain diplomatic relations with the governments of Afghanistan and Nicaragua despite political differences so strong that in each case the United States was concurrently providing military support to those trying to overthrow the government.

Since the reason for wanting a good working relationship is to resolve differences peacefully and effectively, the more serious the disagreements, the more important it is to have a good way to deal with them. Between the Soviet Union and the United States, differences of ideology and perception, and the vast nuclear weaponry that might have been used in any armed conflict, made an effective working relationship important, even if difficult to build. The more dangerous and serious the differences, the more important it was that the two governments had a relationship in which they were able to handle those differences efficiently and with the kind of understanding and honesty that reduced the risk of disaster.

Shared values.

A good working relationship does not require shared values. The more similar our perceptions of the world and our concepts of fairness are to those held by the other side, the fewer differences we are likely to have and the easier it is likely to be for us to deal with them. If we are selecting individuals with whom to have a relationship, we will want to take shared values into ac-

---

[4]From *Getting Together*, p. 13. Copyright © 1988 by Roger Fisher and Scott Brown. Reprinted by permission of Houghton Mifflin Company. All rights reserved.

count. But we do not want to confine our problem-solving abilities to those relationships in which the problems are small or easy to resolve.

U.S. business professionals often find it difficult to work with and
compete with the Japanese because of the two countries' different approaches
to business and different views of what constitutes appropriate conduct. But,
although trade relations between the two countries are filled with serious and
emotional disputes, both countries understand that the success of their efforts to reach economic goals and sound trade agreements depends on their
ability to work with each other despite differing values.

Concessions.

Our strategy for influencing the other side should neither require us
to give in nor demand that others do so.

Permanent "sides."

If our goal involves full understanding and being open to persuasion,
a good strategy should also leave us open to revising our views about who is
on our side and who is not. Just as a neighbor may become a member of the
family, so business adversaries may become joint venturers and former enemies may become military allies. Relationship-building should be open-ended.

Partisan perceptions.

We should take into account the extent to which we and they will see
things differently. The value of our guidelines should not rest on the premise
that we see the truth and they are wrong. Although on each occasion we may
firmly believe that we are right, it is impossible to build a relationship on the
premise that the other side is always wrong.

Reciprocity.

We should not wait for the other side to engage in exemplary behavior, nor should we assume that our example will be followed. Neither "the
Golden Rule" nor "an eye for an eye" is going to be a helpful strategy, and it is
useful to explore why.

The Golden Rule is a useful rule of thumb in helping us understand
how our behavior is likely to affect the other side and how they might want
us to behave. If you, as a middle manager, appreciate being consulted by your
superiors before they make major decisions that affect you, then you can
safely predict that I, a subordinate, would like similar treatment.

But the Golden Rule is not based on the premise that if we behave as
the other side would like, we can safely predict that they will behave as we
would like. If we avoid criticizing them in public, we cannot safely assume
that they will avoid criticizing us. If we try to build a working relationship
based on such an optimistic view—that they will reciprocate our actions—we

will make dangerous mistakes. Examine how such an extreme strategy would apply to each of the qualities we have identified as being important to a good working relationship:

AN EXTREME APPLICATION OF THE GOLDEN RULE

1. **Rationality**   Since we would like them to base their actions on love for us, we will base all our actions, not on reason, but on love for them.
2. **Understanding**   Since we would like them to accept our understanding of the situation as correct, we will accept theirs.
3. **Communication**   Since we would like them not to bother us with problems, there is no need to talk about any of our differences.
4. **Reliability**   Since we would like them to trust us completely, we will trust them completely.
5. **Coercion/Persuasion**   Since we would like them to yield to us, we will yield to them.
6. **Acceptance**   Since we would like them to accept our interests and views as controlling, we will accept theirs as controlling.[5]

No one seriously recommends this strategy—although some who work for better relations are accused of doing so, and others may favor bits of it, such as not talking about differences. To pursue a comprehensive approach resting on the premise that others will follow our example is highly risky and unwise. We might think we want their actions to be based wholly on affection for us, but we will not solve serious differences if we act wholly on the basis of affection for them. We may think that we would like them to accept without question our understanding of a situation, but it will not help us deal with reality for us to accept theirs. As unpleasant as discussing differences may sometimes be, it is the only way to deal with them successfully. And if we were to trust everybody simply because we would like everybody to trust us, we would certainly be disappointed—and vulnerable. Reliance on reciprocal good will is not a sound foundation on which to build a working relationship.

This is particularly true when partisan perceptions are taken into account. If we pursue a strategy that depends on their equivalent behavior, we will probably find that they fail the test. Even if they believe that their behavior is as good as ours, we are likely to see it as worse. We may then become discouraged and turn to a different, more hostile strategy.

To avoid the obvious risks of expecting reciprocity, some analysts and commentators propose using reciprocity as leverage, commonly suggesting that we let the other side take the lead. If and when the other side treats us well, we will treat them the same way. In the meantime, we will do to them whatever they are doing to us. This policy of "an eye for an eye" is also based

---

[5]Fisher and Brown, p. 32.

on an application of the principle of reciprocity. It might be summarized as follows:

AN EXTREME APPLICATION OF AN EYE FOR AN EYE

1. **Reason and emotion** Since anger dominates their thinking, it will dominate ours.
2. **Understanding** Since they misunderstand us, we will put the worst interpretation on what they do—a prescription certain to produce misunderstanding.
3. **Communication** Since they are not listening to us, we will not listen to them.
4. **Reliability** Since they are apparently trying to deceive us, we will try to deceive them.
5. **Noncoercive modes of influence** Since they are trying to coerce us, we will try to coerce them.
6. **Acceptance** Since they are denigrating us, our views, and our interests, we will denigrate them and theirs.[6]

Such an approach may be the result of our asking why we should behave better than they do. Or perhaps it rests on the notion that only by punishing their bad behavior can we get them to behave better. Regardless, such a strategy is no way to turn a poor working relationship into a good one. If we let our conduct in the relationship reflect theirs, we may never break out of a pattern of hostile interaction. If we react to their bad behavior with actions that are equally bad, we end up accepting the destructive tone they have set.

Again, the effect of partisan perceptions makes matters worse. We are almost certain to see their conduct as worse than ours. If our strategy is to duplicate their conduct and their strategy is to duplicate ours, the bias of partisan perceptions will cause our relationship to deteriorate in a downward spiral. We, putting a bad interpretation on their conduct, duplicate it. Then they, putting an equally partisan interpretation on our conduct, follow our lead and worsen their conduct. Communication breaks down, misunderstanding increases, and trust disappears.

In easily quantifiable situations, such as the expulsion of one low-ranking diplomat suspected of spying, an "eye for an eye" policy may not get out of hand. In more important and more ambiguous situations—when, for example, in arms control or divorce negotiations each party is uncertain whether the other is pursuing negotiations in good faith, honestly disclosing relevant information, or advancing proposals seriously—a partisan interpretation of the other's conduct combined with a policy of following suit will cause an ever-decreasing ability to solve problems.

In any event, by behaving as badly as the other side does, we abandon

---

[6]Fisher and Brown, p. 34.

a leadership role. We give up the enormous opportunity we have to set the tone and manner of our interaction. If each side in a relationship waits for the other to improve first, there will be no improvement. Reactive reciprocity makes it extremely difficult to deal well with differences.

The criteria sketched above constitute no miracle approach that will turn criminals into trustworthy friends, business adversaries into reliable colleagues, and enemies into allies. No such strategy exists. What we offer is a framework for thinking about the problem, a general approach that seems to make sense, and some rules of thumb that may prove helpful in many situations.

In any relationship, we want to be able to take steps that will both improve our ability to work together and advance our substantive interests, whether or not the other side responds as we would like. In short, we are looking for guidelines we can follow that will be both good for the relationship and good for us, whether or not the other side follows the same guidelines. In that sense, this strategy is "unconditionally constructive."

To meet these rigorous tests, the strategy cannot be as bold, trusting, and venturesome as some would like. It must be risk averse. (We, the authors, do not know with whom you, the readers, may be dealing.) In some circumstances, it will not be as quick or successful in improving a relationship as a bolder—and riskier—approach might be. In baldest outline, it is as follows:

AN UNCONDITIONALLY CONSTRUCTIVE STRATEGY[7]

Do only those things that are both good for the relationship and good for us whether or not they reciprocate.

1. **Rationality**   Even if they are acting emotionally, balance emotions with reason.
2. **Understanding**   Even if they misunderstand us, try to understand them.
3. **Communication**   Even if they are not listening, consult them before deciding on matters that affect them.
4. **Reliability**   Even if they are trying to deceive us, neither trust them nor deceive them; be reliable.
5. **Noncoercive modes of influence**   Even if they are trying to coerce us, neither yield to that coercion nor try to coerce them; be open to persuasion and try to persuade them.
6. **Acceptance**   Even if they reject us and our concerns as unworthy of their consideration, accept them as worthy of our consideration, care about them, and be open to learning from them.

These guidelines are not advice on how to be "good," but rather on how to be effective. They derive from a selfish, hard-headed concern with

---

[7] Fisher and Brown, p. 38.

what each of us can do, in practical terms, to make a relationship work better. Insofar as these guidelines have a high "moral" content, we prefer to see that as a bonus. We can feel good about improving the way we deal with differences.

In every relationship, we are bound to encounter significant conflicts of interest. But we will almost always share an interest in dealing skillfully with those conflicts. Neither partner in a relationship wants the other to bungle. It is not inconsistent for us to want to advance selfish interests that conflict with theirs and at the same time want to improve our joint ability to deal with those conflicting interests.

We can pursue such a strategy without risk to substantive interests. No matter how they respond to our behavior, we will tend to be better off than if we were to pursue another strategy. And if they do follow the strategy, no matter how we respond to their behavior, they will tend to be better off too.

CHAPTER
—9—

Building a Productive Framework for Negotiation

There is a widespread belief that the negotiating process is irrelevant: "If the parties want to reach agreement, they will; if they don't, they won't." Negotiators and diplomats tend to take process for granted and concentrate instead on substance, on "the bottom line." They make well-considered moves in a negotiating game whose basic assumptions are fixed and largely unexamined. In any conflict we may be caught up doing things that are not the best things to do simply because we have not questioned the working assumptions that underlie our actions.

QUESTIONING ASSUMPTIONS

Negotiators' routine assumptions might include that the *players* in this game are limited to two parties who are adversaries, and that negotiations are to be conducted without the benefit of a mediator or other third party because to use one would be an admission of weakness or incompetence. For each, the goal of the negotiating game is to reach a comprehensive, legally binding agreement in which "we win." The game proceeds according to *standard moves* of proposal, rejection, counterproposal, rejection, argument, concession, argument, concession, and so forth. Everything that falls outside the standard moves is not to be done; this is an *accepted limitation* of the game.

In the ongoing negotiations between Greek and Turkish Cypriots over the fate of Cyprus, for example, negotiations assisted by the secretary-general of the United Nations have been limited to two parties: Greek and Turkish Cypriots. Although everyone involved recognizes that Greece and Turkey have interests in how the situation gets resolved, there has been little question of their involvement in the negotiating process. Moreover, the two parties involved in the negotiating game are seen (by others as well as themselves) as adversaries with few, if any, mutual interests: the Greek Cypriots are seen as wanting a unified Cyprus with themselves at the top, while the Turkish Cypriots are believed to be promoting a permanent division of Cyprus.

The negotiations have proceeded according to the standard minuet: proposals and counterproposals have been submitted by one side and rejected by the other. Arguments justifying proposals have been made emphasizing the past misconduct of the other party. Greek and Turkish Cypriots have concentrated on strengthening their bargaining power both in and outside the negotiation process: Greek Cypriots have imposed a debilitating economic boycott on the Turkish Cypriots, while the Turkish Cypriots have taken more and more steps to divide the island. As for the goals of the negotiation, they have been assumed to be the signing of a comprehensive, legally binding treaty that sets forth in detail the constitutional structure of a reunified island.

As one might expect, twenty-two years of negotiations over the future of Cyprus have produced no agreement. Everyone has bemoaned the substantive differences between the parties, but no one has asked whether the negotiating process they have been using may have contributed, at least in part, to their deadlock. Like many negotiators, Greek and Turkish Cypriot diplomats have continued to bargain the way a traveler might haggle over the price of a small rug in a bazaar. The seller asks a high price, which the buyer rejects as being much too high. The buyer responds with a low offer. There is discussion, after which the seller may make a concession in price; the buyer may raise his offer. And so the process continues until agreement is reached or negotiations broken off. The explicit or implicit assumption is that it is a contest of will to be settled by a trading process: "I will not go up unless you come down." Whoever is more stubborn will "win."

To operate on the assumption that the international scene is like bargaining over the price of a rug is both risky and counterproductive. Such a model includes incentives for the parties to see themselves as adversaries on all issues and to focus their energies on being inflexible. Despite the fact that both parties may look forward to benefiting from a possible agreement, they see the contest as "zero-sum"—where the sum of the wins and losses adds up to zero. What one party loses or concedes, the other party gains. In the real world there are no zero-sum games. *It is always possible for both to lose.*

By viewing their negotiations as zero-sum, Greek and Turkish Cypriots have made it almost impossible to consider the interests that underlie their inconsistent positions. They have turned the negotiation into a contest of will—who will outlast the other—rather than an effort to devise a solution that best reconciles the interests of both parties. Contrast these zero-sum assumptions with the "expanding-sum" approach that the new Nixon administration took in its strategic arms limitations talks with the Soviets in the late 1960s, as discussed in the case study in Chapter 7. While complex negotiations may have isolated zero-sum aspects—there is only so much land or only so many missiles—most have significant expanding-sum aspects as well. In the case of Cyprus, the development of tourism, foreign aid, and banking might represent expanding-sum opportunities. By focusing on zero-sum aspects, Greek and Turkish Cypriots may not only make agreement impossible, but may actually end up creating a situation both want to avoid: Turkish troops remaining on the island and frustrating all Cypriots.

The "rug bazaar" assumption is just plain inaccurate. In the conduct of international relations there are few "one-shot" transactions. Most of the players in the game will be staying around for years and will be there in the future to play other hands. In these circumstances, relationships and reputation may be far more important than any one transaction. In a single transaction, it might be thought a good tactic to call the rug ugly and useless, but where one must inevitably participate in an ongoing relationship it is probably a poor tactic. Taking again our example of Cyprus, haggling might be an expedient strategy if after an agreement is concluded the parties will never have to deal with each other again. But where the success of the agreement, and the success of any reunification effort whatsoever, depends on the development of a good working relationship between the two sides, haggling is likely to produce greater hostility.

All in all, the power of working assumptions to dominate our actions without our being aware of them justifies a significant effort to reexamine those assumptions. Inspecting our working assumptions about the negotiating process is particularly desirable since most parties most of the time pay comparatively little attention to questions of process. They are concerned with substance. Yet the Cyprus problem, like many others, might be better dealt with if each of the four basic assumptions about the negotiating process—two adversarial players; the goal of a comprehensive treaty; standard moves; accepted limitations—were changed. The decisions governments make are a function of the choices they face. Different procedures generate different choices. We will want to be aware of our own and others' working assumptions about those procedures. We will want to take charge of the game that we are playing and turn it into the best game to play. Although we have already considered our own purposes and the interests of the other party, we will want to reexamine them in the context of a negotiating game before turning to the critical question of standard moves.

FOCUSING ON PROCESS DESIGN

What is our objective—not only the direction in which we want to go but a fixed point that we would like to reach? We often assume that what we want is an agreement. We also often assume that we want the agreement to embody as much of our own initial position as possible, that is, that we want in some sense to "win" the negotiation. However, since a treaty is usually subject to termination on short notice—in fact, if not in law—and since there is no supranational authority to enforce compliance with them, it may be a mistake to confine our efforts to treaty-making.

Other objectives may be more attainable and more in our interest. We can, for example, conclude agreements of different strengths. If we cannot agree on substance, perhaps we can agree on procedure. If the United States and Canada cannot agree on fishing in the Atlantic, perhaps they can submit the issue to an arbitrator or to the International Court of Justice. Similarly, where a permanent agreement is not possible, perhaps a provisional agreement is. At the very least, if we and the other side cannot reach a first-order agreement, we can usually reach a second-order agreement—that is, we can agree on where we disagree, so that we both know the issues in dispute. The pairs of adjectives below suggest potential agreements of differing "strengths":

STRONGER	WEAKER
Substantive	Procedural
Permanent	Provisional
Comprehensive	Partial
Final	In principle
Unconditional	Conditional
Binding	Nonbinding
First-order	Second-order

The point of demonstrating these different types of agreements is to provide options in terms of how we frame the decision we are asking the other side to make. These other options may accomplish some of our goals and be more realistic.

Positions versus Interests

As we move from considering the type of commitment we wish to pursue to defining our specific objectives—the substance of the commitment we desire from the other party—we should reconsider our second assumption about our goals in the negotiation. Is the object of the negotiation to win or to reconcile interests? We want to "win" an agreement that satisfies our interests, and we should be careful that our specific objectives do not blind us to our real concerns. The more we focus on our specific objective, clarifying it and defending it against attack, the more committed we may become to it and the more difficult it may become to change it. We may even lose sight of the interests our position was originally designed to serve.

The danger that single-minded pursuit of a specific substantive objective or position will impede a negotiation was well illustrated by the break-down of the 1962 talks under President Kennedy for a comprehensive ban on nuclear testing. A critical question arose: How many on-site inspections per year should the Soviet Union and the United States be permitted to make within each other's territory to investigate suspicious seismic events? The United States proposed that each side be permitted to make no fewer than ten inspections. The Soviet Union offered three. And there the talks broke down, even though no one had tried to define what an inspection was—whether it would involve one person looking around for one day or a hundred people for a month. The parties had made no attempt to design an inspection procedure that would reconcile the United States' interest in verification with the desire of both countries for minimal intrusion. But the formulated goals of "at least ten" and "no more than three" became frozen. It became difficult to look behind these positions and reconcile the interests.

As more attention is paid to positions—the specific objectives we have defined—less attention is devoted to meeting the underlying concerns of the parties. Agreement becomes less likely, and perhaps more arbitrary. Our specific objective needs to be kept open to constant reexamination to make sure that in the pursuit of our positions we are not damaging our interests.

As National Security Adviser Henry Kissinger did in the first, five-week stage of the SALT I negotiations, we should avoid steps that will commit us deeply to our negotiating positions (see Chapter 7). Interdepartmental discussion should not be looking toward government-wide agreement on a position. That practice tends to produce rigidity even when it later turns out that a position was unwise, or that our interests can be well-served by some other option. Internal discussions are better devoted to clarifying the *interests* involved and to inventing a variety of *approaches* that might be tried. Flexibility is also maintained by our having already on hand two or more positions we are prepared to accept. In complex problems there is always more than one package that will be acceptable to us; if we were to have more of this, we could accept less of that; if this took place sooner, that could take place later. Having various options on the table from which the other party can choose keeps us more flexible. We cannot be deeply committed to one outcome.

Who Are the Players (and Who *Should* They Be)?

For purposes of exposition, we have generally assumed that there are two parties in a conflict. In a real situation these simplifying assumptions need to be examined with care. We have seen in our discussion of the goals of the negotiating game that concentrating on "winning" a negotiation can produce an unwise agreement, or prevent agreement altogether. We also noted that where an ongoing relationship exists, viewing the negotiating process as an exercise in haggling may damage interests that transcend the particular negotiation.

A key misconception contributing to this problem is the extent to which we consider the players in the game to be the governments with which we are in conflict. A negotiator on the other side is considered to be an extension of her government, with no interests of her own. Governments, however, are abstractions; governmental decisions are made by human beings. It is a mistake to treat the person with whom we are dealing as a personal adversary, even if the government he represents is in some sense an adversary of our government. It is wise to separate the human being from the problem, from his clients, and from the substance of the cause he represents.

In face-to-face negotiations, it is particularly useful to establish a personal relationship with one's opposite number that is wholly independent of the positions two governments may be taking. Trust between individual representatives quickly becomes an asset of value to both governments. They now have the ability to say things and be believed and, in turn, to rely on things that are said to them.

For example, in November 1967, Lord Caradon, then Britain's permanent representative to the United Nations, was able, to the advantage of everyone, to rely on a personal request of the Soviet ambassador for a two-day delay in a crucial vote on the Security Council Resolution on the Middle East. The Soviet ambassador made it clear that he was making the request on his own account, not at the bidding of his government. In those circumstances Lord Caradon felt confident that the delay would not be used for any purpose that would prejudice him or his government. When the critical vote came two days later, the Soviet Union abandoned its own resolution and voted for the British draft. The Soviet Ambassador had used the time to persuade his government to change its position. The personal relationship between the two negotiators helped to resolve a problem that might have escalated had they considered each other as adversaries.[1]

What we have said about separating the person with whom we are dealing from the dispute at hand applies equally to groups and governments themselves. One of the great mistakes negotiators make is to treat each party as a monolith—as an entity that behaves as though it were a single human being. We often see this phenomenon in media coverage of international conflicts, where issues are framed in terms such as blacks versus whites, Muslims versus Christians, industrialized nations versus developing countries. When a single cleavage becomes prominent, the sides become more important than the issues. Adversaries on one issue tend to be seen as enemies for all purposes. Yet in every international situation there are more than two people, even if there are only two sides. Thinking of negotiation as a two-sided affair can be illuminating, but it should not blind us to the presence of other people, other sides, and other influences.

As the case study on the Antiballistic Missile Treaty emphasizes, governments themselves are complex institutions; they are subject to influences

---

[1]Interview with Lord Caradon cited in I. William Zartman, *The Practical Negotiator* (New Haven, CT: Yale University Press, 1982), pp. 40–41.

and pressures from extragovernmental groups, and even within a government, bureaucracies have different interests and different priorities. The complexity of government decision making opens up the possibility of realigning the players in a negotiating game—establishing a division among players who have been seen as being on one side, and establishing bridges across what has been seen as *the* divide.

Creating a cross-cutting cleavage can quickly produce a radical change in the perceptions of those involved, so that some of those on each side of a previously perceived line find themselves on the same side of a different dividing line. Aristophanes provides us with a good example. In his play *Lysistrata*, the women of Athens and Sparta unite to stop a war by refusing to sleep with their husbands until a treaty of peace is signed. A difference of interest between men and women is used to break down that between Sparta and Athens.

Similarly, a quite different perspective might have been gained in the strategic arms limitation talks between the United States and the Soviet Union if each side had appreciated the fundamental conflict that existed between the peace-through-strength "hawks" (both Soviet and American) who believed that security was best pursued through an unrestricted acquisition of more weapons and, on the other side, "doves" (both Soviet and American) who believed that security for all was best enhanced by a perspective of superpower interdependence that included agreed-upon restrictions on strategic arms. With this new perception of the sides, it would have become easier for arms controllers in the United States and the Soviet Union to work together against the destabilizing effects of new weapons systems, whether in one country or the other. In this context, the arms controller's task becomes one of helping his adversary get new instructions, that is, to help him influence his own government to support arms control.

Another way of promoting such cross-cutting cleavages is to set up subcommittees or working groups of professionals to prepare and jointly recommend a single proposal. Economists from different countries may find that they have more in common with each other's views than they have with the views of lawyers or of the military members of their own delegation who are meeting in a different working group.

Bringing in a third party may also reduce the adversarial nature of the discussions by reinforcing some mutual interests of the parties. The water dispute between India and Pakistan was resolved in 1960 after nine years of negotiation after the World Bank entered the discussions; the parties were challenged to invent new irrigation projects, new storage dams and other engineering works for the benefit of both nations, all to be funded with the assistance of the World Bank.

Acting in ways that establish or accentuate such cross-cutting cleavages is one of the easiest ways to make a significant difference in the working assumptions of the parties as to the game they are playing. When we have the objective of reducing confrontation, we look for various ways of causing the parties to see themselves not as facing each other like two pistol-toting cowboys in a *High Noon* confrontation, but as sitting side by side at a table, facing a common problem.

Changing Some Standard Moves

In any situation, we tend to do what protocol demands or what we think others expect. The standard plays of international relations are not quite as fixed as those of chess or baseball, but there are nonetheless patterns of behavior into which we fall. As we approach an international negotiation we are far more likely to ask members of our delegation, "What shall our opening position be?" than we are to ask members of the other delegation to sit down with us and draft up half a dozen possible solutions that might fairly reconcile the interests involved. As noted, the standard approach toward negotiation derives from a two-person haggling model. Each side takes a position, argues for it, and makes concessions to reach a compromise. Each side can either play a "hard bargaining" game or a "friendly bargaining" game in order to work toward a desired result. Yet neither approach is, on the whole, particularly appealing. Chart 9–1 details some of the standard moves of each of these negotiating strategies.

CHART 9–1
STANDARD MOVES OF TWO NEGOTIATING STRATEGIES

Friendly Bargaining	Hard Bargaining
Make a strong commitment to reach agreement no matter what.	Make a strong commitment to your position.
Put personal relationships above the merits of the case.	Identify people with their case.
Trust your adversary.	Distrust your adversary.
Be easygoing.	Be ruthless.
See negotiations as an opportunity to acquire friends (by giving them expensive presents, if necessary).	See negotiations as a contest of will (as in arm-wrestling).
Disclose your minimum position.	Mislead as to your minimum position.
Demonstrate a willingness to compromise on your position.	Demonstrate an unwillingness to compromise on your position.
Cultivate friendship through making substantive concessions.	Make your friendship depend on receiving substantive concessions.
Treat substantive differences as personally embarrassing.	Treat substantive differences as a personal challenge.
Be passive.	Attack your adversaries.
React amicably; turn the other cheek.	React strongly; strike back.
Ask them to be friendly.	Press them to make concessions.
Insist that we all agree.	Insist that they give in to you.
Offer friendship and good will.	Threaten linkage, leverage, and pressure.
Yield points as needed to avoid a confrontation.	Yield to pressure slowly as a last resort.

Hard Bargaining.   Positional bargaining and the concurrent strategy of taking and giving up has many costs, however. It encourages one's opposite number in the negotiation to bargain harder. Positional bargaining becomes a contest of will, and can quickly become hard bargaining, where parties damage the relationship in attempts to coerce or intimidate. Each negotiator asserts what she will or won't do. And the more she clarifies her position and defends it against attack, the more committed she becomes to it. The more she tries to convince the other side of the impossibility of changing her position, the more difficult it becomes to do so. The negotiator develops a new interest in "saving face"—in reconciling future action with past positions—making it less likely that any agreement will be reached at all. And if the other party plays the same game, the conflict tends to escalate, as does the value of the time and resources devoted to it. The process becomes less and less constructive as each side tries to press the other to the brink.

When attention is focused on positions and pressures, the content of any agreement that is reached is also likely to suffer. As more attention is paid to positions, less attention is devoted to meeting the underlying concerns of the parties. If the negotiating process is viewed as a contest of will, the agreement that is reached, if any, may reflect a mechanical splitting of the difference between final positions rather than a solution carefully crafted to meet the legitimate interests of those involved.

Arguing over positions can also endanger the parties' ongoing relationship as each side tries through sheer willpower to force the other to change its position. Anger and resentment often result as one side sees itself bending to the rigid will of the other while its own legitimate concerns go unaddressed. Positional bargaining can strain and sometimes shatter the relationship between the parties.

The imprudence of routinely balancing one issue against another, irrespective of the merits, or of using pressure tactics can be illustrated by a hypothetical negotiation over the specifications of a building. Suppose a contractor said, "Go along with me on putting less cement in the foundations because I went along with you on stronger girders in the roof." No owner in his right mind would yield. Neither would he yield on the necessary strength of the foundations if the contractor threatened to have the owner's brother-in-law fired, or offered the owner a special favor. Such tactics would all increase the risk that the building—if the bargain were to be agreed on—would be unsound and in danger of collapse. The same often holds true for international negotiations, where "logrolling" trade-offs can help reach closure, but may form a shaky foundation for an agreement.

Friendly Bargaining: Being Nice Is No Answer.   Many people recognize the high costs of hard positional bargaining, particularly on the parties and their relationship. They hope to avoid them by following a more gentle style of negotiation. Instead of seeing the other side as adversaries, they prefer to see them as friends. Rather than emphasizing a goal of victory, they emphasize the necessity of reaching agreement. In a "soft" negotiating game the standard moves are to make offers and concessions, to trust the other side, to be friendly, and to yield as necessary to avoid confrontation. The friendly negotiating game emphasizes the importance of building and maintaining a relationship. Priority is given to reaching an agreement. Indeed, negotiating according to the friendly bargaining model will likely result in an agreement. However, this model has several problems as well.

First, any negotiation that sacrifices substance in an attempt to maintain or improve a relationship runs the risk of producing a sloppy agreement and may not be good for the relationship. Second, pursuing a friendly form of bargaining makes one vulnerable to someone who plays a hard game of positional bargaining. In positional bargaining, a hard game dominates a soft one. If the hard bargainer insists on concessions and makes threats while the soft bargainer yields in order to avoid confrontation and insists on agreement, the negotiating game is biased in favor of the hard bargainer. The process may produce an agreement, but it may not be a wise one. It will certainly be more favorable to the hard positional bargainer than to the soft one. In our hypothetical negotiation over the specifications of a building, the stubborn contractor would gain an agreement that almost exactly reflected his position, but the building would not be sound.

A Third Choice: Congruent Problem-Solving.

The costs associated with bargaining, whether hard or friendly, suggest an alternative: don't bargain at all. When the contractor suggests changing the amount of cement in the foundations, the owner can remain open to reason, but not to bargaining tactics and pressure. He can listen to arguments based on engineering facts, on professional opinion, on precedent or other sound principles, but can decline to bow to pressure or threats. He can ask *why* the contractor insists so vehemently on changing the amount of cement—that is, what interests underlie that position. He can change the game by giving no weight to "negotiating positions." By perceiving his differences with the contractor not as a contest of will but as a problem to be solved, the owner can rely on facts and reasons to resist the pressure of the contractor—criteria in the real world such as wall strength, costs and appropriate margins of safety.

Some standard moves of a congruent problem-solver are compared with those of bargainers in Chart 9–2. Congruent negotiation can be boiled down to four basic points. Each point deals with a basic element of negotiation and suggests what one should do about it.

1. People: Separate the people from the substantive problem.
2. Interests: Focus on interests, not positions.
3. Options: Generate a variety of possibilities before deciding what to do.
4. Criteria: Insist that the result be based on some objective standard.[2]

---

[2]Roger Fisher, William Ury, and Bruce Patton, *Getting to Yes*, 2nd ed. (NY: Penguin, 1991).

CHART 9–2
Illustrative Standard Moves of Three Negotiating Games

Friendly Bargaining	Hard Bargaining	Congruent Problem-Solving
Make a strong commitment to reach agreement no matter what.	Make a strong commitment to your position.	Commit yourself to seek a principled solution.
Put personal relationships above the merits of a case.	Identify people with their case.	Separate people from their case.
Trust your adversary.	Distrust your adversary.	Proceed independently of trust.
Be easygoing.	Be ruthless.	Adhere to principle.
See negotiations as an opportunity to acquire friends (by giving expensive presents, if necessary).	See negotiations as a contest of will (as in arm-wrestling).	See negotiations as a joint search for a principled solution (as with two judges seeking a basis for a joint decision).
Disclose your minimum position.	Mislead as to your minimum position.	Avoid fixing a minimum position.
Demonstrate a willingness to compromise on your position.	Demonstrate an unwillingness to compromise on your position.	Demonstrate a willingness to respond to reason and principle.
Cultivate friendship through making substantive concessions.	Make your friendship depend on receiving substantive concessions.	Treat personal friendship as independent of substantive differences.
Treat substantive differences as personally embarrassing.	Treat substantive differences as a personal challenge.	Treat substantive differences as an objective problem to be dealt with.
Be passive.	Attack your adversaries.	Attack the problem.
React amicably; turn the other cheek.	React strongly; strike back.	Do not react; act purposively.
Ask them to be friendly	Press them to make concessions.	Press them to invent wise ways of reconciling our interests.
Insist that we agree.	Insist that they give in to us.	Insist on objective criteria that both can accept.
Offer friendship and good will.	Threaten linkage, leverage, and pressure.	Direct reasoned argument at the merits of the problem.
Yield points as needed to avoid a confrontation.	Yield to pressure slowly as a last resort.	Do not yield to pressure; respond to principle and to sound arguments on the merits.

The first point, "people," responds to the fact that human beings are not computers. We are creatures of strong emotions who often have radically different perceptions and have difficulty communicating clearly. Emotions typically become entangled with the objective merits of a problem. Taking positions just makes this worse, because people's egos become identified with their positions. Before working on a substantive problem, the "people problem" should be disentangled from it and dealt with separately. Figuratively, if not literally, participants should come to see themselves as working side by side, attacking the problem, not each other.

The second point, "interests," is designed to overcome the drawback of focusing on people's stated positions when the object of a negotiation is to satisfy their underlying interests. A negotiating position often obscures what you really want. Compromising between positions is not likely to produce an agreement that will effectively take care of the human needs that led people to adopt those positions.

The third point, "options," responds to the difficulty of designing optimal solutions while under pressure. Trying to decide in the presence of an adversary narrows your vision. Having a lot at stake inhibits creativity. So does searching for the one right solution. We can offset these constraints by setting aside a designated amount of time within which to think up a wide range of possible solutions that advance shared interests and creatively reconcile differing interests.

Where interests are directly opposed, a negotiator may be able to obtain a favorable result simply by being stubborn. That method tends to reward intransigence and produce arbitrary results. The fourth point, "criteria," responds to the difficulty of countering such pressure tactics. By discussing objective criteria as the basis for an agreement, we can ensure that the negotiation is no longer a contest of will; neither party gives in to the other, but both defer to a fair and objectively justifiable solution. Responding to pressure tactics and stubborn positions by insisting on looking behind the positions of the other side to the interests and principles underlying those positions is itself a negotiating strategy, and a good one.

Instead of rejecting the other side's position and defending our own, we can counter an intransigent negotiator by insisting on examining the extent to which his position meets the interests of both parties, or might be improved to do so. We can explicitly operate on the assumption that any party will of course change a position if a better solution for both can be found, and that therefore all "will nots" and "won'ts" simply indicate a present belief that certain proposals will not adequately serve certain interests. Approaching agreement by discussing interests rather than positions not only increases the chance that an agreement will be reached, but also increases the chance that the agreement will be a stable one. It makes it easier for the parties to change their positions. The parties can insist that their interests be satisfied, but they don't have to remain committed to their positions. And the agreement they reach will likely be a stable one because no one will feel he has been forced to back down by an intransigent and perhaps more powerful negotiator.

The Egyptian–Israeli peace treaty blocked out at Camp David in 1978 demonstrates the advantages of looking behind positions. Israel had occupied the Egyptian Sinai Peninsula since the Six-Day War of 1967. When Egypt and Israel sat down together in 1978 to negotiate a peace, their positions were incompatible. Israel insisted on keeping much of the Sinai. Egypt, on the other hand, insisted that every inch of the Sinai be returned to Egyptian sovereignty. Time and again, maps showing possible boundary lines that would divide the Sinai between Egypt and Israel were rejected by the parties. Compromising in this way was wholly unacceptable to Egypt. To go back to the situation as it was in 1967 was equally unacceptable to Israel.

Looking to their interests instead of their positions made it possible to develop a proposal at Camp David. Israel's interest lay in security; it did not want Egyptian tanks poised on its border ready to roll across at any time. Egypt's interest lay in sovereignty; the Sinai had been part of Egypt since the time of the Pharaohs. After centuries of domination by the Greeks, Romans, Turks, French, and British, Egypt had only recently regained full sovereignty and was not about to cede territory to yet another foreign conqueror.

At Camp David, President Sadat of Egypt and Prime Minister Begin of Israel agreed to a plan that would return the Sinai to complete Egyptian sovereignty and, by demilitarizing large areas, would still assure Israeli security. The Egyptian flag would fly everywhere, but Egyptian tanks would be nowhere near Israel. By looking behind their opposing positions to their motivating interests, Egypt and Israel found an option that met both parties' interests.

We can also counter an intransigent negotiator by insisting that her single say-so is not enough and that the agreement should reflect some external standard independent of the naked will of either side. This does not mean insisting that the terms be based on the standard we select, but only that some fair standard such as market value, expert opinion, custom, or law determine the outcome. By discussing criteria rather than what the parties are willing or unwilling to do, we ensure that neither party need give in to the other; both can defer to a fair solution.

Moreover, an agreement consistent with precedent or some other fair standard is less vulnerable to attack. If a trade treaty contains standard terms or if an international sales contract conforms to practice in the industry, there is less risk that either negotiator will feel that he was harshly treated or will later try to repudiate the agreement.

Approaching agreement through discussion of objective criteria also reduces the number of commitments that each side must make and then unmake as they move toward agreement. In positional bargaining, negotiators spend much of the time defending their positions and attacking the other side's. People using objective criteria tend to use time more efficiently in talking about possible standards and possible solutions.

Independent standards are even more important to efficiency when more than two parties are involved. An episode during the Law of the Sea Conference illustrates the merits of using objective criteria. At one point, India, representing the Third World bloc, proposed an initial fee of $60 million per site for companies mining in the deep seabed. The United States rejected the proposal, suggesting there be no initial fee. Both sides dug in; the matter became a contest of will.

Then someone discovered that the Massachusetts Institute of Technology (MIT) had developed a model for the economics of deep-seabed mining. This model, gradually accepted by the parties as objective, provided a way of evaluating the impact of any fee proposal on the economics of mining. When the Indian representative asked about the effect of his proposal, he was shown how the tremendous fee he proposed—payable five years before the mine would generate any revenue—would make it virtually impossible for a company to mine. Impressed, he announced that he would reconsider his position. On the other side, the MIT model helped to educate the American representatives, whose information on the subject had been mostly limited to that provided by the mining companies. The model indicated that some initial fee was economically feasible. As a result, the United States also changed its position. No one backed down; no one appeared weak—just reasonable. After a lengthy negotiation, the parties reached a tentative agreement that was mutually satisfactory.

The MIT model increased the chance of agreement and decreased costly posturing. It led to a better solution, one that would both attract companies to do mining and generate considerable revenue for the nations of the world. The existence of an objective model able to forecast the consequences of any proposal helped convince the parties that the tentative agreement they reached was fair. This in turn strengthened relationships among the negotiators and made it more likely that the agreement would endure.

Congruent problem-solving is not without its own risks and costs. It does not guarantee that an agreement will be reached, and it involves its own forms of brinkmanship. Nor is it a strategy that is easily mastered. A look at Chart 9–3, a balance sheet comparing hard bargaining and congruent problem-solving, helps to illustrate the pros and cons of these two styles. Commitment to principle serves as the "hard-hearted partner" that protects us from yielding to unprincipled threats and pressures. Just as hard bargaining is a dominant strategy over friendly bargaining, congruent problem-solving tends to be dominant over hard bargaining. When the hard bargainer discovers that pressure does not produce results but that the congruent negotiator is flexible and willing to respond to good arguments on the merits, then he, too, begins to emphasize arguments on the merits. Charts 9–4 and 9–5 serve as a summary to this chapter. Chart 9–4 asks you to set forth the working assumptions under which the parties in a conflict have been operating and some different working assumptions that could be more helpful. Chart 9–5 is a filled-out example demonstrating some of the assumptions we addressed in this chapter and preferable working assumptions based on our advice.

CHART 9–3
What Negotiating Game Should We Play?

Hard Bargaining	Congruent Problem-Solving
+ It is a game people expect.	– It is not the game people expect.
+ We apparently minimize the risk of agreeing to a bad deal.	– It is often difficult to play.
+ Constituents understand and support our adversarial style.	– It requires flexibility.
+ We may win a short-term victory.	– It requires insistence on standards.
	– It requires a solution on the merits.
	– Applicable principles are often difficult to find and difficult to agree upon.
	– It deprives constituents of "victory."

BUT:

Hard Bargaining	Congruent Problem-Solving
– It tends to escalate conflicts.	+ It tends to keep conflicts small and on their respective merits.
– It subjects us to counterpressure.	+ It provides a basis for resisting pressure.
– It exacerbates our relations with those whom we pressure.	+ It rewards the inventing of solutions.
– It exacerbates our relations with those over whom we "win."	+ It encourages candor and cooperation.
– There can be no agreement without someone giving up his position.	+ The process builds better international relations.
– We cannot expect others to play a game in which we win every time.	+ The results set good precedents.
– The game rewards obstinacy, encouraging more obstinacy.	+ We maintain a reputation for integrity.
– It exacerbates the process of conducting international affairs.	+ We gain the power of principled behavior.
– Both the process and the results set bad precedents.	+ When we agree, we have accepted principled argument, not yielded to pressure.

CHART 9–4
Game Analysis Tool
Working Assumptions about the Game Being Played

Case: _____

Our side: _____

Their side: _____

As of: _____

WHAT IS THE GAME AS WE PRESENTLY PERCEIVE IT?	**WHAT MIGHT BE A BETTER GAME TO PLAY?**
(WHAT ARE THE IMPLICIT WORKING ASSUMPTIONS?)	**(SOME POSSIBLE NEW WORKING ASSUMPTIONS.)**
I. *THE PLAYERS*	*THE PLAYERS*
II. *GOALS*	*GOALS*
III. *STANDARD MOVES*	*STANDARD MOVES*
IV. *ACCEPTED LIMITATIONS*	*ACCEPTED LIMITATIONS*

CHART 9–5
Working Assumptions about the Game Being Played
(An illustrative checklist to be used to stimulate thinking in
connection with Chart 9–4)

Case: _____
Our side: _____
Their side: _____
As of: _____

WHAT IS THE GAME AS WE PRESENTLY PERCEIVE IT?	WHAT MIGHT BE A BETTER GAME TO PLAY?
(WHAT ARE THE IMPLICIT WORKING ASSUMPTIONS?)	**(SOME POSSIBLE NEW WORKING ASSUMPTIONS.)**

I. *THE PLAYERS* (*roles, relationships*)

Parties are divided into two sides (we / they)

They are the enemy.

They are evil.

They behave outrageously.

They are untrustworthy.

As a negotiator, I am a combatant.

THE PLAYERS

Among us there are cross-cutting interests and differences.

They are our adversary today, perhaps our ally tomorrow.

They do not understand us.

I do not understand them.

I lack confidence in them.

As negotiators, we are joint problem-solvers.

II. *THE GOALS*

To win.

To establish that we are right.

To impose painful losses on them.

To get an immediate solution.

THE GOALS

To improve the situation.

To reconcile conflicting interests.

To achieve gains for all.

To establish a good working relationship.

III. *STANDARD MOVES*

Make demands.

Justify positions.

Reject proposals.

Argue.

Make threats.

Talk to impress constituents.

Refuse to make any change.

STANDARD MOVES

Express concerns.

Explain interests.

Explore possibilities.

Listen and learn.

Brainstorm, make offers, invent options

Talk to understand each other; acknowledge good points; build on each other's ideas.

CHART 9–5 (continued)
Working Assumptions about the Game Being Played
(An illustrative checklist to be used to stimulate thinking in
connection with Chart 9–4)

WHAT IS THE GAME AS WE PRESENTLY PERCEIVE IT?	**WHAT MIGHT BE A BETTER GAME TO PLAY?**
(WHAT ARE THE IMPLICIT WORKING ASSUMPTIONS?)	**(SOME POSSIBLE NEW WORKING ASSUMPTIONS.)**
IV. *ACCEPTED LIMITATIONS*	*ACCEPTED LIMITATIONS*
They have fixed intentions.	*None of us can be sure of what to do.*
They will remain hostile.	*We all dwell on the same planet.*
Nothing we can do can change them.	*Almost anything is possible.*
We can't do much.	*The only way to know is to try.*
Nothing can be done in a hurry.	*Significant changes can take place in a day (e.g., Sadat's visit to Jerusalem).*

CHAPTER
—10—

Solving the Inventing Problem

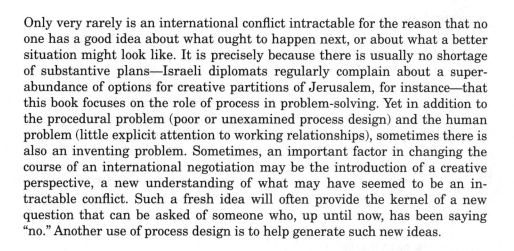

Only very rarely is an international conflict intractable for the reason that no one has a good idea about what ought to happen next, or about what a better situation might look like. It is precisely because there is usually no shortage of substantive plans—Israeli diplomats regularly complain about a super-abundance of options for creative partitions of Jerusalem, for instance—that this book focuses on the role of process in problem-solving. Yet in addition to the procedural problem (poor or unexamined process design) and the human problem (little explicit attention to working relationships), sometimes there is also an inventing problem. Sometimes, an important factor in changing the course of an international negotiation may be the introduction of a creative perspective, a new understanding of what may have seemed to be an in-tractable conflict. Such a fresh idea will often provide the kernel of a new question that can be asked of someone who, up until now, has been saying "no." Another use of process design is to help generate such new ideas.

THE LACK OF NEW IDEAS

Parties to a conflict tend to get stuck because they have been going back and forth arguing about the past and about the merits of their respective posi-tions. The debate has taken on a stale quality, and new ideas are not being generated. Often, those involved simply see no need for new ideas. They know what they are opposed to. They see their primary concern as having their views prevail. New ideas are a threat to existing ideas. Inventing does not take place because parties are content with the ideas they have. Or emotional involvement on one side of a conflict makes it difficult to achieve the detachment necessary to think of solutions that reconcile the interests of all parties.

BUREAUCRATIC CONSTRAINTS

A second explanation for the absence of creative thinking in a conflict lies in the various constraints under which the participants operate. Most of those involved in international conflicts are government people; bureaucracy often accords a cool reception to new ideas. The bureaucrat is taught by his colleagues that any new idea he suggests for consideration may be treated as if it were his considered recommendation. And his colleagues may also teach him that any new idea that is not adopted by the government will be treated as a "failure" and chalked up in their mental record of his batting average. This disastrous confusion of the creative function with the judgmental function encourages a conservative approach that inhibits fresh thinking.

IMPLICIT ASSUMPTIONS

A serious constraint on the inventing process also lies in the extent to which we are unwitting victims of our implicit assumptions. Our minds are tied by traditional and conventional ways of looking at the world. If one of our citizens is mistreated by a foreign government the first response of our government is likely to be a protest, because that is what is done. The text of the last protest is likely to be consulted as providing a model for the present one. There is likely to be little fresh thinking about what we might do to lessen the occurrence of such incidents in the future. We are trapped in our own thinking. It seems almost a foregone conclusion that there is no thought in our heads that was not previously thought.

STATUS OF PARTICIPANTS

Perhaps the most serious constraint on creative thinking in a conflict is the official role of those involved in it. Having authority puts a negotiator in the position where a freely invented option may be mistaken by adversaries as an official position. There is serious risk that she will be seen, at least personally, as committed to accept an idea that she created or helped to create. Something said in a creative context by a negotiator may later be treated as a concession by other negotiators or by critics at home.

LACK OF EXPERIENCE GENERATING NEW IDEAS

A final reason for not coming up with better ideas is that most of us do not know how—we are untrained in the art of generating fresh ideas. Worse than that, the imaginative creativity we start out with as lively preschoolers is typically deadened by years of sitting in a classroom being asked to repeat what we are told and to do things the way they have been done before. In these circumstances, few of those involved in a conflict ever spend much time trying to invent better solutions for all concerned. Parties rarely spend time consciously trying to invent original ways of resolving our differences or formulating principles that will appeal to both sides.

A LACK OF CREATIVE OPTIONS CAN CAUSE DEADLOCK

Chart 10–1 presents a situation that may exist at any point during an internal bureaucratic negotiation or an external negotiation with "the other side." The left-hand column describes an undesirable situation conducive to a deadlock. The right-hand column describes a preferred situation. The problem is the difference between the two. The answer, as the remainder of this chapter discusses in some detail, is to invent options.

CHART 10–1
IS THERE A NEED FOR INVENTING?

Disliked Situation	Preferred Situation
Options on the table are:	*Options on the table are:*
few in number	numerous
narrowly conceived	wide-ranging
reflective of the positions of the parties	objective solutions independent of the positions of the parties
extreme	moderate
reflective of the interests of one side only	designed to reconcile the interests of both sides
unfair enough that if they were agreed to they would probably be short-lived	fair, if agreed to would probably be durable
vague generalities (which even if agreed to would not ensure progress)	operational proposals
sloppily conceived	competently conceived
sloppily drafted	competently drafted
certainly not acceptable to both parties	might be acceptable to both parties

GENERATING NEW APPROACHES

You are the expert on the substance of any particular dispute in which you are a player or advisor. We cannot provide the creative element that may prove determinative to managing or resolving any particular dispute. We have found, however, that third parties—including those acting as advisors to key decision-makers—are often well-situated to add new thinking and fresh ideas. One step or more removed from the heat of battle, an advice giver can often generate a new question to which the parties might say "yes," even though up until now they have been saying "no." We therefore provide approaches to diagnosing and approaching international conflicts that have proved of practical value to practitioners seeking insight on how to generate a new question to be asked of the same or a different decision-maker. There are three basic principles that may help address an inadequate quantity or poor quality of substantive options on the table:

Make the need explicit. The first is to become aware of the need for thinking of new actions that someone might take to lessen the conflict or make it more amenable to solution. Recognizing the limited number of options that are now on the table will force us to think of additional possibilities.

Make the constraints explicit. When we appear to be at a dead end, a useful exercise is to articulate the assumptions within which we are operating. If we do not see how a puzzle might be solved, it helps to make explicit our implicit operating constraints and then question each one carefully: "Must that be so?"

Make a concerted effort to understand different points of view. When a conflict seems intractable, we should change our point of view. Countries that will not come to the table on political questions may well find common ground on religion or education. We can ask from a variety of perspectives, what are the barriers to reaching resolution? What advice would you give to whom for approaching resolution differently?

Designing a Way Out of Constraints

Framing the inventing problem in this way suggests several possible approaches:

Consider listing the substantive options currently on the table. One way of increasing awareness of the quality and quantity of the proposed solutions currently under consideration is to have the parties or a third party prepare a list. Each proposed substantive solution can be listed and then described with a few adjectives of the kind used in the left- or right-hand column of Chart 10–1. In the very preparation of a list of existing options, the parties are likely to find themselves inventing additional ones they believe ought to be on the list.

Consider organizing a brainstorming session. The most straightforward way to reduce constraints is to construct an occasion where those constraints are at a minimum. Brainstorming sessions, when carefully designed, can be just such occasions. In organizing and conducting a brainstorming session, a large number of variables are involved:

Who? While it may be desirable to include the chief negotiators from each side, middle-level people may have more flexibility, as the early stages of the SALT I negotiations showed (see Chapter 7). Experience suggests that a group of, say, five to seven people is large enough to provide a stimulating interchange without being so large as to dampen discussion and limit the freedom to participate.

Where? The objective of freeing negotiators from the constraints imposed by their official positions is likely to be best served by maximizing the number of ways in which a brainstorming session is *unlike* a negotiating session. A brainstorming session might thus be best conducted in a different room, a different building, a different town, or even a different country. A rural retreat can offer an ideal change of pace.

When? The inventing of options should be separated in time and space from the evaluation of those options. An inventing session should certainly be separated from any time at which the parties would be expected to consider accepting any of the options invented.

Purpose? Participants should understand that the sole purpose of the session is to invent a wide variety of ways in which substantive issues might conceivably be addressed. An idea with a 5 percent chance of success might be a fine idea. The purpose of the session is not to judge these options, or to agree to them, or to negotiate about them. It is simply to devise them. The proper response to an idea one doesn't like is to devise a better one.

Atmosphere? The more that can be done to change the environment from that of a negotiating session, the more unfettered thinking may be promoted. Informal sessions on a first-name basis over a glass of wine, with participants from different delegations seated among each other, are common ways of loosening the atmosphere. Less usual devices—such as not wearing watches, skipping meals or preparing meals together, having periods of silence for free-thinking or note-taking—may serve to free participants even more from the constraints that accompany their regular work.

Ground rules? Brainstorming is normally aided by making the entire session off the record, all ideas to be without attribution. An extremely useful rule—useful, that is, in the limited context of brainstorming sessions—is to "outlaw" all negative criticism of any kind. Participants could be invited to precede constructive criticism with: "What I like best about that idea is . . . Might it be better if . . . ?" It will be easier to get the participants to respect the ground rules if there is a third-party facilitator who can get their consent to the rules before the session begins. If someone then breaks the rule, all the third party needs to do is to remind him of the agreement and to ask him if he would like to rephrase his contribution in a positive manner.

A rapporteur? To reduce the sense of attribution, an activist third party may want to designate an assistant as rapporteur of the brainstorming session. The rapporteur is to collect and write up all ideas; all bright ideas are attributed to the "scribe." Other participants in the brainstorming session are simply advising and stimulating the rapporteur, who has full and sole responsibility for what to write up.

Consider using a simple tool to help multiply options.   Often the busy practitioner of international relations is not well situated to develop fresh ideas. He or she does not have the luxury of analysis, but rather must simply react to a given situation. What is urgent will often trump what is important. As Dean Acheson once stated, if the choice is between getting a haircut and going to the bathroom, going to the bathroom will always win out. No matter how important it is to understand and apply theory, the immediate need for action may supersede it. Busy practitioners often have no choice: they must move from problem to solution, without consulting any theory about what they are doing, or ought to be doing.

Academics may have a quite different approach, and yet be similarly constrained from contributing new substantive approaches. They often study specific problems and then generalize about what is happening; or they theorize about what is wrong, and how, in theory, that might be changed. Social scientists often gather as much data as possible, and try to analyze why certain problems occur. Pure theoreticians may identify categories of causes for the ills of this world, and try to suggest some general approaches that could usefully be adopted.

We want process ideas that will supplement the approach of the busy practitioner, who has no time for theory, and the approach of the academic, who has only a limited interest in practice. The thinking about what we as interested activists can offer the real world can be illustrated by a simple chart—Chart 10–2. The task of inventing options can be seen as involving four basic steps. We start with an existing problem in the real world, a disliked factual situation that exists in contrast to a situation we would prefer. The second step is to analyze that present situation in theoretical terms—to diagnose it. Here we sort problems into categories and tentatively suggest causes. The third step, again at the theoretical level, is to suggest what ought, perhaps, to be done. Here we are looking for prescriptions and general approaches. Given the diagnoses that we have made, we consider what might in theory be a possible "cure." The fourth and final step is to apply the theory of what ought to be done in the real world and come up with some specific action ideas and operational suggestions. Chart 10–2—arranging the steps in a circle—illustrates these four steps. Logical problem-solving and the generation of fresh ideas involves activity in all four quadrants.

CHART 10–2
THE CIRCLE CHART[1]
Four Basic Components of Coping With a Problem

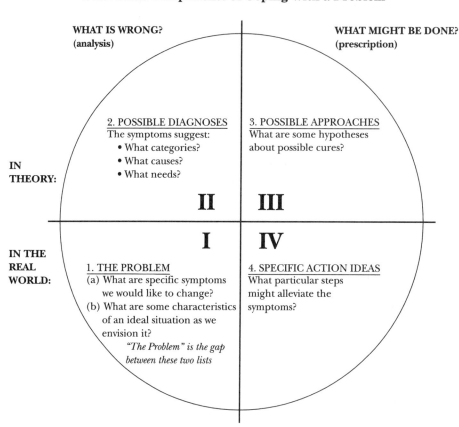

WHAT IS WRONG?
(analysis)

WHAT MIGHT BE DONE?
(prescription)

IN
THEORY:

2. POSSIBLE DIAGNOSES
The symptoms suggest:
• What categories?
• What causes?
• What needs?

3. POSSIBLE APPROACHES
What are some hypotheses
about possible cures?

II   **III**

I   **IV**

IN THE
REAL
WORLD:

1. THE PROBLEM
(a) What are specific symptoms
    we would like to change?
(b) What are some characteristics
    of an ideal situation as we
    envision it?
    *"The Problem" is the gap
    between these two lists*

4. SPECIFIC ACTION IDEAS
What particular steps
might alleviate the
symptoms?

This framework provides an easy way of using one good idea to generate others. With one good action idea before it, a brainstorming session can be asked to go back over the Circle Chart and try to identify the general approach of which the action idea is one example. Given a general, theoretical approach, the brainstorming group can be asked to think of other action ideas that would be applications of the same general approach. Similarly, a group can go back one step further and ask, "If this theoretical approach appears to be a good cure, what is the diagnosis?" Having articulated a diagnosis, one can again go forward, looking for other approaches for dealing with a problem analyzed in that way, and then look for other action ideas that would involve using that approach in the real world. One good option on the table thus opens the door to asking about the theory that makes that option a good one, and then using that theory to invent more options.

---

[1]Roger Fisher, William Ury, and Bruce Patton, *Getting to Yes,* 2nd ed. (NY: Penguin, 1991), p. 68.

There is nothing unusual or original about these four steps; they are simply common sense organized in a clear and schematic way. What is different about them is that they focus on the *process* of coming up with specific tactics to deal with a given problem. An answer to our problem doesn't necessarily pop out at the end when we reach Quadrant IV; often this tool helps us redefine a problem in a more workable way, and sends us around the circle again with a more refined analysis. These four steps also provide a useful outline for an operational memorandum:

    I. Problem
   II. Diagnoses
  III. General Approach
  IV. Specific Recommendation

It is this kind of thinking that we propose to apply to the task of generating fresh ideas, either on our own, within our own negotiating team, among different teams of the same "side," or even during a negotiation with our opposite numbers.

The Circle Chart in action. An example may illustrate the process. In the Northern Ireland conflict it has been suggested that it might be a good idea to have Catholic and Protestant teachers prepare a common workbook on the history of Northern Ireland for use in the primary grades of both school systems. The book would present that history as seen from different points of view, and would give the children exercises that involve role-playing and putting themselves in other people's shoes. This idea appears to have some merit, and is in fact being worked on in Northern Ireland. But what if we want to use this basic idea to generate more ideas? We start with the initial idea and then look for the theoretical approach that underlies it. Looking for theory we might find such propositions as:

- "There should be some common educational content in the two school systems."
- "Catholics and Protestants should work together on small manageable projects."
- "Understanding should be developed in young children before it is too late."
- "History should be taught in ways that illuminate partisan perceptions."

Working with such theory we may be able to invent additional action suggestions, such as a joint Catholic and Protestant film project that presents the history of Northern Ireland as seen through different eyes (perhaps like the Japanese film *Rashomon*). Other action ideas might be teacher exchange programs or some classes or functions for primary-age children in the two systems.

Or we might first go back even further and look for the analysis or diagnosis that lies behind the approaches suggested above. In the upper left-hand quadrant of the Circle Chart we might offer a diagnostic statement such as:

> "The Protestant–Catholic division is exacerbated by the fact that all major cleavages (where people go to school, where they live, where they work, where they go to church, where they shop, the pubs they use, etc.) fall along the same line and reinforce each other—they are coordinated."

Working from that diagnosis, we might generate new approaches and new action suggestions intended to establish cross-cutting cleavages within each community and new alliances or associations across the sectarian line. In such a way the Circle Chart can be used to generate new substantive options based on the approach or diagnosis implicit in those substantive options that are already on the table.

Consider looking through the eyes of different disciplines.
One final suggestion for breaking out of an existing mode of analysis and thinking about problems in new ways is to run them through the Circle Chart using the different "lenses" offered by different academic or professional specialties. In trying to invent new options that may be worth considering, it may help to look at all or parts of a conflict as it would be seen by someone with a specialized point of view, such as an economic planner, a transportation expert, or a military officer. If one were to look at Northern Ireland, or at Cyprus, or at the administration of Jerusalem purely as a question of economic planning, what might one do? Would an economic planner have any suggestions to make that might be worth including as part of a settlement?

Military views are taken into account in a partisan fashion by the parties to a conflict, but it may be stimulating to look at a situation through the eyes of an intelligence officer or military planner from a neutral country. What military arrangements for the two sides could be designed, so that such an officer would be equally happy to serve on the force of either side? Further, could such an expert design mutual military arrangements that would be inherently stable; could they be such that whichever side made the first military move would thereby be more likely to lose the engagement?

Similarly, new ideas might be stimulated by looking at the emerging relationship between the Palestinian administrative units on the West Bank and the rest of Israel as a transportation problem. Might an elevated highway with controlled underpasses help address security concerns while reducing the need for checkpoints? If one looks at Northern Ireland through the eyes of an educator as a problem of education, what possible options might be suggested? If Northern Ireland is seen through the lens of psychological disciplines, or as a problem of institutionalized religion, what ideas might come to mind? If looked at as a legal problem, what suggestions might a lawyer generate? Looking at a conflict through the eyes of a particular discipline or profession provides no easy answers but does provide a way of stimulating fresh thinking that will in some cases produce new options to put on the table.

This chapter offers a rationale for devoting as much sustained and creative attention to process as to issues of substance. In addition, we offer some practical process ideas for generating new thinking on the substance of a dispute. Our ultimate purpose is to gain new insight on a conflict, and to develop a framework of analysis that can move us from a vague sense of what's wrong to a fresh idea that could be presented to decision-makers in the conflict. We do not mean to suggest that these are the only approaches to generating a new and better question for a decision-maker. We do mean to suggest that parties to the conflict—and their advisors—ought to be spending more time examining how they plan to get results, as well as what variations on those results might best accomplish their purposes.

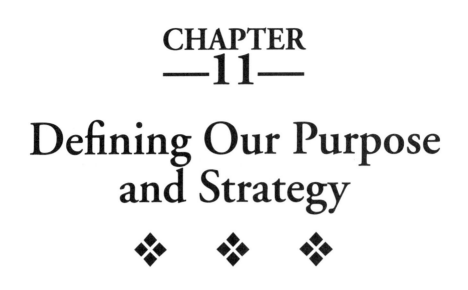

CHAPTER
—11—

Defining Our Purpose
and Strategy

❖   ❖   ❖

In the spring of 1979, the United States Senate chose to engage directly in a bit of foreign relations. It unanimously adopted a resolution condemning the postrevolutionary government of Iran for the more than 200 executions conducted by that government in the previous weeks. Following the overthrow of the Shah, there was uncertainty and confusion over the conflicting authority of the religious leader (the Ayatollah Ruhollah Khomeini), the Cabinet in Teheran, and various revolutionary groups and leaders. During this period in Iran, courts were set up, those charged with having committed political crimes against the people under the Shah were tried, and scores were executed. The U.S. Senate responded to the executions by adopting its resolution. Why?

SEEING CHOICES THROUGH A REAR VIEW MIRROR

The word "why" asks either for a cause or for a purpose. An appropriate answer can begin either "Because . . ." or, "In order to . . . ." That is to say, the answer can either explain the event as being a consequence of something that happened before, or it can explain the event as a purposeful act intended to achieve something in the future. The Senate Resolution condemning the executions in Iran was reactive—a response to those executions—and not purposive—a forward-looking act thoughtfully designed to further some interest or concern. It implies no affection for the revolutionary government of

Iran to say that we have a better chance of accomplishing an objective if we make our actions purposive rather than reactive. Of course, this means knowing what our purposes are.

In June of 1979, what were the objectives of the United States in Iran? The United States government, which had provided the recently overthrown Shah with extensive military and political support, was politically unpopular in Iran. It was arguably in the interest of the United States to establish a working relationship with the new government of Iran and to avoid driving that government toward the Soviet Union. Presumably, a U.S. goal was to develop patterns of cooperation with the new Iranian government that would deal with practical problems and to avoid the kind of political confrontation that would fuel anti-American feeling. The United States had avoided confronting the Shah over the thousands of political prisoners who were detained under him or over the killings by his secret police. Despite that record, the United States government did have some concern for human rights in Iran.

In this situation, it is difficult to believe that any of the 100 U.S. senators could, if they had given it five minutes of thought, have concluded that a good way to further the interests of the United States would be for the Senate (which had never condemned the Shah) immediately to condemn the new government of Iran for executing people, many of whom had been engaged in torture and the killing of political prisoners. However unjustified the Iranian executions may have been, the Senate resolution was a reactive and not a purposive act. To the extent that it may have had a future-oriented purpose, it was not well designed to achieve it: within forty-eight hours the largest anti-American demonstration ever held in the Middle East was held in Teheran. The policy of executions continued, strengthened by a desire to demonstrate Iranian independence in the face of United States pressure.[1]

Actors on the international scene frequently fail to look where they are going because they are too busy looking back over their shoulders. As with the U.S. Senate, they fall into the trap of reacting to recent actions by others that are upsetting and that engage the emotions of their constituents.

Often the pace of action and reaction is so swift that all concerned ignore both the original cause and the subsequent chain of events; each simply responds to the latest move by someone else. Israeli bombing raids on Palestinian camps in southern Lebanon have been explained by the Israeli government as part of a program designed to make the Palestinians more peaceful and less violent, but are probably seen by the Palestinians on the receiving end as purely retaliatory.

Another version of this tit-for-tat approach is policy-making by reacting to perceived historical injustice. People who believe that they are historical victims often become frustrated, angry, and violent. Palestinian guerrilla

---

[1] Roger Fisher, Elizabeth Kopelman, and Andrea Kupfer Schneider, *Beyond Machiavelli* (Cambridge, MA: Harvard University Press, 1994), p. 12.

raids into Israel can hardly be the consequence of a rational strategy intended to make Israelis more willing to accept Palestinians as peaceful neighbors. Looking backward rather than forward is tempting, even though it is most unlikely that we will end up where we want to be if we have not thought enough about exactly where that is, and have not directed our actions toward getting there.

Finally, our purpose has been inadequately considered if we are pursuing an objective that is simply impossible to attain. People who fight on for lost causes can create a great deal of bloodshed to no avail. It is often difficult to know when a goal is beyond hope and should be abandoned for something more realistic. A diplomat who says, "I know we are going to lose, but we must fight on," or, "It is hopeless to restore the empire, but we must try," could usually benefit from strategic advice.

Many European diplomats, for example, have unfavorably compared the 1995 Dayton Peace Plan for the former Yugoslavia with the Vance-Owen Plan of 1993. An important difference, however, was that the otherwise desirable goals of avoiding partition along ethnic lines and avoiding the rewarding of aggression and intransigence with territorial concessions had come to be seen as hopeless. Different analysts will disagree about the value of accomplishing minimal goals (such as "end the shelling") when important principles are seen to be at stake. Realizing that a particular goal is impossible to achieve, however, at least in the short term, is an essential step toward redefining our purpose so we can make progress, even if different decision-makers disagree about what "progress" means in the newly defined context.

Where the difficulty is caused by lack of purpose or confusion of purpose, the prescription is simple: clarify our purposes by thinking them through. Look forward, not back. We are more likely to achieve our ends at minimum cost if we first identify those ends and then design our efforts to achieve them, rather than driving with our eyes on the rearview mirror.

GETTING ORIENTED: WHOSE PURPOSE?

A purpose is always *somebody's* purpose. As conflict analysts, we may be in a good position to step back from the partisan perceptions of the parties and see where purposes may have become muddled, or where there is a disjuncture between ends and means. Developing a diagnosis of how the parties see their own purposes can be a good starting point. This does not mean that we will ultimately take the disputants' statements of purpose at face value, however. Much of the value added by our role as advice-givers may turn out to be a result of improving on the parties' purposes based on clear analysis, and of exploring their enlightened self-interest. A key skill of good lawyering is helping a client refine and prioritize his or her interests. Similarly, the notion of helping an advisee to an "enlightened self-interest," while lending itself to abuse and manipulation in some instances, is a goal we explore in Section IV of this text when we turn to the more operational details of advice-giving. For now, we need a clear sense of where the parties' minds are at present if we hope to change their minds in the future.

WHAT DO THEY WANT?

The kinds of international relations problems we may be trying to manage or resolve can usefully be analyzed under three broad categories. These categories are set out in Chart 11–1.

First, there are the substantive problems relating to meeting people's physical and psychological needs. These are matters having to do with ignorance, poverty, environmental pollution, homelessness, and other problems of injustice. The first group of symptoms in Chart 11–1 illustrates this category. The essential quality of these substantive problems is that they represent something "wrong" or something lacking. When our purpose is to deal with such problems, we would like to "win" something that we want, for ourselves or others, such as territory, money, or food. Such purposes are like the stakes in a game of cards that each player wants to win.

The second category of problems in Chart 11–1 relates to status. People, as individuals or as a group or state, often find that they—or others—are too weak and powerless to win their substantive objectives. To remedy this situation, they want power. They want to be in a position to control their own individual lives, to control what takes place within their country, and to exert influence on what happens in the rest of the world. The breakaway republics of the former Soviet Union saw a chance to assert their national identity and autonomy on the international stage and acted to seize that chance. One of the major purposes states have in the conduct of international relations is the acquisition and maintenance of power—the ability to affect the future.

The third kind of problem in Chart 11–1 relates to affecting the way in which people pursue their sometimes conflicting purposes of winning and gaining power. As separate states pursue their respective ideas of what they want, they come into collision. When one government pursues the substantive goals of justice, well-being, security, and power for itself and its people, it must inevitably deal with other governments that similarly are pursuing such goals for themselves and their people. The ways in which they interact can be more confrontational, violent, and costly, or more orderly, peaceful, and efficient.

The governments of the European Community provide one such example. Each government has an interest in having its interactions with other governments take place efficiently and at a minimum level of friction consistent with the pursuit of its other goals. No matter how serious the differences, each government has an interest in having those differences dealt with at a minimum cost. These three types of problems can be summarized by reference to three types of purposes: victory, power, and peace.

CHART 11–1
POSSIBLE PROBLEMS

Some Disliked Symptoms	Some Preferred Situations

Victory

hungry	well-fed
ill	healthy
poor	prosperous
in pain	comfortable
unequal	equal
rejected	accepted

Power

denied	recognized
fearful	confident
in danger	secure
oppressed	free
dominated	self-governing

Peace

violence	no violence
confrontation	joint problem-solving
no diplomatic relations	easy working relationship
coercive threats	good-faith negotiations
misunderstanding	mutual understanding
conflicts are being dealt with ineffectively, and at high cost.	conflicts are being dealt with efficiently at low risk and low cost

Why Distinguish Victory, Power, and Peace?

Some of the world's problems result from the way in which people carry on their disputes: there are protracted quarrels where there might be speedy agreement; resources are devoted to arms that might better be devoted to human needs; there are threats where there might better be offers; there is political violence where there could be productive discussion; there is war where there could be peace. As with the player in a game of cards, each government has an interest in having the game carried on with some degree of order, and in seeing that nobody kicks over the table or turns a friendly contest into a gunfight. We will always be better off if we distinguish how we carry on our disputes from that which we are disputing about—even when we have disagreements under both headings.

The Purpose Tool, Chart 11–2, is intended as a simple device for helping identify problems and relate them to purposes. To use the tool, select the case that you as an advisor are analyzing, and the parties whose respective points of view you are considering. Fill in a sheet for each party to the dispute by formulating short phrases that will identify the essence of the three kinds of problems that may exist in that situation: wrongs to be righted; weaknesses to be strengthened; and procedures to be improved.

Chart 11–3 is a filled-in Purpose Tool using as an example a clarification of the purposes the United States government had in October 1962 during the Cuban Missile Crisis. The Purpose Tool forces us to look forward, not back, in order to sort out and look more closely at purposes we have in mind.

CHART 11–2
PURPOSE TOOL
Clarifying Our Purposes by Sorting Them Out

Case: _____
As of: ___(date)_____
Our side: _____
Their side: _____

PROBLEM	PURPOSES
I. Victory Substantively, what is some wrong that should be righted?	**I. Victory** Substantively, to the extent that our purpose is to right the wrong, what constitutes "winning"?
II. Power What is the matter? What is at risk? Who is weak? Who should be stronger?	**II. Power** Whom do we want to be in a stronger position? What elements of power should be strengthened?
III. Peace Procedurally, how are differences being dealt with unwisely?	**III. Peace** Procedurally, how do we want the process of coping with conflict improved?

CHART 11–3
PURPOSE TOOL
Clarifying Our Purposes by Sorting Them Out

Case: *Cuban Missile Crisis*
As of: *October 1962*
Our side: *U.S. Government*
Their side: *Soviet Government*

PROBLEM	PURPOSES
I. Victory Substantively, what is some wrong that should be righted?	I. Victory Substantively, to the extent that our purpose is to right the wrong, what constitutes "winning"?
• *Soviet missiles are being secretly installed in Cuba.*	• *Get Soviet missiles out of Cuba. Have no more installed.*
II. Power What is the matter? What is at risk? Who is weak? Who should be stronger?	II. Power Whom do we want to be in a stronger position? What elements of power should be strengthened?
• *U.S. will be more vulnerable to Soviet military power.* • *U.S. prestige is at stake.* • *U.S. political bargaining might be weaker.*	• *Postpone the day when U.S. is so vulnerable to Soviet missiles.* • *Look strong.* • *Look successful.*
III. Peace Procedurally, how are differences being dealt with unwisely?	III. Peace Procedurally, how do we want the process of coping with conflict improved?
• *Soviet Union has been lying to U.S.* • *Soviet Union is secretly trying to gain a military advantage.* • *U.S.–Soviet relations are dominated by military considerations.*	• *Avoid nuclear war.* • *Avoid armed conflict.* • *Move away from military crises toward resolving differences by peaceful political means.*

Although purposes and goals cannot always be separated, it is often helpful to think of a purpose as identifying the direction in which we would like to proceed, and a goal as constituting a specific place on that road. If the problem is seen to be that the United States is militarily vulnerable to the increasing capability of stray Third World nuclear missiles, then the purpose may be to make the United States less vulnerable to a first strike, and the goal may be to have by a given year a retaliatory missile system of which at least a given number of missiles would survive any foreseeable attack. If the problem is seen as widespread illness and death from AIDS that spreads from country to country, our purpose is to reduce suffering and the risk of the disease's spreading, while our goal may be to find a vaccine, or to eliminate AIDS completely.

As noted, we need to examine whether a party's purpose, which may have become identified with a fixed goal, may be unattainable. The single most important ingredient to accomplishing one's goal is to formulate a goal that can be accomplished. In clarifying our objectives we are likely to do better if we formulate a purpose, at least to ourselves, in terms of a direction in which we would like to go, rather than starting by formulating a goal in terms of a fixed point that we "must" reach. Public statement of an absolute goal such as "end violence," "unconditional surrender," "abolish hunger in the world," "worldwide equality," and "freedom from fear" can raise people's sights, can elicit great efforts, and can serve as a highly valuable political strategy. But when privately formulating the advice we are going to give a decision-maker, we need to be utterly candid. We should first decide on the direction in which we want to go; we can later formulate specific goals and action programs for trying to get there.

Focus on One Purpose at a Time

Every actor on the international scene must constantly have in mind the three kinds of purposes—victory, power, and peace—but our analysis will be clearer if we think about trying to change one variable at a time. Even the most powerful decision-maker cannot fix all the problems in the universe, and conflicts that have built up over many generations may need many steps or phases to manage them. Looking at Bangladesh, for example, a United Nations officer might wisely formulate a single purpose: improve the economic and social lot of the large proportion of its people who have as yet received almost no benefit from the Industrial Revolution. Focusing on the single substantive purpose of improving the welfare of the majority of the population, our hypothetical UN officer would still want to bear in mind that ways of improving their economic welfare should not adversely affect some important power interests: the power of the local people to have a substantial say about their own way of life; the power of Bangladesh to govern itself; and the power of the United Nations.

Further, still limiting her affirmative purpose to that of improving the welfare of the inhabitants, our UN officer would want to have in mind how that purpose could be advanced without adversely affecting some important peace interests: any aid contemplated for Bangladesh should not be handled in ways that might damage relations between Bangladesh and its neighboring states, between Bangladesh and the United Nations, or between Bangladesh and those countries providing assistance. We try to keep all three kinds of interests in mind, even though our present actions are intended to further only one purpose.

Analyzing one purpose at a time will also reduce the risk of unintended consequences. Even when we act purposively, we may adversely impinge on other purposes that we have not taken adequately into account. Every country, and every other significant international actor, such as a business or large organization, has multiple concerns. Trying to teach another country "a lesson," like trying to teach a child a lesson, may both damage a relationship and set a bad precedent. The U.S. invasion of Panama in 1989 met the immediate objective of extracting a troublesome local "strongman," General Manuel Antonio Noriega. Longer-term interests, such as a thriving and independent Panamanian economy, mutual confidence among members of the Organization of American States, and support in Central America for moderate political parties seen to be "pro-U.S.," all suffered continuing damage. Great concern with short-term interests often leads to actions that damage longer-term interests. In such instances an action may have been taken purposively, but its impact on other purposes may have been insufficiently considered.

In complex situations, we may want to advise a decision-maker to pursue a strategy that simultaneously advances more than one purpose. With respect to South Africa, for example, a Scandinavian government might want to pursue the purpose of improving the economic and social conditions of South African blacks, pursue the purpose of helping them to gain additional political power, and also pursue the purpose of reducing the risk of a breakdown of civil society before new democratic traditions can take root. In such a complex situation where a decision-maker would like to deal with substantive problems, with problems of a lack of power, and with problems of a risk of violence all at the same time, it will be useful first to look at each purpose separately, and consider how it might best be pursued in ways that would not adversely affect the others, before trying to consolidate the strategies.

The best approach seems to be to identify at a given time the area in which one is trying to produce change, and then try to pursue that purpose in ways that do not impose undue costs in terms of other purposes. Within any one kind of purpose, it is appropriate and often necessary to consider comparative merits and trade-offs. If we are allocating money to the acquisition of military power, for example, we will need to consider the comparative utility of nuclear weapons versus conventional aircraft. If we are pursuing peace through the negotiation of an international agreement, should we focus on a short-term interim agreement or should we seek a more comprehensive and lasting agreement? Having thought broadly about the conflict and specifically about the interests of the parties, we can concentrate our efforts on the purposes that seem most relevant.

DESIGNING A STRATEGY TO REALIZE OUR PURPOSE

In considering how to pursue an international purpose, parties often focus on the difference between military means and political ones. This distinction can be treacherous. Decision-makers may sometimes conclude that first they will try a political strategy, and if that does not work they will rely on military means. Military personnel often express the wish that "politicians" would "stay out of" military matters, which are deemed to be inherently nonpolitical. This false distinction runs the risk of leading officials to conclude that if they are relying on military means, and if they have superior military force, then they can accomplish their objectives. It also suggests that if military force is being used, the critical choices are military rather than political.

The United States' experience in Vietnam over the decade from 1965 to 1975 amply illustrates the dangers of dividing our thinking between military and political means. Of all the explanations for the disastrous conduct of the United States in Vietnam, one of the simplest lies in the false distinction that was drawn between "fighting the war" and "negotiating the peace." The United States had decided not to attempt to conquer all of Vietnam, South and North, acre by acre. The risk of getting involved in a land war with China was too great. In other words, the war was not being fought in order to impose our will physically on Vietnam; it was being fought to affect the decisions and thinking of our opponents. We were going to fight until they decided "to leave their neighbors alone." We were fighting "to teach them a lesson."

The Communist government of North Vietnam was engaged in helping overthrow the government in the South, hoping to unify all of Vietnam on its terms. The United States government, by a variety of military actions in South Vietnam and by bombing in the North, was attempting to exert influence on the government in North Vietnam. Because military hardware was used, this was a "military strategy." But North Vietnam would of course continue to fight on until it saw some alternative that was more attractive. To construct and offer such an alternative was seen as a "political strategy." In effect, the Department of Defense told the U.S. President that they could make it terribly costly and painful for North Vietnam, but that the North would probably fight on until it saw a better choice. Meanwhile, the Department of State was in effect telling the president that it was "too early" to offer North Vietnam a draft cease-fire agreement; that after the military had "won the war" the State Department would be happy to "negotiate the peace."

So the North Vietnamese were never offered a choice that looked better to them than the bloody and painful choice of fighting on. The United

States did have a choice: leave—an alternative that over time looked increasingly attractive to more and more Americans. In hardware terms, the United States had superior military force. But unless we are physically going to impose a result independent of what anyone else decides to do, the "military" outcome will depend on "political" choices. The political aspects of any strategy and its military aspects are intimately interrelated. To think of pursuing one means *or* the other is a limited and dangerous way of organizing our thinking.

What Is Our Strategy: Self-Help, Education, or Influence?

As we think clearly about our choice of strategies, we need categories more useful than military and political. The single most important distinction is between those measures that can succeed by bringing about a desired result independent of anybody else's choice, and those measures where success depends on our affecting somebody else's thinking. Can we impose our will irrespective of what they think? Or do we need to change their mind to get what we want? A second important distinction divides these latter measures into those where we are seeking to "educate" people (by affecting their knowledge, attitudes, skills, or perceptions), and those where we are seeking to "influence" them by persuading them to make a particular decision we desire. It can accordingly be useful to consider the strategies available to us under three broad categories: self-help, education, and influence.

Self-Help.   One basic way for a party coping with a dispute to get something done is to do it himself or herself. Within a country, when the government wants to achieve a particular result it often relies on physically doing the job itself. If the government wants a new kind of hybrid corn developed, it might simply do the job itself within its Department of Agriculture, as opposed to promoting various regulatory or incentive schemes that would encourage other people to decide to develop such a strain of corn.

Foreign affairs differ from domestic affairs because most issues that come up in international relations are not within our exclusive control; they are not such that we can solve them by self-help. Yet sometimes we can cope with an international problem by self-help—we can improve the situation from our point of view without having to work through the medium of affecting how other people think.

A critical international problem, for example, may be the increasing worldwide demand for energy contrasted with a limited supply of petroleum resources. International cooperation will be required to deal with many aspects of the world energy situation if we hope to avoid future conflict over petroleum deposits. Yet it is useful for each country to ask itself, "What can we accomplish through self-help?" Without having to affect the thinking or the decisions of any other government, what can we do within our own country that will reduce the seriousness of that problem? For the United States, which consumes per capita many times more energy than other countries, one answer is direct: do what we can by ourselves to reduce consumption. This strategy does not depend on the assent of any foreign government.

The problem of escalating levels of international arms traffic offers another example. Again, unilateral action cannot solve the whole problem, but each government concerned with the dangers inherent in an increasing proliferation of military hardware should consider what might be accomplished through independent national action. Stopping the direct sale of arms by the United States government and imposing restrictions on arms exports would impinge on other American interests. It would adversely affect the U.S. balance of payments, and it would no longer be as easy to please the leaders of another government by selling them large amounts of U.S. arms. But the benefits of trying to acquire and maintain international friends through selling them arms are doubtful, at least over the medium-to-long term. Both the United States and the people of Iraq might have been better off if we had sold their government fewer military jet aircraft and more irrigation pipe, schoolbooks, and equipment for building roads and processing food. The same may well prove to be true of Syria.

The most clear-cut form of self-help is the use of military equipment to impose a physical result on others outside one's own territory. In the final phase of World War II, the Allies defeated Germany by physical self-help. Some German soldiers and units had decided to stop fighting and surrender, but the government of Germany did not. The strategy against Germany was not designed to succeed through affecting the thinking or decisions of the German government, but rather through the physical, acre-by-acre conquest of Germany no matter what the German government thought or did.

This use of force to accomplish a victory by self-help is in sharp contrast to the way military force was used to influence the government of Japan to make its decision to surrender in August of 1945. There, the U.S. objective was to persuade the Japanese cabinet that it would be futile to fight on. Although the United States used massive military force, success was dependent on what was going on in the heads of those Japanese cabinet members—whether they had been persuaded to choose unconditional surrender. Using atom bombs at Hiroshima and Nagasaki was seen by the U.S. government as an alternative to the self-help strategy of conquering the Japanese home islands inch by inch. This is an example of an influence strategy being pursued by military means. The fact that military force is being used thus does not mean that a strategy is based on a theory of self-help.

The government of Israel has used military force to achieve desired results through self-help in several instances: it participated in the kidnapping of Nazi war criminal Adolf Eichmann from Argentina, bringing him to Israel for trial; it sent assassins into Lebanon to kill certain Palestinian officials whom Israel wanted dead; and it sent a military team to Entebbe, Uganda to rescue Israeli citizens who were being held aboard a hijacked airplane. In each of these cases the strategy was accomplished by self-help. Its success did not depend on what went on in the minds of others.

In any conflict, it is useful first to consider what we might be able to accomplish through self-help. Self-help, as noted, avoids depending on successfully affecting what other people are thinking and deciding. But self-help in international affairs often produces fresh conflict as a byproduct.

Education.   The second broad strategy to consider is that of investing resources to alter the attitudes, perceptions, or knowledge of others. Here we are working through the minds of others but do not depend for success on producing a specific decision in the near future. Rather, we hope to establish a reputation, convince people of the merits of democracy or the evils of pollution, or otherwise affect the thinking of others with the hope that in the long run they will do things differently. Many foreign policy actions are concerned with such educational objectives.

The problem to which an educational strategy is the answer is essentially ignorance or misperception. Having identified the parties' perceptions on a diagnostic level, we should examine them to see whether there are specific areas of ignorance, misperception, or attitude that we might want to try to change. As we use the word, "education" refers to intentional changes in what is in someone else's mind, not to some near-term decision. When we are concerned with educating decision-makers we are interested in making an investment in what other people know and in how they think.

In exploring this possibility, the first task is to identify with some clarity who these decision-makers are. If Canadians want "China" to know more about Canada, or to consider the Canadian approach to free markets and federation of diverse cultures as a worthy model, just who is it in China that the Canadians want to think that way: 100 members of the elite or 100 million of China's one billion plus population? Voice of America radio broadcasts around the world are aimed at educating a broader audience than those diplomats and officials with whom the United States deals directly. The more democratic and open the society, the broader the constituency in which another government is likely to be interested.

Having identified a target audience with a current mental attitude, level of knowledge, or set of perceptions that we believe it may be in our interest to change, we should then identify those specific attitudes or perceptions that we would like to target. Chart 11–4 is intended as a simple device for helping to identify such attitudes or perceptions. Chart 11–5 illustrates one way of approaching this problem by considering what aspects of the thinking of politically mainstream German citizens some community leaders of recent nonwhite immigrants to Germany might make it their purpose to change, and how.

Education is a two-way street. Chart 11–5 looks at some elements of the educational strategy that the immigrant community leaders might want to pursue vis-à-vis German public policy (and private attitudes) affecting them. Charts 11–5 and 11–6 illustrate the gap between present and desired perceptions, and also help clarify the relationship between proposed actions and desired perceptions. Even simple charts such as these can ultimately help fine-tune proposed actions.

CHART 11–4
TOOL ON EDUCATIONAL ENDS AND MEANS

Case: _____
As of: ___(date)_____
Our side: _____
Their side: _____
Prepared: ___(date)_____
By: _____

A	B	
Present perceptions, attitudes, beliefs, etc. of _____ that we might want to change.	Perceptions, attitudes, and beliefs that we might want them to have instead.	Specific action programs that might move them from (A) to (B).

CHART 11–5
TOOL ON EDUCATIONAL ENDS AND MEANS

Case: _Native German–Recent Immigrant Relations_
As of: ___1996_____
Our side: _____
Their side: _____

A	B	
Present perceptions, attitudes, beliefs, etc. of _German public_ that we might want to change.	Perceptions, attitudes, and beliefs that we might want them to have instead.	Specific action programs that might move them from (A) to (B).
1. Many Germans know no individual nonwhite immigrants, yet are exposed to stereotypes of them as dirty or dishonest.	_Better knowledge of the facts._	_German citizens get tax breaks if they volunteer in immigrant communities; films, television specials, lectures attacking stereotypes are widely disseminated._
2. Mainstream media routinely feature jokes, caricatures, etc., about people of non-Caucasian descent.	_That racial slurs against any group are outrageous._	_Cooperation with editors at TV stations, papers, magazines, etc._
3. Many Germans are wholly ignorant of the extent to which immigrant labor has supported the German economy and high standard of living.	_That native-born Germans see the symbiotic relationship their economy has with the immigrant labor pool._	_A documentary series on immigrant contributions to the economy._
4. Many ordinary Germans may feel that it is easier to keep silent than to take action.	_That the cost of keeping silent is high. That anti-immigrant violence negatively affects Germany's international image._	?

CHART 11–6
TOOL ON EDUCATIONAL ENDS AND MEANS

Case: _Native German–Recent Immigrant Relations_

As of: ___1996_____

Our side: _____

Their side: _____

A	B	
Present perceptions, attitudes, beliefs, etc. of <u>immigrant communities</u> that we might want to change.	Perceptions, attitudes, and beliefs that we Germans might want immigrant communities to have instead.	Specific action programs that might move them from (A) to (B).
1. _"Nativist groups will attack us whatever we do."_	_"Nativist groups are small and vulnerable enough that we can mobilize to undercut their support."_	_Publicize the impact of nativist attacks on their victims in the local, national, and international press._
2. _"We will never be accepted as Germans, and there is nothing we can do as a community that will ease our adjustment."_	_"There is a great deal that the Germans do not understand about us, and that we do not understand about them."_	_Joint activities across communities; exhibits and media coverage of immigrant contributions._
3. _"Moderate German political parties will abandon us and let us down."_	_"Our communities and moderate political parties share many interests."_	_Joint discussions among community leaders about ways to build a broad, antiracist political base._
4. _"Ordinary Germans will remain silent or secretly support our attackers."_	_"German people will respond to principled arguments and examples that help them feel less threatened."_	?
5. _"The German government should force rightists to abandon the streets and their cause."_	_"In a democratic society, all voices must be heard. Suppressing rightist agitation could bolster their cause."_	?

Educational objectives and strategies are often closely tied to other strategies. To return to the use of nuclear weapons in 1945, one aspect of that strategy may have had little to do with the Japanese cabinet, emperor, or public. Some historians and social scientists now maintain that the Nagasaki bombing, in particular, was actually targeted at educating the Soviet Union about the extensive inventory of powerful hardware in U.S. arsenals. They also argue that the lesson was designed to be a deceiving one: while the use of a second bomb was meant to imply the existence of more, in fact the United States in 1945 had no more.

A negotiating strategy, which is by definition designed to exert influence and produce a specific decision, may have an educational component; for example, we often want to lower another party's expectations. But such elements are so closely tied in with influence that it is probably better to consider them as part of the third way of pursuing our objectives, namely to exert influence.

Influence.   If parties are in a conflict there is almost always some decision that each wants the other to make—or to refrain from making—in the near future. The rational pursuit of conflict is carried on for the purpose of exerting influence—for the purpose of causing an opposing party to make some decision that we would like them to make. Most of this book is therefore focused on the advice that we would give one decision-maker so that we can cause another decision-maker (perhaps on "the other side") to be faced with a new choice.

A party to a conflict may seek to acquire power through self-help—through the unilateral acquisition of military hardware. They may also seek to enhance their power through education—through behaving in ways that establish a particular kind of reputation. If they are using military power to establish a reputation, it is well to recognize and make explicit that it is being used for such an educational purpose. A decision-maker can also combine all three strategies, employing a self-help strategy together with an education strategy when taking unilateral steps to do what is best for his or her own side, while simultaneously hoping to lead others by example. The United States government protects its own people by refusing to manufacture or import certain products that do not meet basic safety or environmental standards. Such a self-help strategy may raise the safety and environmental standards in other countries as well, by showing them how seriously the United States takes these standards. The success of such a strategy may also depend on influencing other manufacturers to make a specific decision—by letting them know that they will not sell in U.S. markets unless they raise their standards.

When we consider the role of individuals seeking to have an impact on the conduct of foreign affairs, self-help and education strategies may well be beyond any one individual's personal means. A given decision-maker may, however, be able to influence others to use self-help or education.

The balance of this text focuses on influence—negotiation and persuasion strategies for realizing limited and defined objectives. Influence is itself such a broad strategy that we need to think quite clearly about just how anyone might propose to change a situation in order to make it likely that the relevant decision-makers might consider making some different choices going forward. As the previous few chapters of this book have discussed in detail, there are a wealth of tactical options at our disposal. In canvassing the details, however, it is always useful to step back and ask: "What's our purpose?" and to follow that key question with, "What's our theory about *how* to proceed?" Sorting through the trade-offs among ends—victory, power, or peace—and means—self-help, education, or influence—will help guide our smaller, tactical choices as we pursue our objectives.

CHAPTER
—12—

Case Study—
The Bombing Campaign
in Vietnam

Any book on international negotiation written in the United States is almost required to discuss Vietnam. Vietnam is often seen as a watershed in U.S. history, changing U.S. views of the world and of its own power. Vietnam is also used by many scholars as an example of how international conflict shifted in the latter half of this century from full-fledged world wars to more localized conflicts requiring entirely different ways of fighting and thinking.

This particular study of the bombing campaign in Vietnam focuses on the years 1964 to 1966 and is designed to help illustrate some of the miscommunication and missed opportunities between the United States and North Vietnam. It provides the background material necessary to understand the application of the tools in Chapters 13 through 17. The materials chosen for this case study are designed to demonstrate the communication between the parties and interpretations that each side gave to the other side's actions. Consequently, the quotations, examples, and stories in this case study usually reflect a partisan, rather than a neutral, point of view. Additionally, the bibliography for this case study is an eclectic collection of these points of view, rather than a comprehensive list of sources on the Vietnam conflict.

HISTORICAL BACKGROUND

Early in World War II, in September 1940, Japan took over Vietnam (then French Indochina), but allowed the French colonial administration to con-

tinue. In 1941, Vietnamese leader Ho Chi Minh (who had attempted to petition U.S. President Woodrow Wilson in 1919 at the Versailles Peace Conference for the self-determination of Vietnam) returned secretly to Vietnam after
having formed the Indochinese Communist Party in Hong Kong in 1930. In
Vietnam, he formed the Vietminh to fight the colonial French as well as the
Japanese presence. On March 9, 1945, the Japanese took over the administration of Indochina from France. Two days later, the last Vietnamese emperor, Bao Dai, declared independence for Vietnam under Japanese auspices.
The Allies decided at the Potsdam Conference in July 1945 that the British
would disarm the Japanese in southern Vietnam, while the Chinese Nationalists would do the same north of the 16th parallel. Three days after Japan
surrendered, the Japanese transferred power in Indochina to the Vietminh,
on August 18, 1945. Five days later, Bao Dai abdicated. On August 29, Ho Chi
Minh proclaimed a provisional government in Hanoi, with Bao as his
supreme counselor. On September 2, 1945, Ho declared independence for all
of Vietnam. Nevertheless, on September 13, 1945, the British landed in
Saigon, and soon returned authority over the South to France, which had
claimed Vietnam as part of its colonial empire since the 1860's.

In 1946, China withdrew its forces from Vietnam, and in March,
France recognized the nation as a "free state" within the French Union and
French troops were authorized to replace the departing Chinese. Ho signed
an agreement to end hostilities with the French in September 1946, but the
agreement was soon violated when French warships attacked Haiphong (the
main northern port) on November 23, 1946. In December, the Vietminh de-
parted Hanoi and formed a rural base. This marked the beginning of the
French–Indochina Conflict in Vietnam.

In March 1949, Bao Dai signed an agreement with France, making
Vietnam an "associated state" within the French Union, and he returned to
Vietnam in April after three years of self-imposed exile. On January 14, 1950,
Ho Chi Minh challenged Bao Dai's power to make such an agreement on behalf of the country, declaring that the Democratic Republic of Vietnam (DRV)
was the only legal government and the only legal representative of the wishes
of the people of Vietnam. The DRV was recognized by the Soviet Union and
China. On February 7, 1950, the United States and Britain recognized the
government of Bao Dai, while Chinese Communists on the Vietnam border
began providing the Vietminh with modern weapons. In July of that year, the
United States contributed $15 million in military aid to the French for the
war being waged in Indochina. However, three years later the French were
still struggling.

In early 1954, the strategically important French garrison at Diembienphu came under siege by the Vietminh. Although the United States had
been providing monetary aid to the French, the United States refused to provide direct military intervention to save the garrison. On May 7 the garrison
fell to the Vietminh.

The next day, after Ho had confirmed his willingness to undergo
peace talks, the Geneva Conference was convened on May 8, 1954 to resolve

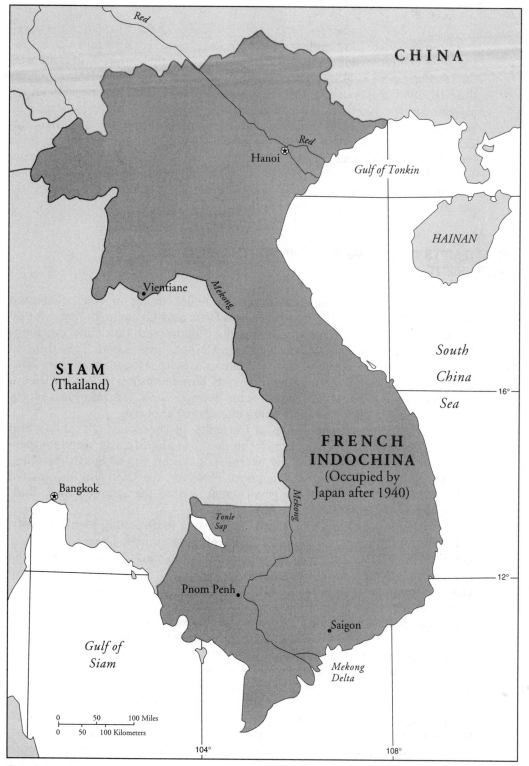

French Indochina

the French–Indochina Conflict. The conference issued an agreement that provided for the redivision of Vietnam at the 17th parallel, while it also allowed for elections to be held by July 20, 1956, leading to reunification. However, on July 16, 1955, the South (with U.S. approval of their decision) rejected an invitation by the North to discuss reunification elections, and the issue was never discussed by the two halves of the separated nation. By that time, the U.S. was directly sending aid to the South Vietnamese and had given their leader, Ngo Dinh Diem, $100 million in aid in late 1954. The United States had decided that Vietnam provided an important arena for the fight between communism and capitalism, and therefore did all it could to strengthen the government and economy of the South.

U.S. ATTEMPTS TO STRENGTHEN THE SOUTH VIETNAMESE GOVERNMENT

After the Geneva Agreements, many Catholics living in North Vietnam crossed the border into the South because Diem was Catholic. In fact, over 80 percent of the 900,000 Vietnamese who came south were Catholics; this number constituted two-thirds of the Northern Catholic population. Once they arrived in the South, many of the Northern Catholic refugees who were educated received high-level administrative or bureaucratic positions in Diem's government. Their arrival caused some tension with the Southern officeholders, who felt that the Northerners often acted superior.

The increased population of Catholics in the South (the influx had doubled the number of Catholics in the South to slightly over a million people, constituting 7 percent of the overall population in the South) provided Diem with his strongest base of support. However, the Catholics also caused political tensions outside of the government, within the largely Taoist, Buddhist, and spiritualist Southern population.

Diem's popularity faltered as he became increasingly identified with not only the Catholics, but the Northern refugees and the United States, especially since U.S. support had been so crucial to massive migration of the Northern Catholics. Partly because it thought that the refugees would provide a strong power base for its ally, Diem, the United States spread propaganda throughout the North about the Virgin Mary departing for the South. The migration of Catholics to the South had also been facilitated by the transportation provided by the U.S. government in the form of the U.S. Navy's Seventh Fleet, as well as by $93 million provided for the relocation. Apparently, the U.S. and Diem had not realized, or perhaps had chosen to overlook, the impact of such an influx on domestic politics.

In 1957, the Communist insurgency began in the South, with guerrillas assassinating almost 400 minor South Vietnamese officials. Two years after the Communists in the South had begun their own rebellion, North Vietnam formed Group 559 to begin infiltrating weapons and men into South

Vietnam via the Ho Chi Minh Trail. The Trail was a highly organized series of routes through Laos and Cambodia into South Vietnam along which flowed constant material to support the insurrection in South Vietnam. In 1960, the leaders in Hanoi formed the National Liberation Front for South Vietnam (NLFSV, or Vietcong, as they were called by Saigon) to parallel Ho's organization in the North, the original National Liberation Front (NLF).

By the end of 1961, "rebel" activities were increasing in South Vietnam, so the government of South Vietnam asked the United States for increased military assistance to fend off the rebels as well as their threatening neighbor to the North. On February 6, 1962, the U.S. Military Command was formed in South Vietnam, with the number of advisors there growing by the middle of that year from 700 to 12,000. Tension concerning Diem continued to increase as several coup attempts failed. Finally, with U.S. support, a coup was successful on November 2, 1963, and Diem was murdered after surrendering. By the end of December, the number of U.S. military advisors in the South had increased to 15,000 and more than $500 million in aid had been provided in that year alone. The United States' involvement in the war had become larger and larger, but the U.S. was soon to become more directly involved.

DIRECT U.S. INVOLVEMENT BEGINS—BOMBING CAMPAIGNS

On August 2, 1964, North Vietnamese patrol boats attacked the *Maddox*, a U.S. destroyer in the Tonkin Gulf. In response, five days later the House and Senate overwhelmingly passed a resolution (the Gulf of Tonkin resolution) permitting the president to take all necessary measures to repel attack on U.S. forces and to prevent further aggression in the region. Later that month, after somewhat disputed reports of a second attack in the Gulf, U.S. aircraft directly bombed North Vietnam for the first time, in retaliation for the events in the Gulf. On October 30, 1964, the Vietcong attacked a U.S. air base in Bienhoa in South Vietnam; however, President Lyndon B. Johnson rejected proposals to bomb again in retaliation. Two months later, on Christmas Eve of 1964, the Vietcong bombed a U.S. military camp in Saigon, and Johnson once again refused retaliatory air raids against North Vietnam.

However, when the Vietcong attacked U.S. installations on February 7, 1965, Johnson approved Operation Flaming Dart, a series of air raids against North Vietnam. Flaming Dart consisted of three air strikes on February 7, 8, and 11, 1965. During the lull in bombing, which would resume on March 2, the United States issued a "White Paper" on February 27, outlining its conditions for settlement of the conflict. The Americans' key components for a peace agreement were North Vietnam's acceptance of South Vietnam as a separate and independent nation, and the complete withdrawal of North Vietnamese forces from the South.

Between the end of Flaming Dart and the inception of Operation

Rolling Thunder (another bombing campaign that will be described below), the North Vietnamese government was very receptive to peace initiatives presented to it by UN Secretary-General U Thant and French President Charles de Gaulle. The North Vietnamese assumed that during the pause in bombings, negotiation possibilities should be explored. However, the United States was not of the same mind-set, declining all offers for a conference and resuming bombings on March 2, sending Marines into South Vietnam a few days later. Such actions led the North Vietnamese government to believe that the U.S. was not receptive to an early settlement based on compromise. Therefore, the North Vietnamese government expressed no further interest in negotiations without preconditions, believing that the U.S. had already rejected such a format.[1]

On March 22, Ho Chi Minh's NLF countered the U.S. "White Paper" with its own five points, which stipulated the removal of U.S. troops located in the South as a condition for their cooperation in efforts to settle the conflict peacefully. Three weeks later, the North Vietnamese government in Hanoi softened this requirement in its four points, which declared that a promise from the U.S. to withdraw all of its troops would be acceptable as a prerequisite to negotiations.

On April 4, South Vietnam issued a reply to the seventeen nonaligned nations that had appealed for a negotiated peace, in which the Saigon government expressed its opinion "that negotiations in view of restoring peace could only have a chance of success if the Communists show their sincere desire of putting an end to the war, of which they are the authors, by withdrawing beforehand their armed units and their political cadres from South Viet-Nam territory."[2] The battle of positions had begun, several months after the true battle had started to blaze for the United States.

Aside from diminishing North Vietnamese faith in the American desire for a peaceful settlement to the conflict, another unfortunate result of the U.S. choice to begin bombing was that it thwarted Soviet Premier Kosygin's attempts to bring North Vietnam to the negotiation table, because the Northerners could now claim to be victims of U.S. imperialist aggression. In the circumstances, the Soviets felt it necessary to provide unconditional military aid from that point on, in keeping with their own anti-imperialist stance.

At its inception, the decision to resume bombing (known as Operation Rolling Thunder) constituted a U.S. plan for an eight-week series of bombing raids. This sustained bombing of North Vietnam began on March 2, 1965 and would not end for another three years, with the exception of a few brief pauses discussed below. Some saw the initiation of Operation Rolling Thunder as the solution to the mounting fighting between North and South Viet-

---

[1]George M. Kahin and John W. Lewis, *The United States in Vietnam* (NY: Doubleday, 1969), p. 207.

[2]South Vietnam's Reply to the Seventeen Nonaligned Nations; April 4, 1965; Article 5. Cited in Marcus G. Raskin and Bernard B. Fall, eds., *The Viet-Nam Reader: Articles and Documents on American Foreign Policy and the Viet-Nam Crisis* (NY: Random House 1965), p. 271.

nam. Critics now argue that if the Johnson administration had consulted history (other incidents of bombing for political reasons include Mussolini's bombing of Ethiopia, the Japanese of China, and Hitler's of Britain), they would have seen the pattern of failure of such an avenue.[3]

On March 2, 1965, U.S. Secretary of State Dean Rusk announced the following as the three purposes of the bombing campaign: (1) to build South Vietnamese faith in U.S. intentions by penalizing the North Vietnamese for their aggressions; (2) to provide barriers to the path of supplies and enemy forces flowing from North to South Vietnam; and (3) to demonstrate to North Vietnam that their support of the insurgency within South Vietnam would continue to result in punishment.

While President Johnson saw the bombing as a means to stop Communist aggression in South Vietnam, as well as to provide a psychological boost to the Saigon government to help it attain stability, he overlooked the psychology of the North. Paul Warnke, who was an assistant secretary of defense in the United States at the time, viewed the crucial error in the policy toward Vietnam as not realizing the North Vietnamese determination to resist: "The trouble with our policy in Vietnam has been that we guessed wrong with respect to what the North Vietnamese reaction would be. We anticipated that they would respond like reasonable people."[4]

General Maxwell D. Taylor, former ambassador to Vietnam, stated regarding the Hanoi government's reaction to the bombing: "Thus far, Hanoi has shown no interest in opening negotiations but concentrated propaganda emanating from every Communist capital to get us to stop the bombing of the North is a persuasive testimonial to its effectiveness."[5] In actuality, the bombing merely served to harden Hanoi's position on negotiations, moving it from the position that the NLFSV should be a *part* of any negotiation process, to the assertion that the NLFSV was the only true representative for South Vietnam.[6]

PRESIDENT JOHNSON'S SPEECH AT JOHNS HOPKINS UNIVERSITY[7]

A speech given by President Johnson at Johns Hopkins University on April 7, 1965 represented one of his major statements regarding the situation in Viet-

---

[3]For example, see Ernest R. May, *"Lessons" of the Past* (New York: Oxford University Press, 1973).

[4]Paul Warnke, quoted in "Chronology" abbreviated from *Vietnam: A History* by Stanley Karnow, p. 396. Copyright © 1983 by WGBH Educational Foundation and Stanley Karnow. Used by permission of Viking Penguin, a division of Penguin Books USA Inc.

[5]Association of the U.S. Army, *Vietnam in Perspective: A Time for Testing* (Washington, D.C., 1968), p. 11.

[6]Kahin and Lewis, p. 210.

[7]Excerpted from remarks made at Johns Hopkins University, Baltimore, MD, April 7, 1965. Cited in Raskin and Fall, p. 344.

nam. One comment in it set the tone for the remainder of the speech: "We hope that peace will come swiftly. But that is in the hands of others besides ourselves." In other words, peace had to result from a North Vietnamese initiative to end their aggression, basically terminating their support for the Vietcong in the South. While seemingly leaving any move toward peace up to the North Vietnamese, Johnson simultaneously offered an incentive to the North in the form of a $1 billion aid program for Southeast Asia once peace had been achieved in Vietnam.

Johnson argued: "We must fight if we are to live in a world where every country can shape its own destiny, and only in such a world will our own freedom be finally secure." Later in the speech, Johnson characterized North Vietnam's primary goal as "total conquest" of the South. Ho Chi Minh argued that his true goal was "complete national liberation and the reunification of the country"[8]—a country that was supposed to reunite, according to the Geneva Agreements discussed above, through elections to be held in 1956. Yet, as explained earlier, the South did not cooperate with arrangements for such elections, and therefore they did not occur.[9]

In defense of U.S. motives, Johnson also asserted that Americans "want nothing for ourselves—only that the people of South Viet-Nam be allowed to guide their own country in their own way." And yet, the U.S. had, in his own words, "helped to build" the nation, from its government to its army.

Johnson also outlined the essentials of any peace agreement in this speech: "an independent South Viet-Nam—securely guaranteed and able to shape its own relationships to all others—free from outside interference—tied to no alliance—a military base for no other country." Yet Johnson was unclear on the way to achieve such a settlement, saying that "There may be many ways to this kind of peace."

Johnson further limited the options for negotiations in his comment that the United States would be willing to hold talks with all of the "governments involved," implying that Ho Chi Minh's NLF and the NLFSV would not be included in any negotiations. In a later address, on July 28, 1965, Johnson once again mentioned "any government" as a possible party to negotiations, effectively overlooking the immediate adversary, the Vietcong. However, in a press conference following that address, Johnson stated that the views of the NLFSV could be represented at a negotiation table. The U.S. government contradicted itself a few months later when, on December 7, Secretary of State Rusk declared that the U.S. would not give the NLF any political influence or status in South Vietnam.

---

[8]Letter to the Cadres from South Viet-Nam regrouped in the North by Ho Chi Minh; 19 June 1956; cited in Bernard B. Fall, ed. *On Revolution: Selected Writings, 1920–1966* (NY: Praeger, 1967).

[9]In fact, in the same letter quoted above, Ho Chi Minh asserted that the Americans were at fault for preventing the elections: "They are scheming to divide our country permanently."

BREAKS IN THE BOMBING AND ATTEMPTS AT NEGOTIATION

When the U.S. government initiated the first break in its bombing of North Vietnam on May 13, 1965, the hope was kindled that the government in Hanoi would take the opportunity to express a desire for communication. A U.S. Army statement asserted that the government in Hanoi had called the pause a "trick" after it had been in effect for only three days.[10] Therefore, the U.S. government resumed the bombing on May 17, 1965.

Another interpretation of the events resulting from this pause has been offered: the North Vietnamese received what they viewed as an ultimatum from U.S. Secretary of State Dean Rusk, demanding that the Vietcong cease fighting in exchange for an end to the bombing. However, the short span of the pause (only five days) did not allow sufficient time for consultations between Hanoi and the Vietcong, and then subsequent reductions in armed actions. The U.S. reinstated its bombing campaign, claiming that North Vietnamese military action had not slackened during the break—but the amount of time allotted had been insufficient for the government to consult with the military and change any initiatives already begun.[11]

In fact, there had actually been a preliminary response from North Vietnam that seemed receptive to the U.S. demand, though the administration denied this for more than seven months. For example, a few months after the pause in May, on July 13, 1965, President Johnson asserted that there had not been "the slightest indication that the other side is interested in negotiation"; his withholding of the fact that Hanoi had indeed responded a few months earlier merely served to further convince North Vietnamese leaders that the U.S. was not looking for compromise. While the U.S. seemed to have offered the North Vietnamese a viable option—agree to stop aggressions and bombing will cease—it subsequently revoked the offer too soon for any feasible decrease in military maneuvers by the North to occur and ignored the verbal response given by Hanoi. Actions such as these served to heighten preexisting mistrust of U.S. intentions in North Vietnam.

In addition, in November 1965, the U.S. State Department admitted that President Johnson had declined an opportunity for peace talks secretly arranged by U.N. Secretary General U Thant in 1964, because the North Vietnamese had attached unacceptable conditions. North Vietnam had rejected U.N. jurisdiction over the war because of its mistrust of that institution, feeling that it was dominated by the United States and that it had unfairly denied membership to North Vietnam and to Communist China. Therefore, U Thant had been counting on the Soviet Union to convey his message to North Vietnam in 1964. At that time, Soviet Premier Khrushchev was

---

[10]Association of the U.S. Army, *Vietnam in Perspective: A Time for Testing* (Washington, D.C. 1968).

[11]Kahin and Lewis, p. 214.

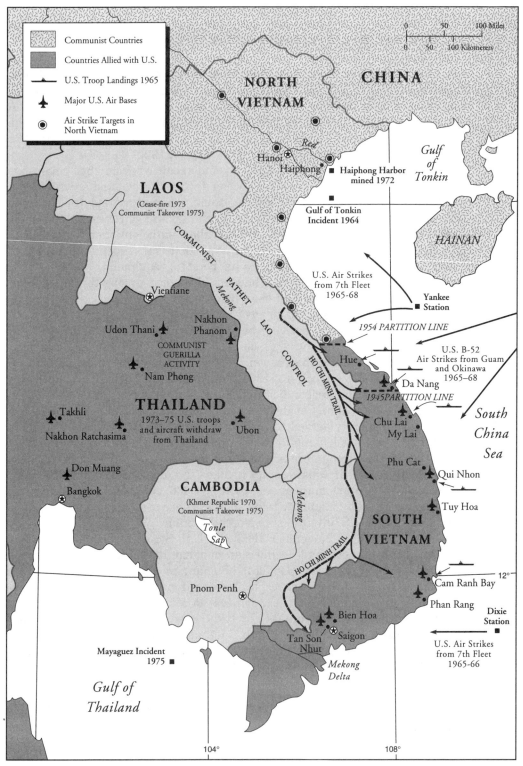

Legend

Communist Countries

Countries Allied with U.S.

U.S. Troop Landings 1965

Major U.S. Air Bases

Air Strike Targets in North Vietnam

CHINA

NORTH VIETNAM

Red

Hanoi

Haiphong

■ Haiphong Harbor mined 1972

Gulf of Tonkin

Gulf of Tonkin Incident 1964

HAINAN

LAOS
(Cease-fire 1973
Communist Takeover 1975)

COMMUNIST

PATHET

LAO

CONTROL

Mekong

U.S. Air Strikes from 7th Fleet 1965-68

■ Yankee Station

1954 PARTITION LINE

Vientiane

Udon Thani

Nakhon Phanom

COMMUNIST GUERILLA ACTIVITY

Nam Phong

HO CHI MINH TRAIL

Hue

U.S. B-52 Air Strikes from Guam and Okinawa 1965–68

Da Nang

1945 PARTITION LINE

THAILAND
1973-75 U.S. troops and aircraft withdraw from Thailand

Takhli

Nakhon Ratchasima

Ubon

Chu Lai

My Lai

South China Sea

Phu Cat

Qui Nhon

Tuy Hoa

Don Muang

Bangkok

CAMBODIA
(Khmer Republic 1970
Communist Takeover 1975)

Tonle Sap

Mekong

SOUTH VIETNAM

Pnom Penh

Cam Ranh Bay

12°

Phan Rang

Dixie Station

HO CHI MINH TRAIL

Bien Hoa

U.S. Air Strikes from 7th Fleet 1965-66

Mayaguez Incident 1975 ■

Tan Son Nhut

Saigon

Mekong Delta

Gulf of Thailand

104°

108°

Vietnam During the War

also attempting to get North Vietnam to the negotiating table, by promising more aid if it agreed to negotiate. However, this glimmer of hope died when Khrushchev was overthrown in October 1964 and Soviet aid to North Vietnam was increased by his successors.

Immediately prior to the second break in bombing, in December 1965, U.S. Secretary of State Rusk claimed to be seeking "clarification" of a message expressing a North Vietnamese desire for peace conveyed by two Italians who claimed to have spoken with Ho Chi Minh and the North Vietnamese premier, Pham Van Dong. The message included the conditions that the North Vietnamese would want met before negotiations could occur. These included: a cease-fire throughout Vietnam, the termination of belligerent operations, prevention of the arrival of further U.S. troops in South Vietnam, and a declaration comprising the four points outlined by Hanoi earlier in the year. The two Italians concluded that Hanoi was ready to negotiate without requiring the removal of U.S. troops prior to talks.

However, rather than exercising some patience in awaiting the promised clarification from the Italians, the U.S. launched its first air strike on a major industrial area on December 15. This attack destroyed 15 percent of North Vietnam's power output, as well as whatever negotiation possibilities had existed when the Italians spoke with the North Vietnamese leaders. In fact, Hanoi's response over Hanoi Radio a few days later, on the 18th, reflected their disillusionment with repeated U.S. offers of negotiations, saying, "each time the U.S. imperialists jabbered about peaceful negotiations, they intensified and expanded the war in Vietnam."[12]

The second break in bombing would end in much the same way. During the Christmas truce (as it was called because it began on December 24, 1965), the U.S. told North Vietnam that if they would reduce their military action in South Vietnam in some concrete way, then the pause would be extended. However, North Vietnam did not choose this option. Rather, it demanded that the U.S. recognize the NLFSV as the only true representative of the South Vietnamese people, and again called for the withdrawal of U.S. troops from the South.

This suspension of bombing was much longer than the first, lasting more than thirty days, ending on January 30, 1966. During this time, U.S. diplomats traveled the world with a set of fourteen points to be included in the peace agreement. Basically, the U.S. said that everything was on the negotiation table, with the exception of the surrender of South Vietnam. At the same time, military activities by the Northern forces did indeed decrease, with almost no contact between the Northern and Southern or U.S. forces for about a month. This fact indicated that the North Vietnamese had actually called for a halt to aggressive acts during the U.S. peace initiative. However, this apparent cessation of hostilities was not an adequate response to the peace initiative, in the view of the U.S. government.

---

[12]Kahin and Lewis, p. 217.

Although the bombing had ceased, the U.S. troop buildup continued, as did artillery and air attacks on Vietcong positions in South Vietnam throughout January. These actions increased Hanoi's skepticism about the supposed U.S. peace initiative. In addition, the South Vietnamese government never stated that it would agree to negotiations. Since the South did not seem to be supporting the U.S. initiative, and U.S. military actions continued (as did its uncompromising position denying the NLF any role in possible negotiations), Hanoi and the NLF did not believe that the U.S. would make any concessions to permit a compromise.[13] For its part, Hanoi continued to request that NLF representatives be allowed to participate in any negotiations as equal members of the process. In response, the U.S. reaffirmed that it would never recognize the NLF, and that if that body wanted representation at negotiations, it would only be allowed to do so as a part of the North Vietnamese delegation.[14]

There was some internal debate within the United States about the wisdom of such a stance, led by Senator Robert Kennedy. Kennedy seemed to understand that the inclusion of the NLF was key to any peaceful settlement. He was opposed by, among others, Vice President Humphrey, who said that the U.S. should not reward the NLF for its aggressions. Kennedy supported free elections in South Vietnam because he did not believe that a Communist group, such as the NLF, could ever emerge victorious in a "free" election. On the other hand, Kennedy also realized that the NLF would not accept the results of any elections run by a South Vietnamese political system of which it was not a part, and therefore suggested that the NLFSV be allowed to participate in a coalition government in Saigon until elections could be held. Humphrey responded that the Communists were unfit to share the reins of government.

Indeed, the role of the NLF was at the crux of the debates over peace negotiation in Vietnam, as well. In a letter written on January 24, 1966, Ho Chi Minh responded to the U.S. peace initiative. While he did not request withdrawal of U.S. troops prior to negotiations, he did question whether the U.S. would ever be willing to depart. However, the most contentious part of his letter for the U.S. had to do with the very issue of the NLFSV. Ho asserted that the U.S. would need to recognize the NLFSV as the only true representative of the South Vietnamese, and include them in negotiations, in order for peace to occur.

Basically, the parties' views on the Vietcong ranged from Ho's (the only true representative) to Rusk's (that they were a fraction of the South Vietnamese people) to Saigon's (refusing to recognize them at all). These indeed seemed to be irreconcilable differences, and provided the main obstacle to negotiations. The NLF would not agree to negotiations if all they could ex-

---

[13]Kahin and Lewis, p. 219.

[14]According to Secretary Rusk's statement to the House Foreign Affairs Committee on January 26, 1966.

pect was a request for their unconditional surrender. As the war continued to escalate, the hope of a compromise settlement became increasingly remote. All sides had become unwilling to compromise because of the mistrust that had gradually built up among them.

ALTERNATIVES TO ARMED AGGRESSION

Many experts had come to the conclusion that the main reason the guerrilla movement in the South was thriving was that it had the active support of the population. Therefore, it seemed that if the Vietcong's popular base of support were eroded, then the Vietcong would find it increasingly difficult to carry on its insurgent activities. Some Marines had moderate success with initiatives in the Southern villages to win the peasants away from their support of the Vietcong.

Bill Corson was a Marine who set out to approach the villagers in a new way.[15] Many before Corson had indeed attempted welfare programs by distributing food, clothing, and toys, but none had been successful, partly due to the fact that the Vietnamese culture did not produce reciprocity or gratitude, as the U.S. expected.

Corson focused on the importance of the peasant to the Vietcong, and therefore to the U.S.—a connection he believed others had overlooked. Corson believed it was important to understand the Vietnamese culture in order to approach the peasant, and discovered something central to their lives—the game of "elephant chess." This game was actually a status symbol to the Vietnamese, in that skill at "elephant chess" was a reflection of a man's cultural prowess. Once he realized the importance of this game to the society, Corson organized a tournament, with a championship to be held during the harvest festival in Phong Bac (the village in which he was stationed). Over a thousand people appeared for the championship and were impressed by the Americans' interest in the game. Corson then taught twelve of his Marines the game, and it was used to cross the cultural and language barriers. Soon, the Marines had been accepted in Phong Bac society.

Corson went on to train the town in the uses of more modern fishing tactics and developed a town fund, while the Vietnamese villagers elected a town council to decide what to do with their money. As their prosperity increased with more commercial endeavors (such as pig farming and bee breeding) encouraged by the Marines, the appeal of the Vietcong subsided. In fact, some of the new entrepreneurs of Phong Bac later became willing to inform on the NLFSV for fear that the Marines would get into a battle near one of their pig farms and destroy it. In Corson's view, the Marines, because they were successful in winning the loyalty of many of the villagers, had offered the Vietnamese of Phong Bac an attractive alternative to the Vietcong. Corson's goal was to make the community strong enough to resist the appeal of

[15]William R. Corson, *The Betrayal* (New York: W. W. Norton, 1968).

the NLFSV, and he apparently accomplished it. This raises the question of whether the United States might have had a larger degree of success in pacifying southern villages if more such initiatives had been followed.

REASSESSMENT OF BOMBING

It was revealed several months after the initiation of Operation Rolling Thunder that the bombings were not accomplishing the goals they had set out to attain. In the Jason reports issued in the summer of 1966 from the Pentagon, it was established that the bombings had not had any "measurable direct effect on Hanoi's ability to mount and support military operations in the South." Basically, the reason for this was that any damage caused by the bombings was counteracted by a steady stream of military and economic aid from the U.S.S.R. and Communist China.

The Jason report also asserted that the bombings had not proven very detrimental to North Vietnamese morale. The report continued that the North Vietnamese decision to continue fighting was in no way impacted by the bombings, and that any effect of the bombings was marginal, since the North's two primary considerations were the chances of winning the war in the South and the continued aid from its Communist allies. And, in fact, its relations with its allies were actually strengthened by the U.S. bombing, with the result that the U.S.S.R. provided more material support than it might have been inclined to prior to the bombings, which made North Vietnam able to portray itself as a victim of imperialist aggression. In conclusion, the Jason report declared that U.S. decision-makers had not taken into consideration the well-documented historical fact that when a society is faced with a direct attack (such as the bombings), popular support for the existing government tends to increase, social bonds of the nation strengthen, and the determination on the part of the government and its people to fight back is augmented.

After the release of this report, which was kept very secret because the contents were so damaging, the Johnson administration admitted that it did not seem possible to bomb the North Vietnamese to the negotiation table. It was also acknowledged that the progress of the ground conflict in the South, and not the air attacks in the North, seemed to determine the North's willingness to continue the fighting. Therefore, the bombings had indeed been fruitless—if anything, they had done more harm than good to the U.S. and South Vietnamese cause.

END OF U.S. INVOLVEMENT

Large antiwar protests spread throughout the United States in the late 1960s and early 1970s, and U.S. troop strength was decreased starting in 1969. On January 27, 1973, cease-fire agreements were signed in Paris by the U.S. and

North Vietnam, and the U.S. secretary of defense announced the end of the draft. The last U.S. troops left Vietnam on March 29, 1973. Over the next two years, North Vietnam planned the takeover of the South, culminating, for the U.S., on April 29, 1975, when Option IV was initiated to evacuate the last Americans from Saigon. They left by helicopter from the roof of the U.S. embassy. The next day, Communist forces captured Saigon, reuniting Vietnam under Communist control after more than two decades of fighting.

CHRONOLOGY OF U.S. INVOLVEMENT IN VIETNAM[16]

1930   Ho Chi Minh forms Indochinese Communist Party in Hong Kong.

1940   Japan occupies Indochina.

1941   Ho returns to Vietnam and forms Vietminh to fight France and Japan.

1945   **March 9**—Japanese take over administration of Indochina from France.

  March 11—Vietnamese emperor, Bao Dai, declares independence of Vietnam under Japanese auspices.

  July—Allies split Vietnam at sixteenth parallel at Potsdam Conference.

  August 18—Japanese transfer power to Vietminh.

  August 23—Bao Dai abdicates.

  August 29—Ho proclaims provisional government in Hanoi.

  September 2—Ho declares independence of Vietnam.

  September 13—British forces land in Saigon and return authority to French.

1946   **March**—French and Vietminh agree to recognize Vietnam as "free state" within the French Union.

  September—Ho agrees to cessation of hostilities with France.

  November 23—French warships bomb Haiphong.

  December—Vietminh leave Hanoi and Ho forms rural base. French-Indochina war begins.

1947   Bao Dai negotiates with French to recognize Vietnamese independence.

1949   **March 8**—Bao Dai and president of France agree to make Vietnam an "associated state" within the French Union, with France retaining control over Vietnam's defense and finances.

  April—Bao Dai returns to Vietnam from self-imposed exile.

1950   **January 14**—Ho declares DRV as only legal government of Vietnam, and is recognized by U.S.S.R. and China.

---

[16]Chronology abbreviated from *Vietnam: A History* by Stanley Karnow. Copyright © 1983 by WGBH Educational Foundation and Stanley Karnow. Used by permission of Viking Penguin. A division of Penguin Books USA Inc.

February 7—U.S. and U.K. recognize Bao Dai's government. Chinese Communists on Vietnam's border start to provide Vietminh with modern weapons.

July 26—President Truman signs bill to grant $15 million in military aid to the French for the war in Indochina.

1954   **April**—President Eisenhower decides against U.S. intervention on side of French when the British reject his proposal for joint action.

May 7—The French garrison at Diembienphu falls to the Vietnamese.

July—Geneva Agreements call for cessation of hostilities and divide Vietnam at 17th parallel, to be reunited through nationwide elections. Bao Dai's government denounces agreement.

October 9—French forces leave Hanoi.

1955   **January**—U.S. begins to send aid directly to Saigon government and agrees to train South Vietnamese army.

July 16—Diem refuses to participate in elections and denounces Geneva Agreements, decision backed by U.S.

July—Ho Chi Minh receives promises of Chinese and Soviet aid and assistance.

October 23—Diem defeats Bao Dai in referendum.

October 26—Diem proclaims the Republic of Vietnam, with himself as president.

1957   More than 400 minor South Vietnamese officials assassinated by Communist insurgents supported by the North.

1959   **May**—North Vietnam forms Group 559 to begin infiltrating weapons into South Vietnam via the Ho Chi Minh Trail.

1960   **November 11**—South Vietnamese army units unsuccessfully attempt to overthrow Diem.

December 20—Hanoi forms NLFSV, later dubbed the Vietcong.

1962   **February 6**—U.S. military assistance command formed in South Vietnam, number of U.S. advisors grows from 700 to 12,000 by middle of year.

1963   **November 1**—South Vietnamese generals stage a coup and murder Diem when he surrenders the next day.

By end of year, 15,000 U.S. military advisors are in South Vietnam, and $500 million, aid has been given.

1964   **August 2**—North Vietnamese boats attack U.S. destroyer Maddox in the Tonkin Gulf.

August 7—Gulf of Tonkin resolution passed.

Late August—U.S. aircraft directly bomb North Vietnamese targets for first time.

October 30—Vietcong attack Bienhoa air base.

1965   Johnson authorizes Flaming Dart, U.S. air raids against North Vietnam.

March 2—Operation Rolling Thunder, sustained U.S. bombing of North Vietnam, begins.

April 7—President Johnson gives speech at Johns Hopkins University.

December 25—Christmas truce in bombing begins.

1966   **January 31**—Johnson resumes bombing.

September—French President Charles de Gaulle calls for U.S. withdrawal from Vietnam.

1967   **August**—Secretary of Defense McNamara testifies before a Senate subcommittee that U.S. bombing of North Vietnam is ineffective.

1969   U.S. troop reduction begins.

1970   Large antiwar protests spread across U.S.

1973   **January 27**—Cease-fire agreement formally signed in Paris.

March 29—Last U.S. troops leave Vietnam.

1975   **April 29**—Option IV initiated to evacuate last U.S. officials from Saigon, including Ambassador.

April 30—Communists capture Saigon.

BIBLIOGRAPHY

ASSOCIATION OF THE U.S. ARMY. *Vietnam in Perspective: A Time for Testing.* Washington, D.C., 1968.

BURCHETT, WILFRED G. *Vietnam: Inside Story of the Guerrilla War.* New York: International Publishers, 1965.

CORSON, WILLIAM R. *The Betrayal.* New York: W. W. Norton, 1968.

FALL, BERNARD B., ed. *On Revolution: Selected Writings, 1920–1966.* NY: Praeger, 1967.

GETTLEMAN, MARVIN E., JANE AND BRUCE FRANKLIN, MARILYN YOUNG, eds. *Vietnam and America: A Documented History.* New York: Grove Press, 1985.

HALBERSTAM, DAVID. *The Best and the Brightest.* New York: Ballantine Books, 1992.

HEARDEN, PATRICK J. *The Tragedy of Vietnam.* New York: HarperCollins, 1991.

"THE JASON SUMMER STUDY REPORTS," in *The Pentagon Papers: The Defense Department History of United States Decisionmaking on Vietnam.* Boston: Beacon Press, 1971.

KAHIN, GEORGE M. AND JOHN W. LEWIS. *The United States in Vietnam.* New York: Doubleday, 1969.

KARNOW, STANLEY. *Vietnam: A History.* NY: Penguin Books, 1983.

MAY, ERNEST R. *"Lessons" of the Past.* New York: Oxford University Press, 1973.

OLSON, JAMES, ed. *Dictionary of the Vietnam War.* Westport, CT: Greenwood Press, 1988.

RASKIN, MARCUS G., AND BERNARD B. FALL, eds. *The Viet-Nam Reader: Articles and Documents on American Foreign Policy and the Viet-Nam Crisis.* New York: Random House, 1965.

SHEEHAN, NEIL. *A Bright Shining Lie.* New York: Vintage Books, 1989.

SUMMERS, JR., HARRY G. *Vietnam War Almanac.* New York: Facts On File, 1985.

CHAPTER
—13—

Analyzing Threats
and Sanctions

International conflicts exist because one government is unhappy with what another government is doing or is planning to do. We can therefore think of a conflict as an attempt by one government to influence another to do something or not to do something.

In international conflict as elsewhere, a party's first reaction to another party's doing something it doesn't like is to think of doing something unpleasant to that party. In South Africa, we do not like apartheid; we promptly think of stopping future investment in South Africa. The UN opposes Iraq's invasion of Kuwait, so it sends troops. The United States wants the North Vietnamese to stop the military and political support they are giving to the Vietcong, so it bombs them. A government typically cuts off trade, stops aid, stirs up public opinion, passes resolutions of censure in the United Nations General Assembly, and institutes retaliatory bombing. Whether it thinks it through or not, the implicit goal of its action is to cause the other government to make some decision. The government wants to cause the other government to change its mind.

Raising the cost to an adversary of pursuing a course of action we do not like, however, may not be a good way to exert influence. This is particularly true when the international adversary is a government, which necessarily means a group, a committee, a bureaucracy. Obviously, cost is not wholly irrelevant and is most persuasive where we are trying to prevent a decision that has not yet been made. But a present conflict, as contrasted with a potential one, involves an attempt to change a government's mind. We want it to stop doing something it is doing, or to do something it is not doing. As a means of bringing about a change of intention, a foreign policy that concentrates on raising costs to an adversary is likely to prove both ineffective with regard to our adversary and costly for us.

THE LIMITED EFFECTIVENESS OF INFLICTED PAIN

The Other Side Probably Anticipated Some Cost

Inflicting pain on the other side is, for a number of reasons, likely to be a poor way of getting it to change its mind. First, the other side probably anticipated some costs when it decided to do something we do not like. And the anticipated costs were apparently insufficient to deter it. For us to inflict pain may simply be to impose costs that it has already taken into account. To act as it expected is hardly likely to cause it to reverse its position.

The theory of inflicting pain on another country rests upon the premise that its government will change its mind in order to avoid further pain. Bombing power plants and other targets in North Vietnam, insofar as it was initiated for the purpose of producing a political decision, was carried out in order to make credible the threat of additional bombing. Present sanctions exert influence only if they communicate something about the future. They are intended to convey a convincing message that unless the decision we desire is made, the situation will get worse. As in a labor strike, each day's infliction of pain is primarily for the purpose of communicating a vivid threat to inflict additional pain in the future. If the costs being imposed are no worse than those that had been feared, the other side is given no reason to reverse its position.

To be sure, pain and costs in actuality may be more impressive than they were in contemplation. The other side may have underestimated the actual consequences of economic sanctions or of a bombing program. It is equally probable, however—perhaps more so—that imposed costs will seem less onerous in actuality than in contemplation. People adapt quickly to adverse circumstances. A future that might have looked intolerable is proved to be tolerable. The bombing of North Vietnam by the United States probably did more to convince the leaders of Hanoi that their economy could cope with the consequences than it did to make the costs seem impossible to bear. The threat of B-52 bombings was perhaps more awe-inspiring than the bombings themselves.

Pain Equals Investment

Other considerations also suggest that inflicting pain upon an adversary may be worse than useless. There is a common tendency to treat sunken costs as invested capital. The greater the costs we impose on our adversary, the greater the amount they will regard themselves as having committed to their present course of action: "Having invested this much in the war of liberation, we cannot quit now. Having lost so many lives and most of our power plants, we should not now abandon the effort."

Imposing additional costs may be like implementing a threat to kill hostages or prisoners of war: each cost imposed reduces the amount that could be saved by yielding to the demand. Suppose an adversary has twenty power plants. We bomb ten and say, "Will you quit now to save the remaining ten?" They refuse. We knock out five more and say, "Will you quit now to save five?" Although the marginal value of the remaining plants will have risen, our adversaries are likely to conclude that if they would not quit before to save twenty plants they should not quit now to save five.

Increasing the Pain Is Also Ineffective

To overcome these difficulties we are tempted to increase the amount of pain we impose. "So," we think, "they thought they could get away cheaply; we will show them how high the costs are really going to be." Can we, by thus imposing unexpectedly high costs, expect them to change their minds?

The first problem is that the higher costs also may be expected. Our adversaries may have foreseen better than we what we would do. We are likely to be optimistic and to hope that modest efforts will be sufficient. They are likely to think the worst of us. This appears to have been the situation during the early stages of the bombing of North Vietnam. At a time when the bombing was still light and far removed from Hanoi and Haiphong, the government of North Vietnam spent a great deal of effort in building bomb shelters in Hanoi and in dispersing industry and population. The United States had made no decision to bomb Hanoi and presumably did not expect to do so. While the U.S. was presenting the North Vietnamese with the vague threat of pain tomorrow if they did not change their mind today, the North Vietnamese had in fact already decided not to change their mind even though the level of destruction increased substantially. As the United States stepped up its bombing program, it simply reached levels that had already been anticipated. The U.S. should not have been surprised that it was an ineffective way of producing a change in North Vietnam's conduct.

Even where a change has been unexpected, a marginal increase in the costs we are inflicting is not likely to appear to them sufficient to justify reversing their decision. At any one time, incurred costs are water over the dam. It is the increase in the threat that matters, and there, too, marginal changes are likely to be insignificant.

Reversing a Decision through Pain Is Unlikely

With a group or a government, the problems are even more than dealing with a single decision-maker. First, there is a natural inertia that tends to prevent the reconsideration of decisions already made; a past decision will continue to govern future conduct even though some of the facts change. Governments cannot reconsider a decision every day. And marginal changes in the cost rarely appear to justify putting a matter back on the agenda at all, since the new problem seems so much like the one already considered and disposed of. We may think that by increasing the pain a little bit every day we have made our adversaries reconsider their actions every day. But they may never have seen a new decision as coming up for consideration at all. Their old decision simply continues to govern.

Even if increasing pain puts the matter back on their agenda, making the decision we want will look to them not like a new question but rather like the reversal of a decision already made. We will be asking them to change their mind and back down because of a little more pain.

It is even more difficult for a committee to abandon a course of action to which it has become committed than for an individual to do so, particularly in the face of what is sure to appear as blackmail. No individual in the group wants to be the one who says, "It didn't work so let's change our policy. We made a mistake. Let's try something else." His status and his reputation among his colleagues are likely to be more important to him than any marginal contribution he might make to the national interest by sticking his neck out. Particularly in response to foreign pressure, any one member of the group may find it personally costly to suggest that the government ought to yield or otherwise to reverse its course. Each may keep his views to himself until it appears that the current of opinion for a change is running strong within the group. Under these circumstances, actual support for a change may never be disclosed.

There is another and somewhat peculiar factor that makes it difficult for a government to reverse a decision taken in the face of a threat. A group that has decided to launch a project despite the *chance* that there will be high costs tends to confuse that decision with a decision to complete the project despite the *certainty* that the costs turn out to be high. A decision to start doing something that takes into account certain risks will be confused with a decision to proceed even though the risks materialize.

THREATS ARE COSTLY TO US

Not only is threat-making likely to be ineffective in persuading the other side to change its mind, it is likely to be unduly costly to us. It may seem as if we pay only modest costs in making a threat. However, most of the threats we are discussing are "action threats," threats of carrying out future action that are communicated by the actions we are now taking and the pain we are now inflicting. Economic sanctions communicate a credible threat of further sanctions, bombing a threat of further bombing, and the breaking of diplomatic relations the threat of international isolation. These threats by action involve greater immediate costs to us.

Economic Costs.   First, there are out-of-pocket costs. Economic sanctions cost the imposing country lost trade and lost opportunities for future trade. It is expensive to maintain a huge military arsenal at the ready, or to mobilize and transport troops in order to show that a country can and will use military force. The program of bombing in North Vietnam cost the U.S. economy a great deal. These out-of-pocket costs also represent opportunity costs—there are other useful ways to spend the resources, both at home and abroad.

Reputation Costs.   Second, since it is generally regarded as immoral to inflict pain simply to prove that you are willing and able to inflict it, we damage both our reputation and our self-esteem. Deliberate pain whose only justification is to extort a decision bears too close a resemblance to torture. This immorality is so compelling that we will always advance some other justification for an action threat: we refer to it as interdiction, or retaliation, or even self-defense. If the United States had not had the interdiction rationale for the bombing of North Vietnam—the contention that its bombing of the North was not only to exert influence but also physically to prevent military supplies from reaching the South—the bombing would have been intolerably immoral both at home and abroad. This necessary gap between the primary motive of threatening future costs and the alleged justification resulted in a third cost to the U.S.—an almost inevitable "credibility gap," resulting from multiple and inconsistent explanations of military or other measures.

Precedent Costs.   There are other costs of threat-making inherent in the international system. There are styles in international conflict: countries follow the precedents of others in the ways in which they seek to exert influence. A retaliatory raid by Israel may have more impact as an example to be followed than as a deterrent. Threats by one become a justification for threats by others. Reciprocal escalation is the consequence of two countries trying to influence each other by threats of demonstrated credibility. This style is costly and destructive to international order. It does not easily lead to solutions.

Distraction Costs.   Another cost of threat-making is that it diverts our attention from exactly what it is that we would like to have an adversary do. Britain devoted almost all its attention in the first year after Rhodesian independence to making economic sanctions "effective." Effectiveness was being measured in terms of the extent to which trade was being impeded, not in terms of the extent to which Rhodesians were being influenced to make a decision that Britain wanted. Almost no attention was devoted to the process by which a reduction in Rhodesia's economic welfare was supposed to convert that country into a functioning biracial democracy. Similarly, the United States spends far more time ensuring the effectiveness of the embargo against Cuba than it does trying to figure out a plan for converting Cuba to a democracy.

Our High Cost Gives Them Hope

Because these threats hurt us as well, the other side may well expect that we will quit before they do. The same thinking that leads us to believe that imposing costs on our adversaries will cause them to change their mind leads them to believe that the costs we are imposing on ourselves are likely to make us change our mind.

The bombing of North Vietnam from mid-1965 to mid-1967 cost the United States at least $4 billion in airplane equipment alone. Whatever the monetary value of the destruction the U.S. inflicted on North Vietnam during that period, it was almost certainly less than that. The U.S. looked at the destruction it had caused and could not understand why the rising cost of the war did not influence the North Vietnamese to change their mind. The North Vietnamese undoubtedly looked at the costs to the U.S. and were led to believe that the costs were so high that at some point the U.S. would change its mind.

A DECISION TO THREATEN BECOMES A DECISION TO IMPLEMENT

A decision to threaten and the later decision to implement that threat if the adversary fails to respond as we wish are two quite different decisions. What exerts influence on an adversary is the risk of unpleasant consequences. They do not need to be certain that we will carry out a threat, nor do we. The fact that it may be wise to make a threat does not mean that if our attempt to exert influence fails it will also be wise to carry it out. This is one reason why a decision to threaten is seductively attractive. The postponed costs are not immediately evident. We hope that the threat will be effective, in which case we will get something for very little. If it is not effective, it appears that we will still have open the choice of what to do then. Since that choice need not be made until later, it is easy at the outset simply to make the threat.

The real costliness of threat-making lies in the fact that the postponed bills are likely to be large. If the threat fails, both courses open to us will probably be costly. Failure to implement our threat may reduce our credibility. We can afford to bluff occasionally without ruining our capacity to exert influence, but we cannot bluff every time without making future threats worthless.

On the other hand, there are heavy costs in implementing the threat. The out-of-pocket costs are likely to be much larger than the costs of making the threat in the first place. There are, of course, some kinds of threats that we would like to carry out anyway: implementing that kind of threat, like quotas on imports, may give us some actual benefit. But most of the threats we make in attempting to influence an adversary are threats of action we do not particularly want to take, such as stopping trade or aid, cutting off diplomatic relations, or taking military action.

A bias in favor of implementing threats is another result of the inherent ambiguity of a decision that takes some future risks into account. The decision to make a threat presumably took into account the possibility that the threat would not work and that in such an event we might implement it. But a government will tend to treat that decision as a decision to carry out the threat if the occasion arises. People will not realize that there is an opportunity for a new decision to be made in the light of new circumstances.

Further, a governmental threat (for example, "If Cuba seizes the oil refineries, the U.S. will cut off all trade") sounds like a governmental decision. Subordinate officials will see themselves as having the power to implement such a policy but not to change it. There is no automatic occasion for a new decision. The bureaucracy is likely to proceed day by day toward carrying out the threat.

Confusion between the decision to make a threat and the decision to implement it is particularly costly where the threat is to do something for an indefinite period in response to some one-shot action. An example illustrates how one thing is likely to follow another without reexamination. Suppose a foreign government proposes to nationalize some U.S.-owned property. In an effort to deter them, the U.S. threatens to cut off all trade if they seize the property. To make the threat credible, the U.S. suspends trade immediately. If the property is nationalized, the initial decision to make the threat will be taken by most people in the U.S. government as a decision to cut off, and to keep cut off, all trade. Any official can continue the trade embargo for another day. That appears to be the "policy."

A decision not to carry out the threat that failed will be regarded as a reversal of a prior decision. It will be difficult for someone to say: "They nationalized the property. That's water over the dam. Our threat failed, and we should now resume trade. We should now try for a different objective, such as compensation or some arrangements to protect other property not yet nationalized, and make threats or offers appropriate to our new purpose." Any termination of the embargo will be left to higher authority within the government. These open-ended punishments, which include things like nonrecognition and the breaking of diplomatic relations, are likely to continue indefinitely with no real purpose in mind and with no advance consideration of the circumstances in which we would expect to stop imposing them. It is highly unlikely that any U.S. official in the early 1960s actually envisioned that the U.S. embargo against Cuba would continue well into the 1990s and long after the cold war ended.

ANALYZING INFLICTION OF PAIN

All of the preceding examples indicate that infliction of pain will not automatically result in changed behavior by the other side. The cost to us of pursuing such a strategy can also be significant. Decision-makers would therefore benefit from an analysis of a strategy of inflicted pain even before the first threats are made. If it best meets our interests, it should be considered; but if it does not, another strategy will need to be pursued.

A variety of factors will influence the effectiveness of a strategy of inflicted pain. Some of these are set out in Chart 13–1:

CHART 13–1
THE EFFECTIVENESS OF INFLICTED PAIN

Will Be Higher If:	*Will Be Lower If*
our action is threatened to deter behavior	our action is carried out to change behavior
there is little real cost to us	our action is, or is perceived as, costly to us
there is high real cost to them	our action is, or is perceived as, not costly to them
there is low net cost to us	there is, or they perceive, high net cost to us
it is a one-shot action	it is an ongoing action
our reaction was not adequately anticipated	our reaction was accounted for
continuation of our action is believable	continuation of our action is unlikely or in doubt
there are low sunken costs for them	there are high sunken costs for them
it is inconsequential whether or not our action actually works	it is perceived as a failure for us if the action does not achieve the desired effect
our action is directly related to the desired behavior	our action is unrelated or only tangentially related to the desired behavior
our action sets a good precedent	our action sets a bad precedent or invites reciprocal threats
our action leaves our options open	our action forecloses options
the consequences of our action are immediate	the consequences of our action are delayed
our action is tangible or important symbolically to them	our action is intangible and has no symbolic meaning to them

A first step in analyzing threats and sanctions would be simply to lay out, with as much detachment as possible, the factors that might make a strategy of inflicted pain more likely to change the other side's behavior, and those factors that would make it less likely for such a strategy to be effective. Had this been done before U.S. bombing of Vietnam began, for example, the chart of the most important factors might have looked something like Chart 13–2.

CHART 13–2
THE EFFECTIVENESS OF INFLICTED PAIN
Will Inflicting Pain on North Vietnam Make It Stop Its Support of the Vietcong?

Case: _Vietnam_
Us: _The United States_
Them: _North Vietnam_

Factors That Make This More Likely:	*Factors That Make This Less Likely:*
The consequences of our action will be immediate and tangible.	*Our action is to change behavior already in motion.*
There will be high real cost to Vietnam in terms of material destruction and human life.	*It is hard to imagine that North Vietnamese planners did not anticipate a violent reaction on our part, and decide, on balance, to go ahead anyway.*
Our action leaves some options open (we can always stop bombing later).	*It will be evident that bombing costs us much, in terms of both real dollars and international credibility. The net cost to us will be high.*
	To be effective, bombing must continue indefinitely. It will be perceived as a failure for us if the action does not achieve the desired effect, and so waiting may be an effective strategy for North Vietnam.
	North Vietnam has high sunken costs; it will be hard for them to justify backing down.
	Other countries are unlikely to take away the lesson that we intend.
	Our action closes some options (it will be hard for us to pursue cooperative strategies, both because they won't be inclined to and because it will look as though we backed down).

We might hope that even a cursory analysis would be enough to give decision-makers on our side pause. It might help, however, to engage in some more deliberative balancing. Thus, it could be of assistance to lay out more explicitly the costs and benefits to each side. In Chart 13–3, we have attempted to lay out the two or three most important costs and benefits to each side.

CHART 13–3
COSTS & BENEFITS CIRCLE

Case: _North Vietnam_

Date: _1965_

Benefits to North Vietnam Gov't.

> They claim victory when the U.S. bombing does not stop them
>
> We prove their view of the U.S. to their own people (and some other parts of the world)

Benefits to U.S. Gov't.

> We may set some precedent or achieve some deterrence for future conflicts
>
> We look consequential to parts of the U.S. population

> Some loss of military capability (but not expected to be debilitating)
>
> Economic loss (but the government is primarily politically, not economically, driven)
>
> Loss of life (but the government is ideologically prepared for this)

> Loss of military prestige that may lower our deterrent abilities later
>
> Enormous economic cost that is higher than the economic cost inflicted on N. Vietnam
>
> Loss of life that is extremely unpopular at home

Costs to North Vietnam Gov't.

Costs to U.S. Gov't.

We can then plot, along the outside edge of the circle, the net costs and benefits to our side of pursuing a strategy of inflicted pain. By net costs we mean a rough calculation of whose costs or benefits are higher than the other party's. In the example on p. 203, although North Vietnam's costs are high, the United States' costs are probably even higher. This is a net cost to the United States. We can show this graphically by plotting the net cost point closer to the U.S. side of the cost semicircle:

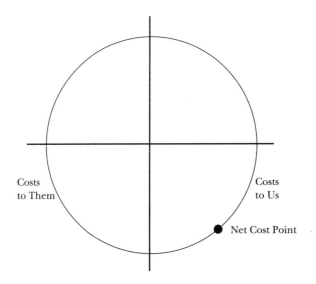

We now do the same for the net benefits—how the benefits to us look in relation to the benefits to them. Assume that our best analysis tells us that there is marginal if any benefit to either party. We would therefore plot the net benefit point near the neutral point of the benefit semicircle:

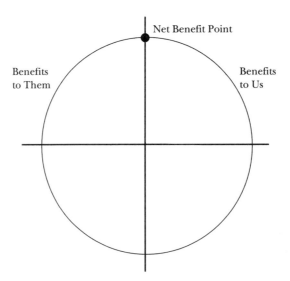

We can then create a kind of "compass" to help us consider how effective a strategy of inflicting pain is likely to be. We do this by drawing a line from the net cost point through the net benefit point:

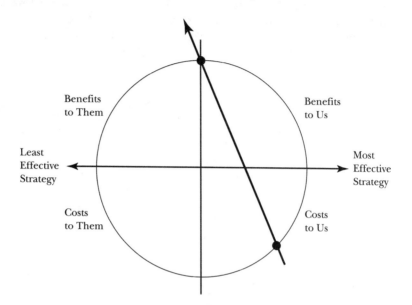

The most effective strategy, from our perspective, would point due east. That graph would indicate high net costs to them and high net benefits to us. The strategy most detrimental to us points due west: high net costs to us and high net benefits to them. In between—say, between NW and NE on the compass—are a number of strategies that are probably merely ineffectual (although possibly quite costly to us). In our case study, the bombing of North Vietnam by the United States, an analysis of net costs and net benefits indicates a strategy that was at best ineffectual and at worst detrimental to U.S. interests.

Net cost/net benefit analysis does not exclude the possibility of a successful strategy of inflicted pain. In 1985, for example, France was attempting to secure the release of two of its agents by New Zealand. Both agents had been implicated in the bombing of the Greenpeace vessel *Rainbow Warrior*, which was being used to bring attention to French nuclear weapons testing by sailing into French territorial waters in the South Pacific during planned nuclear tests. The sabotage of the *Rainbow Warrior* had resulted in the death of one person, a Dutch photographer. New Zealand apparently intended to put the two agents on trial for murder. International sympathy ran strongly in favor of Greenpeace and the New Zealand government.

France threatened New Zealand with restrictions of imports into the European Community if the agents were not released to French custody. This action threatened extremely high cost to New Zealand, whose sheep industry depended on access to European markets. France would incur negligible costs in implementing the threat. New Zealand would garner little benefit from the implementation of the threat, while France was in the position of threatening action that it in any case would have wanted to take, in order to protect French farmers from foreign competition. Thus, net costs to New Zealand were high, and net benefits to France were high:

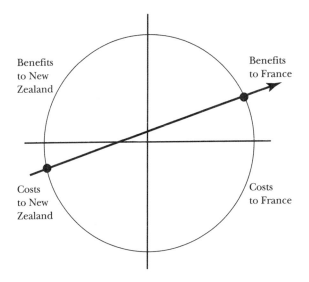

The strategy in fact proved effective, and the French agents were released to French custody within weeks.

Decision-makers who contemplate strategies of inflicted pain often consider the costs to the other side and any benefits to their own side, without considering the relative costs and benefits to each side. Like the other tools in this book, the factors affecting a strategy of inflicting pain and the compass of net benefits and costs cannot provide a certain answer to the question of whether a particular strategy will in fact prove effective or ineffective. By asking a more complete and more meaningful set of questions, however, it can provide a framework for fuller reflection and decision.

Of course, the effectiveness of these tools will turn on our honest research and analysis of the underlying conflict, and on our dispassionate assessment of actual costs and benefits. There is nothing we as authors can do to keep you from drawing a skewed compass arrow in order to reach a predetermined result; such *post hoc* analyses are all too common in real-world foreign ministries and departments of defense. As with all of the tools in this book, we recommend that you discuss your perceptions and conclusions with as many knowledgeable parties as possible and with people from as many different perspectives on the conflict under analysis as possible.

THE DIFFERENCE BETWEEN THREATS AND WARNINGS

We also want to distinguish between *threats* and *warnings*. Both threats and warnings are kinds of commitments. Both are announcements to other parties of what we intend to do or not do under certain conditions. There is a subtle but significant difference between communicating to the other side the course of action that we believe will be in our interests to take should we fail to reach an agreement—a warning—and locking ourselves in to precise terms that the other side must accept in order to avoid our taking that course of action—a threat.

In the 1980s, if the United States honestly believed that deploying 100 MX missiles was a vital part of its national security, then letting the Soviet Union know that in the absence of a negotiated agreement it intended to deploy them would have appeared to be a sound way of exerting influence. In these circumstances, the United States remained open to considering any negotiated agreement that would be better for it than the MX deployment. The U.S. was not trying to influence the Soviet Union by committing itself to refuse to accept an agreement that would in fact have been in its interest. It would have been simply trying to influence them with the reality that deployment seemed to be its best option in the absence of agreement. U.S. action in this case was not a threat—if we do not reach agreement, then we will cut off trade, for example—but rather a warning.

Considering Our Alternatives

We can also distinguish threats from warnings with the concept of BATNA—our Best Alternative To a Negotiated Agreement.[1] To a significant extent, power in a negotiation depends on how well a party can do for itself if it walks away. A negotiator should develop and improve his BATNA, or alternative "away from the negotiating table." One kind of preparation for negotiation that enhances one's influence is to consider the alternatives to reaching agreement with this particular party, to select the most promising, and to improve it to the extent possible. This alternative sets a floor. A party can be clear to itself and clear to others under what conditions it believes it is in its interest to negotiate, and the extent to which it is open to influence. By understanding the other party's BATNA, a party can also understand the extent to which they may or may not be open to influence.

An example may help illustrate this concept. One of the reasons negotiations between Greek and Turkish Cypriots are not making much progress as of 1996 is that Turkish Cypriot leader Denktash seems to feel that his BATNA—sitting tight under the status quo—is simply better than anything a negotiated agreement with the Greek Cypriot President Vassiliou could offer

---

[1]Roger Fisher, William Ury, and Bruce Patton, *Getting To Yes: Negotiating Agreement Without Giving In*, 2nd ed. (NY: Penguin Books, 1991), pp. 97–106.

him. Now he is the president of Northern Cyprus, even if few countries will recognize him as such. Under any kind of plan for federation, whatever position he goes on to hold will likely be something less than president. The way he sees his choice now, his BATNA is better than any options he can see on the table, so it makes sense for him to keep saying "no."

We can strengthen our BATNA by asking ourselves what we can do by self-help. We can communicate our BATNA to other parties as an indication of where it is in our interest to reach agreement. We can also think about how to make the other side's BATNA appear less attractive to them. The less attractive their BATNA is to them, the stronger our influence.

Military defenses enhance a country's negotiating power by making a nonnegotiated solution—the other side's BATNA—less attractive to a hostile neighbor. With adequate defense forces, Country A can say to Country B, "Let's settle our boundary dispute by negotiation; if you try to settle it by military force, you will fail." Country A has lowered Country B's BATNA in a way that makes it less likely that Country B will attempt to pursue an end to the conflict away from the negotiating table.

When we credibly communicate that we can better meet our interests away from the negotiating table—that we have a strong BATNA—we are issuing a warning. The U.S. warning was unsuccessful in the Gulf War, when the U.S. communicated to Hussein that, absent his cooperation, the U.S. would retake Kuwait by force. NATO's warning that U.S. and allied troops would defend NATO members' territorial integrity rather than negotiate with a potential aggressor has proved itself effective over time. The warning is a communication of our BATNA, what we will do to meet our interests absent another party's cooperation.

As the varied examples indicate, we cannot categorically state that threats will never work, or that credible warnings will always be effective. We have hoped to communicate that

- the effectiveness of a strategy of inflicting pain is contingent on a broad range of factors, many of which are in the realm of the parties' tolerances and perceptions;
- a strategy of threats that does not take into account the net costs and benefits to each of the parties is unlikely to succeed;
- we will improve the agreement into which we will be willing to enter with another party by enhancing and credibly communicating our BATNA;
- we will enhance our ability to influence another party by understanding their BATNA.

CHAPTER
—14—

Changing
the Demand

Thus far in the book, we have tried to understand conflict by examining the parties' partisan perceptions and how they currently view their choices. We have examined our own purpose and looked at structural negotiation issues. The next step in formulating our proposal to a decision-maker is to return to the question of what we are asking them to do. In order to exert influence on them, we must change some aspect of the choice with which they see themselves as being faced. We may want to reassess our previous offer as a result of studying our purposes and strategy toward the conflict, toward the relationship, and toward the process of negotiation.

In the last chapter, we suggested that changing the threat—the consequences we promise them if they do not make the decision we are asking for—may be ineffective or worse, for it may involve serious costs to ourselves. Rather than trying to change the threat, we may be more successful if we change the decision we ask them to make. By presenting them with a different proposed decision, we can present them with a decision that we want and that they are more likely to make.

We do not know the exact reasons they did not make the decision yesterday. It may be that what we wanted was so odious to them or so inconsistent with their own objectives that they will never make that decision, no matter how much we can offer them to be "good" or how much we threaten them if they are "bad." In such a case, changing the demand to one that is more internally acceptable to them is the only way to get something we would like. Whether or not that is the case, there are persuasive reasons for changing the decision we are asking them to make.

BENEFITS OF CHANGING THE DEMAND

A New Question Requires a New Answer

First, we can put the matter back on their agenda. We have seen that a government tends to conform to a policy decision to pursue a certain course of action, even though the costs change. A government that has made a decision is unlikely to reconsider the wisdom of that decision every day. If Spain has decided not to negotiate with the Basques, a change in the casualty rate will probably not cause any one Spanish official to reopen that decision. On the other hand, if a fresh proposal comes in, a new decision is required.

Consider the example of an organization that goes to a congresswoman with a proposed bill and a petition signed by a thousand voters asking her to support the bill. The congresswoman says no. The organization will not be likely to achieve success by simply coming back with another 200 names. But if it comes back with a revised Paragraph 6, the congresswoman has a new decision to make. Likewise, if General de Gaulle were to have invited the North Vietnamese to send a representative to a conference in Paris to discuss the Vietnam situation, the government of North Vietnam would have had a slightly different decision to make than the one they had previously made "not to negotiate." The matter would have been up for reconsideration. The whole question of negotiating would have been raised anew because a different demand had been made. The chances of a favorable decision would have been greater than otherwise simply because a new choice—whether or not to send the representative—would have been required.

A New Question Does Not Require Reversal of an Earlier Decision

Second, changing the demand means that a favorable decision now does not require a reversal of a previous decision. The matter is not only back on the agenda, but in order to decide our way the other side need not admit that their prior decision was wrong. We know from our analysis in Chapter 6 that it is extremely difficult for a government to reverse itself. Individuals who now believe the decision was wrong when made, or realize they have been proved wrong by events, often feel bound to respect the decision nevertheless. Coming in from the outside with a different proposal tends to get around this bureaucratic reluctance to reverse prior decisions.

A New Question Frees Us from Domestic Constraints

A third reason for a government's changing its demand is to keep itself unfettered by domestic opinion and free to pursue objectives that seem wise in the light of developing circumstances. By holding rigidly to a particular demand, such as "Fifty-four forty or fight" or "Withdraw from Kuwait immediately," a government can more readily convince the public that the objective is important and that the government is committed to it; however, the longer we go forward with our demand unchanged, the more difficult it becomes to change it.

There are some advantages to this. In one sense, U.S. public opinion, dead set against recognizing Cuba, strengthened the government's hand. But it did so by tying the hand up. There is reason to believe that at times over the past thirty-five years the government would have adopted a more flexible policy toward Cuba had it not been for domestic opinion. And a little flexibility on our part makes possible greater flexibility on theirs.

DISADVANTAGES TO ASKING A NEW QUESTION

There are disadvantages to changing the demand. By changing it we indicate a willingness to change it again. The other side may believe that if they hold firm we will ultimately make a demand that is even more attractive to them. During 1945 the Allies demanded unconditional surrender from Japan. In hindsight, it is apparent that the Allies were asking for more than they needed to, and that on such questions as the emperor's future they had made it unnecessarily difficult for the Japanese government to yield. If, in early 1945, the Allies had shifted and offered a package proposal that embodied the substance of the MacArthur Constitution—the proposal actually imposed on Japan—it would have been more attractive to the Japanese. In theory, it would have been easier for Japan to yield. But for the Allies to move from a demand for unconditional surrender to one for acceptance of a more modest demand might have caused Japan to believe that the terms would continue to improve with time. So long as the Allies remained rigid in their demand for unconditional surrender, there was little chance of the Japanese thinking they might make a better offer.

REFRAME THE SAME DEMAND

As we have suggested, the decision we would like to have an adversary make is not something we can find *a priori* from examination of the problem, or from asking ourselves what it is that we do not like about the situation. The decision must be carefully formulated so that those with the power to decide perceive a choice that is open to them and so that we can arrange that the consequences of making that choice appear more favorable to them than the consequences of not making it. In order to escape some of the common errors of formulating a decision and exerting influence, we should at a minimum define our objective so that the other side perceives a choice open to them and so that it is within the realm of the possible that they will make the choice we desire. Usually the other side has little idea of the range of decisions that would be acceptable to us; often, they will put the worst possible interpretation on our objectives.

Improve the Offer in Their Eyes

The primary way to improve our offers is to make them look better to the other side. If little thought is usually given to the way an adversary looks at the decision we are asking him to make, even less is given to the attractiveness in his eyes of making it. The fact that we think, "Going along with us on this is a pretty good deal for them; they don't lose much," does not mean that they look at it the same way. The other side may not find the consequences of making the desired decision as attractive for them as we do. We should be sure that if we foresee an advantage to them of going along with us, they will be attracted by this advantage and really see it as a plus.

In April 1965, the U. S. offered $1 billion in aid to both Vietnams if peace could be restored. But the idea of a $1 billion U.S. aid program may not have seemed attractive to the North Vietnamese. Political leaders who saw themselves as risking their lives to further national independence, socialism, and anticolonialism may have regarded the prospect of extensive and indefinite economic involvement by a capitalist country in the affairs of Vietnam as more of a threat than a promise. By changing the style of this offer, the U.S. might have made it much more attractive to the North Vietnamese. The U.S. could, for example, have turned $1 billion over to the Asian Development Bank to be used for reconstruction and development in all of Vietnam, it being understood that North Vietnam, if it wished, could consider its share as compensation for damage done by U.S. bombers and artillery fire. The entire program could have been set up to be administered by Asians. Such a scheme could have been far more attractive to North Vietnam and therefore could have exerted, for the same dollar price, far more influence.

Reduce the Disadvantages of Making the Decision

Perhaps more important to the adversary are the minuses in the offer: the disadvantages to them of going along with the decision we want. One way to improve the offer is to lessen the costs the adversary will incur in making the decision. It is not sympathy for an adversary, but common sense, that says we should make it as easy and attractive as possible for them to do what we would like them to do.

A government is often deterred from making the decision we want by the high political costs they anticipate. In particular, governments are often concerned with the bad precedent that they fear a particular action will establish. It may be important to reduce the precedential effect of the decision we seek.

Consider the case of the Basques, a people who live in the border region between France and Spain, many of whom wish to have a Basque country independent of Spain. Arguably, the economic value of the Basque region to Spain is outweighed by the costs of stationing troops there and dealing with continuing terrorist violence. The Basque region is small and has been difficult to govern. But the political costs of allowing independence to one small part of Spain, a country in which other, larger geographical areas have strong separatist tendencies, would be enormous. One seeking to influence the Spanish government to accept self-government for the Basques would seek to distinguish its particular case sharply and clearly from the cases of other areas of Spain. One could reduce the cost by presenting Spain with a case that relied on unique historical facts applicable only to the Basques and that avoided arguments based on language or similar considerations available to other Spanish regions.

Make the Demand Procedural

We can also reinterpret our demand in procedural rather than substantive terms. Instead of a government partial to our side, we might seek a government freely elected by the people. Having as an objective the reaching of some result by a fair procedure, rather than the reaching of a particular result, usually broadens the acceptability of the demand.

Simply restating our objective in procedural terms may alter their perception of what we are asking for. At the outset of U.S. involvement in Vietnam, the U.S. government spoke of its objectives in terms like "teaching the Communists a lesson" and demanding an end of North Vietnamese efforts to take over the South. Later, at various times, U.S. officials referred to their government's objective as the implementation of the Geneva Accords of 1954, an objective also nominally adopted by its adversaries. There can be no doubt that to have stated its objective in such terms would have made it easier for others to accept it and, hence, have increased the chances that the U.S. would get what it wanted.

Ask for a Promise to Act Rather than an Action

Although ultimately we are not as interested in what another government says as we are in what it does, in the short run our objectives might best be satisfied by getting a promise from it—a decision to say something rather than a decision to act. No matter how much we distrust an adversary or think that it is action we want, we should consider whether we might better be asking them to promise something, offer something, or talk about something.

In World War II the immediate objective during the summer of 1945 was to get the emperor of Japan to say he was willing to surrender. If the emperor had said nothing, gone into retirement, and had nothing more to do with the war, various generals would no doubt have continued fighting. The actual laying down of arms by Japan was easier to accomplish once the promise of surrender had been given. The promise was worth more to the Allies than any conduct.

In other cases, a promise may be easier to get than an act, but not worth as much. In changing from one to another we are not necessarily abandoning our former objective, but we can make a different type of demand. The following list suggests the different qualities of conduct we may seek from an adversary that would still move the conflict forward:

> Do what we want you to do.
> Stop doing what we don't want you to do.
> Make us a promise.
> Make us an offer.
> Respond to our offer.
> Negotiate toward an agreement.
> Explain your position.
> Describe your position.
> Say something.
> Don't do something that you are not now doing.

A promise is far better than nothing, and it will make the act more likely; it gives us another tool with which to exert influence. As a standard practice we should try to write out the terms of a promise, such as a draft cease-fire agreement, a draft press statement, or a draft letter, which we could reasonably expect from the other side.

Ask the Other Side *Not* to Act

Often the easiest type of objective to achieve is to have a government continue to refrain from doing something they are not now doing, and we may wish to change our demand to one of that kind. Differences of view within their government, red tape, and the difficulties of bringing about a change in government policy would all be on our side. There is no need for a government to admit or indicate that they have been influenced by others; they need only continue not to do what they have not been doing. For example, if our goal is to influence China to maintain freedom of speech and assembly in Hong Kong after 1997, we can frame our request by asking them *not* to act. The demand would be, "Do not change the local laws in Hong Kong" or "Do not arrest and prosecute those who critize the government in Hong Kong."

DIVIDE THE PROBLEM INTO SMALLER COMPONENTS

When we want the other side to change its behavior, we usually have no trouble in identifying the core of the conduct to which we object. The problem is to define for ourselves the amount and kind of objectionable conduct we should try to stop at one time with the means at our disposal. In selecting a working objective, we have to consider how much of what is going on we can realistically expect to change within a given period of time. Our effectiveness in stopping any action may depend upon not trying to stop too much at one time.

Limit the Scope of the Dispute

One way to look at the problem of formulating objectives is in terms of size: how much shall we try for, now? We cannot eliminate a conflict of interest that exists, but by defining the size of a given dispute—what is included and what is not—we can affect it significantly. In August 1961, a civil aviation agreement between the United States and the Soviet Union was negotiated. The United States might have signed the agreement, treating it as a separate matter. The U.S. chose to treat it as part of the then-pending Berlin confrontation and refused to sign. In 1968, on the other hand, both the United States and the U.S.S.R. were prepared to treat the New York–Moscow air route as unrelated to Berlin or to Vietnam, to sign the agreement, and to put it into effect.

After Brazil expropriated a U.S.-owned telephone company in 1962, there were suggestions in Congress that because of this fundamental dispute between Latin America and the United States, the U.S. should give no further aid to the Alliance for Progress. President Kennedy at a press conference, however, defined the dispute as one between the governor of a province and a single American company over the form and amount of compensation due.

Divide the Conflict into Smaller Issues

In any conflict we should consider changing the situation through dividing up the issues and specifying the distinct things we would like our adversary to decide. For example, the following is a list that could have served for many years as an itemization of things the U.S. might like to have happened in Cuba

—with respect to the Soviet Union:

    1. withdrawal of all Soviet military personnel
    2. no base for Soviet submarines or military "trawlers"

—with respect to Latin America:

    3. no shipment of arms from Cuba
    4. no training for export of militant revolutionaries
    5. some form of OAS inspection of a nuclear-free Latin America

—with respect to the United States:

    6. some steps toward compensation of property taken by Castro
    7. acceptance by Cuba of general international obligations

—inside Cuba:

8. free speech and other civil liberties
9. elections
10. public assertion of an independent ideology, drawing from Jefferson and Lincoln as well as Marx and Lenin

When the United States really wanted to exert influence on Cuba, it defined the issues even more narrowly. In the latter part of October 1962, the U.S. was keenly interested in the removal from Cuba of particular Soviet weapons. It prudently stopped talking about ousting communism from the Western Hemisphere and concentrated on the removal of forty-two weapons. When the U.S. wanted to obtain freedom for the prisoners captured at the Bay of Pigs, it separated that aim from other outstanding issues and bargained using food and medicine. When the U.S. and the Soviet Union became serious about the arms race, both stopped demanding complete and general disarmament and got to work on specific proposals to limit particular arms.

Use Small Steps to Accomplish a Larger Goal

In most cases a government increases its chances of getting something by asking for less. Since it will be easier for the other side to take the first step, there is greater likelihood of getting something rather than nothing. This is the strategy of the camel that concentrated first on getting its nose inside the tent. Setting a limited objective may also make future success in resolving the bigger issues more likely because one success at influence may set a psychological background for bigger demands. More important, splitting the issues asks our adversary to consider each issue on its merits rather than in a broad ideological scheme.

Dividing up a problem makes it possible for countries to agree on issues on which they have common interests, limiting disagreement to those issues on which they truly disagree. This was certainly true of the partial test-ban treaty originally signed by the U.S., the U.K., and the Soviet Union in 1963. Unable to agree on large issues, the countries with nuclear capability made an effective agreement on what they could agree on. This treaty probably helped rather than hindered the negotiation of further agreements.

TAKE ADVANTAGE OF TIMING

Give Them the Benefits Sooner

Both sides in a conflict are naturally concerned about the time when the consequences of making a decision are going to materialize. Changing the timing of an offer may be an important way to exert influence. The more quickly the other side can expect the benefits of making a decision to come home to them, the more influence those benefits will exert. We should try to advance the delivery date of remote benefits so they appear more immediate, and therefore more important, to our adversary. And we should try to postpone, if we cannot eliminate, the drawbacks, as they see them, of making the decision.

Give Them a Fading Opportunity

Those who control the agenda exert influence not only by formulating the questions but also by affecting the timing of decisions to be made about them. Part of our offer should make it much more attractive to the adversary to decide today than to delay. We should try to present the other side with a fading opportunity. They ought to perceive the decision we are asking them to make as an opportunity they will lose if they fail to act soon.

Unless there are persuasive reasons for acting today, the tendency is always to wait and see. Postponing a decision enables either side to attempt to get better terms today and still to keep open the option to decide tomorrow. In most international conflicts the stakes are high. Possible benefits to be gained by improving the terms are likely to exceed the cost of waiting one more day. This tendency is likely to recur day after day.

Rather than stating an offer that is good forever, we should try to arrange offers or opportunities for decision that have an automatic expiration time. There is a great difference between saying "We are always willing to negotiate" and saying "We invite you to send a representative at the ministerial level to meet our representative in Colombo at 11 A.M. local time on Monday the 25th of this month." A fading opportunity undercuts the argument within the other government that by failing to decide they can keep their options open.

In order to avoid the problem of confronting the other side with a public ultimatum, we can have the time limits set by a neutral third party, by secret communications, by ambiguity about the deadline, or by constructing the deadline so that it appears to result from facts outside anyone's control.

MAKE THE DEMAND MORE CREDIBLE

In addition to changing the substance of an offer, we can exert influence by making it appear more likely that what we say will happen will in fact happen. There is necessarily some element of uncertainty in any statement about the future. To the extent that we are seeking to exert influence by holding out attractive consequences for a government if they should make the decision we want them to make, the more certain we can make those consequences the more successful we will be. We will increase the impact of our offers if we make them more credible.

Unless the Offer Is Credible, It Will Not Work

Although even a small chance of having to pay a great cost can be an adequate basis for a governmental decision, a small chance of a fairly large benefit is not. It is easy for a political leader to justify to his government and his own domestic audience taking a course of action because there was a 20 or 30 percent chance that, if he did not, the country would be heavily bombed. Political leaders are not, however, prone to take an action on a small chance—a bet—that it will produce very good consequences.

Ho Chi Minh might have believed that if the North Vietnamese stopped fighting and withdrew there was a small chance of a highly favorable outcome: the United States would honor its promise to withdraw completely within six months. But no matter how favorable the outcome, so long as the chance of it appeared small, it would be politically indefensible for him to take that chance. He would not be able to go back to his people and say, "We accepted the U.S. promise because we believed there was a 30 percent chance we could get what we wanted at no further cost. It was a sound bet under the circumstances. It was a worthwhile risk to take. It just didn't go our way." A government wants to be highly certain that if they make a decision in order to derive some benefits, those benefits are going to materialize.

We Should Have a Reputation for Credibility

One way to make our offers credible is to keep our reputation high. A great deal is said about the importance of implementing our threats in order to preserve the credibility of later threats. Yet there is little if any discussion of what happens to our credibility when we fail to implement an offer. The consequences of a broken promise are serious enough even if the promise was intended to be kept at the time it was made. If the adversary discovers that we never had any intention of keeping the promise—that there was deliberate deception—then our ability to exert influence will be seriously weakened for an indefinite future. As a general rule, it is wise to promise only what we have the capability to deliver.

Credible Offers Exert More Influence

Another reason why it is important to make offers credible is that we want to get the maximum influence out of a given offer. If we offer free elections or troop withdrawal within six months, and are committed to those offers, we are clearly willing to pay such costs for their making the decision we want. Unless we convince them of our degree of commitment, our decision to pay a given cost will have been made in vain. Since we are making the offer for the purpose of producing an impact, we ought to do all we can to get that impact.

To improve the credibility of a given offer is a far more economical way of exerting influence than to improve the content or generosity of the offer. It is as if we were offering a seller a check for $100, but the seller is reluctant to let us have the goods because he fears that the check will bounce. One way to try to influence the seller in such a case is to increase the amount of the check until he is persuaded to take the chance. A far less costly way, assuming we intend to keep our promise, is to improve the credibility of the check, by establishing our good credit, by getting the check certified by a bank, by putting money in escrow, or by some other such device. Similarly, in political negotiations it will usually be more economical to remove doubts about the genuineness or sincerity of an offer than to try to exert influence by improving the content of an offer about which such doubts exist in the first place.

Do Not Ask for More Than is Reasonable

Governments regularly ask for more than they can reasonably expect to get. There are some obvious advantages to "padding" a demand. If we get anything at all, we are likely to get more than we would have got without padding. We have room to retreat, and at the same time it will seem more politically acceptable and more profitable for an adversary to accept a demand that is lower than our initial one. Padding, however, has clear disadvantages which, as outlined, usually outweigh these advantages.

Padding May Harm the Negotiation Process. If we add too much to the price, we may scare off the customers: they will not even be interested in talking. For example, a letter that President Johnson sent to Ho Chi Minh in the spring of 1967 suffered from too much padding. It was meant as an opening gambit in negotiations. Although the president said, "We will stop the bombing if you stop all infiltration and demonstrate that you've done so," he also meant "and if this is not satisfactory, what will you do?" This was an offer on the part of the U.S. not to increase U.S. troop levels in exchange for a demonstration on the part of the North Vietnamese that they had abandoned their troops and left them without supplies or replacements. Although this was a specific proposition, it was so well padded that it elicited no interest. In fact, Ho Chi Minh published it to the world to gain a propaganda advantage demonstrating that, in his eyes at least, the world would not rate the U.S. proposal as that of a government sincerely seeking some mutually satisfactory arrangement. No negotiations took place for a year, during which time thousands of U.S. soldiers were killed. A more realistic proposal might have been to the United States' advantage.

Padding Put Us in a Weak Position. Padding often results in our maintaining a position that is politically weak. Our adversary, rather than entering into negotiations, may concentrate on subjecting us to a propaganda attack to which we have made ourselves vulnerable. We may suffer a political cost in third countries for insisting on an unrealistic demand: Britain's insistence on unconditional surrender by Ian Smith in Rhodesia (not even offering him immunity from prosecution for treason) pleased some African countries in the short run, but Britain then began to pay high long-run costs for that exaggerated demand.

Padding Limits Our Options.   Domestically, we risk tying our own hands. In a situation in which the public has no previously formed view about a proper outcome, its government's first demand sets an objective. As that demand is repeated, it tends to become increasingly difficult for the government to draw back from it. What starts out as fat may end up as bone. In the unsuccessful negotiations for a ban on underground testing of nuclear weapons, the United States publicly adopted the position that a satisfactory treaty would require that each major nuclear power be given a quota of at least ten inspection trips every year. No one knew what constituted an inspection—how many men could visit how large an area for how long a time. But the number ten took on a political life of its own. Senators and columnists argued that the United States could not retreat from ten to three. Whatever the merits of the position, it was clear that by starting out at one point identifiable in numerical terms the government had created strong domestic resistance to their shifting to a lower point.

Padding Harms Our Reputation.   Padding may also be positively harmful. Once we begin to retreat from a padded position, we begin to acquire a reputation for retreating. An adversary might reasonably conclude that if we came down once, we will come down again. They may not believe us when we say that we have come to the end of the padding.

MAKE THE DEMAND MORE SPECIFIC

Specificity increases the credibility of an offer. For one thing, a specific offer shows that we have thought about what we would be prepared to do and have worked out the details. It is a demonstration of our present intentions. Greater specificity also demonstrates greater commitment and therefore makes for greater credibility. The political cost to us of backing out of a specific promise is greater than that of backing out of a loose or ambiguous one. The more explicit the promise, the more difficult it is to find excuses for nonperformance. By being specific, we buy influence at the cost of flexibility.

Ambiguous Offers Have Limited Benefits

There are some clear advantages to being ambiguous about the decision we would like another government to make. Through ambiguity we can avoid confronting our adversary with something that will look like an ultimatum. If the demand is ambiguous, the other side incurs less political risk in meeting it and is therefore more likely to go along in the direction suggested. Ambiguity also allows the other side to meet our general desires in the manner that is most convenient and least costly to them. The demand may be easier to go along with if an adversary can formulate the details himself. Being specific is also likely to put a ceiling on what we can hope to attain. We are unlikely to get anything more favorable. An adversary is likely to start at that point and try to bargain us down. It is often said that being specific at the outset is just poor bargaining.

The disadvantages of ambiguity in communicating international demands are, however, often greater, and usually go unrecognized. These disadvantages are particularly acute if we are seeking to influence a government to take some affirmative action. Any ambiguity about what we want that government to do makes it that much less likely that they will do it. Communication between the sides is often difficult. The level of hostility is likely to be high. Messages are often misunderstood.

Consider the situation in Vietnam in March of 1965, as discussed in the case study, as it might have looked to the North Vietnamese. At that time the United States was asking North Vietnam to "stop its aggression" in the South and indicated that U.S. bombing of the North would stop as soon as that happened. The ambiguous nature of the demand to "stop aggression" undercut any pressure on North Vietnam to stop its support for the South. First, even those in North Vietnam who wanted to do something that would end the bombing probably put the most pessimistic interpretation on what it would take to satisfy the U.S. Second, having left up to them the selection of an appropriate action that would constitute "stopping aggression," the U.S. made it unlikely that all of the different North Vietnamese groups would be able to agree upon the specific action they would be willing to do.

North Vietnam could, perhaps, be certain that the United States would stop the bombing if they, North Vietnam, did everything that could conceivably fall within our definition of aggression: stop all infiltration of men and supplies, recall all "regroupees" born in the South and trained in the North, order them to destroy all equipment already infiltrated, stop all further propaganda and political support for the National Liberation movement, and publicly repudiate the Vietcong program. They could, however, be almost equally certain that something less than that would be sufficient to get the United States to stop the bombing.

But how much less? In taking any particular action, they would risk doing more than the U.S. would have regarded as sufficient (paying too high a price) or not doing enough (paying a price and getting nothing for it). Since time was not of utmost importance, the choice of waiting at least one more day for the situation to clarify itself naturally looked more attractive to them than the choice of paying a price in the dark. It was as though the U.S. had offered to sell a horse for "a reasonable sum," the buyer being required to pay his money over the table first: if he paid enough the first time, the U.S. would give him the horse; if not, no sale and the U.S. would keep the money. Any amount offered by the buyer would be either almost certainly too high or run a great risk of being too little.

The U.S. was in the position of trying to buy the horse when the U.S. embassy was seized in Iran. The Iranian students holding American hostages in Teheran in 1979 said for months that they would not release the hostages until the United States had adequately atoned for its sins and met an ambiguous set of additional demands. No clear offer was given by Iran, and accordingly the United States was under no great pressure to do any particular thing in order to negotiate for the hostages' release.

Ambiguous Offers Do Not Result in Action

Being ambiguous about the decision we would like may get us nothing at all. By 1966 the U.S. seems to have recognized the bind into which it had put the North Vietnamese. So the U.S. began to say, "Just do the minimum. Any assurance regarding a willingness to de-escalate would be sufficient to justify our stopping the bombing. Almost any assurance." It would have been instructive had the U.S. tried to write out some hypothetical assurances that it could realistically have expected Ho Chi Minh to make if he were interested in having the bombing stop.

It turns out that most of the promises he might have made do not look very good. Suppose the North Vietnamese had said, "All right, we'll cut infiltration by 30 percent. Now stop the bombing." The U.S. probably would have said, "Hold on, let's clarify this a little. Thirty percent of what? Last month's infiltration? Next month's infiltration? How will we verify this 30 percent reduction? Will it continue? For how long?" Certainly Hanoi would have realized that U.S. reaction to such an assurance would probably be equivocal. Anyone in the inner councils of the North Vietnamese government would have had a hard time convincing the whole Central Committee that all they had to do was say "30 percent" and the bombing would stop. The apparent generosity of the U.S. in saying "almost any assurance" was designed to influence spectators to the conflict, not its adversaries. The U.S. did not think through the kinds of specific decisions that North Vietnam would know would be adequate to stop the bombing. President Johnson's broad offer to negotiate with North Vietnam "anywhere at any time" suffered from similar vagueness and proved difficult to convert into an operational decision.

Another difficulty of ambiguity is illustrated by the first Security Council cease-fire resolution in the Arab–Israeli war of June 1967. That resolution called on the parties to take "forthwith" all measures for an "immediate" cease-fire. This was a clear proposition but one into which a certain amount of ambiguity was inserted to meet a confused situation. It only made the situation more confused. Since individual military units received word of the truce call at different times, for each unit "forthwith" meant something different. Each unit, as it got word of the demand, apparently justified continuing combat because the other side continued firing. Fighting did not stop.

(The next Security Council resolution tried to meet this problem by demanding that the governments concerned "discontinue all military activities at 2000 hours GMT on 7 June 1967.") The more specific the arrangements for any cease-fire, the more likely it is to be successful.

In the present style of conducting foreign policy, governments too often define demands generally, giving an adversary a great choice in selecting action in which it could engage to satisfy those demands. ("We hope Russia will undertake some reciprocal measures that will further reduce tension in Chechnya." "We hope ethnic cleansing in Bosnia will stop.") Seldom do we identify specifically and narrowly some bit of conduct in which we would like them to engage ("remove forty-two weapons from Cuba"). Yet one of the most effective ways of getting action is to come up with a specific proposition. The easier it is for the other side to make a decision, the more likely they are to make it.

Specificity Is Not Rigidity

Becoming specific about decisions that we would like the other side to make will not rigidify our position, so long as we communicate more than one proposal. Illustrative specificity can indicate the kind of decision that would satisfy us. It should stimulate their thinking and open lines of communication. It will also indicate that we are searching for a solution and are not tied to one plan. And it will give an adversary several propositions while encouraging them to work out more for themselves.

Both before and after President Johnson's letter to Ho Chi Minh in the spring of 1967 there were public statements that there were any number of things the U.S. would have accepted from the North Vietnamese. Yet the letter immediately began to be referred to as "the" U.S. position of what the North Vietnamese would have to do: cut off all infiltration of men and supplies and demonstrate that they had done so. The U.S. had failed to identify specifically more than one assurance. And bureaucracies tend to see a single illustrative example as a fixed minimum requirement: what should be labeled an example tends to become something we insist on. In order to avoid this, it is helpful to have two or more suggestions on the table at the same time. This combines flexibility with the advantages of confronting an adversary with a specific choice.

At Least We Should Be Specific in Our Own Thinking

There is a difference between being specific in our own minds about the kind of decisions we would like another government to make and communicating those decisions specifically. Although in most cases we would be more successful by being more specific in our communication, circumstances sometimes call for a degree of ambiguity. But no matter how ambiguously we decide to communicate with an adversary, we should internally do the necessary staff work to develop in precise words and phrases some illustrative decisions we would like our adversary to make. We are unlikely to get what we want unless we know what that is. We also need a clear idea of what that decision is in order to arrange the consequences of their making or not making the decision. We ought to understand just what they do to get the "carrot" and what they do to get the "stick."

As the Paris negotiations over Vietnam started, the United States should have had in mind drafts of possible joint communiqués that it would have liked and that it could realistically expect the talks might produce. What might be the wording of acceptable joint statements about the bombings, about reciprocal de-escalation, about negotiations among the South Vietnamese, and about Laos? By being specific internally we get the benefits of clear thinking without committing ourselves to a specific position in public.

There will be opposition to this kind of thinking, of course. It requires the bureaucracy to spend time and effort working out specific examples of what we would accept although they may never be communicated. This process will often engender internal conflict among departments and officials on our side, with little apparent reward. Working on actual drafts is, however, a useful and educational experience. Again, it will be helpful to develop several specific proposals, this time to avoid internal rigidity. Such work is bound to stimulate our own thinking about what it is we are trying to get our adversary to do.

HOW TO MAKE THE OFFER MORE CREDIBLE

Increase the Probability That the Offer Will Be Implemented

One way to increase the perceived credibility of our implementing an offer is to increase its actual probability. By making a commitment from which we cannot back down we can show an adversary that we will have to come through on the offer. Even if the North Vietnamese believed that President Johnson was personally committed to the offer of $1 billion in aid, they probably correctly believed that a different administration would feel less bound. They might have thought the offer implausible because it would be difficult to get it through Congress in the event of peace. If the United States had actually appropriated the money and given it to the Asian Development Bank to be distributed when peace was established (perhaps with the interest to be paid to the U.S. in the interim), it would not only have been more attractive because of Asian administration; it would also have been far more credible. North Vietnam would have known that if peace came, the U.S. could not prevent the implementation of the offer. By committing itself, the U.S. could have exerted more influence.

Implementation Plans Demonstrate Commitment

Another way to improve the credibility of an offer is to show the adversary that we have detailed plans for implementing it. This factor is even more striking the other way around: a lack of detailed planning makes an offer look inconceivable. The absence of an effort on our part to prepare to implement an offer usually demonstrates that we ourselves do not take it seriously. On the other hand, if an adversary knows that we have contingent plans for carrying out an offer, that we have actually thought about what we are going to do and how we are going to do it, he will be more likely to believe that the offer is serious.

A general offer to make sure that the rights of the white minority in South Africa were protected did not carry as much weight as a specific constitution that both the African National Congress and the government of South Africa would be willing to sign. Part of the U.S. offer to North Vietnam was to hold free elections under a strengthened International Control Commission. But how was the commission going to be strengthened? The notion that the commission was going to become strong and capable of supervising free elections was implausible in large part because the United States had suggested no plans for strengthening it. The lack of detailed planning undercut the promise that internationally observed elections were ever going to take place.

Implementation Plans Demonstrate Capability

Implementation plans lend credibility to our offers not only because they indicate something about our present intentions, but also because they demonstrate a present capability. An offer will exert little influence if the adversary cannot see how we would be able to implement it. Even if they believe that we are fairly serious about our offer and that we will not look for a way out if they make the decision we are asking them to make, the offer will not exert influence if we appear unable to follow through. Demonstrated capability is just as important with offers as with threats. The white minority of South Africa for many years did not perceive the capability on the part of any government to guarantee white rights should democratic majority government be instituted.

Visible contingency planning for carrying out our offers would involve administrative work, but modest cost. It may well be argued that such efforts would represent a substantial effort to prepare for a situation that may never arise. That is true. But it is equally true that far greater expenditures and efforts are regularly made for military capability that is never used. We have come to recognize that substantial effort is justified in demonstrating a capacity to inflict pain, because that capacity exerts influence. It would be equally worthwhile to develop and demonstrate a capacity to carry out offers, particularly when it could be done at a fraction of the cost.

INCREASING COMPLIANCE MECHANISMS INCREASES CREDIBILITY

The credibility of our proposal is increased when we increase the likelihood that both sides will comply with any agreement. The most significant and troublesome disputes arise among parties who deal with each other again and again. Mexico and the United States will need to negotiate about waters from the Rio Grande for as long as they share a river border; closer economic integration among European states will result in greater rather than fewer occasions on which their interests conflict. In resolving any single conflict, we should also consider possible changes to the system that would reduce the incidence of future conflict and provide for more efficient resolution of those disputes that do arise.

Improving First-Order Compliance

Just as we want a driver to stop her car at a red light, we also want a government to respect the provision of the Antarctic Treaty prohibiting arms in Antarctica. This kind of compliance we call *first-order compliance*—respect for existing agreements and for the standing rules of law. Diagnosing on a systemic basis why a government or other actor fails to comply can lead to a new approach to resolving a conflict and can add important elements to our proposal. Chart 14–1 sets out some considerations for improving the chances that governments will comply with existing norms and rules.

CHART 14–1
ELEMENTS OF FIRST-ORDER COMPLIANCE: Helping the Parties Obey the Rules

ELEMENTS	DIAGNOSTIC QUESTIONS
Compliance as a Function of the Rule	*Does the rule conform to common sense? Could a party's constituent explain the reason for the rule?*
	Does the rule conform to notions of fairness and morality? Is it balanced in its application to the parties?
	If the rule is an agreement, are there fair procedures for renegotiating or changing it under changed circumstances?
	Is it clear when and under what conditions it no longer applies?
	Is the rule clear and specific?
	Was the rule established by means of a fair procedure? Did the parties have a hand in shaping the rule?
Compliance as a Function of Enlightened Self-interest	*Have the parties adequately considered the positive consequences of example and of having other parties follow the rule? The difficulties in reestablishing a rule once it has been broken?*
	Could negative consequences of breaking the rule be made more immediate and real to the party considering it?
Compliance as a Function of Verification	*Are problems of information and verification interfering with compliance?*
	Have the parties balanced the benefits of more perfect verification against the costs of not reaching an imperfectly followed agreement?
Compliance as a Function of a Rule's Place in the Legal Order	*Do parties feel free to violate the rule? Is the desired conduct clearly identified as an agreement or law?*
	Are domestic means of enforcing compliance stronger than international ones? Can the rule be incorporated into the domestic legal order?
	Is compliance with the rule entrusted to a particular person or organization? Can a constituency be created in organized support of the rule?

Improving Second-Order Compliance

In addition to designing a structure in which rules are less likely to be broken, we are also concerned with what happens *after* there has been a violation of standing rules or when there is a dispute about whether a violation has occurred. Returning to our driver, we want to be sure that if she is caught and fined for going through a red light, she will pay the fine or dispute it according to set rules, and then pay the fine if she loses. This is *second-order compliance*—compliance with decisions that settle disputes by interpreting rules and applying them to the facts of a particular case.

Frequently the distinction between first-order and second-order compliance is blurred. Yet it is crucial, especially in the international context, where governments are constantly disagreeing over what the law is and what conduct constitutes compliance with the law. One of the reasons the European Community has been able to function so well in the creation of a common market is its compliance mechanisms. When a country or company violates any of the laws under the Treaty of Rome, a citizen of any member country affected by the violation can bring a court case in his or her national court. Additionally, a country or the Commission of the European Community can bring a case against another country for violating the Treaty of Rome directly before the European Court of Justice. Thus, a clear procedure is set out for second-order compliance. Chart 14–2 sets out some further considerations for reducing the incidence or severity of conflicts we can predict will occur.

CHART 14–2
ELEMENTS OF SECOND-ORDER COMPLIANCE:
What Happens When a Rule Is Broken

ELEMENTS	DIAGNOSTIC QUESTIONS
Compliance as a Function of Foresight	*Could the parties predict in advance the types of conflicts likely to arise in their interactions? Should they explicitly recognize the probability of future disputes?*
	How concretely can the parties plan for disputes that will arise? Should an agreement include a dispute resolution clause? Should it detail the steps to be taken or third parties to be involved?
	Can the parties minimize the risk of misunderstanding? Might they schedule a regular time to discuss issues of compliance? Might they minimize the risk of escalation through early planned interventions?
Compliance as a Function of the Dispute Resolution Regime	*Can jurisdictional questions be agreed to in advance? Is it clear who can hear a dispute, under what conditions? Does the decision-maker have the authority to decide its own jurisdiction, or does that become another dispute of the parties?*
	Is the relief that can be ordered clear to the parties? Would it be more easily acceptable if relief were limited to foward-looking decrees?
	Are the rules and standards for deciding whether noncompliance has occurred sufficiently clear? Are the procedures to be followed agreed on?
	Is any decision renered sufficiently executable? Should relief ordered, for example, be enforceable in national courts?
	Is any party sufficiently invested in compliance with agreements? Should monitoring and compliance procedures be entrusted to a specific organization?

CHART 14–2 (continued)
ELEMENTS OF SECOND-ORDER COMPLIANCE:
What Happens When a Rule Is Broken

ELEMENTS	DIAGNOSTIC QUESTIONS
Compliance as a Function of the Decision	*Does a decision change the demand made on the noncomplying party? Is it sufficiently specific and objectively measurable?*
	Do decisions change the offer made to a noncomplying party? Can compliance be based on an incentive system rather than threats of punishment?
	Do decisions change the threats made to a noncomplying party? Can negative consequences of noncompliance be legitimately increased?

When one is involved in a specific conflict, it is usually difficult to focus attention on the next iteration or the next dispute. It is easier for a country to protest the taxation by a foreign country of a specific national company abroad—and to do so again and again—than it is to negotiate a comprehensive investment treaty with procedures for dispute resolution. Yet as we diagnose the reasons why a conflict has not been settled and develop new approaches for its resolution, we find that the most promising avenue is often to look ahead to more constructive treatment of future disagreements. In a dramatically more complex world, where trade and investment, migration and environmental degradation, interest rates and employment, require increasing global cooperation, a better system for dealing with future conflict may be more important than an answer to any particular problem. Close attention to issues of first- and second-order compliance can help focus our plan of action toward a more systemic solution.

CHAPTER
—15—

Legitimacy
and International Law

❖   ❖   ❖

One critical element in any government's decision is its judgment about what it "ought" to do, reflecting its own notions of decency, fair play, morality, order, precedent, international law, and history. We are more likely to be successful in getting an adversary government to make a decision if our adversary believes that it is legitimate—that it has the quality of being the right thing to do. Governments are moved by their own ideas about what is right. We should, therefore, formulate a decision we desire in such a way that it will strike our adversary as a legitimate request.

Margaret Mead has said that the first thing to remember when dealing with other countries is that they think of themselves as being on the side of the right; they see themselves as the good guys. They may be engaged in conduct that we think is evil. But they do not look at it that way. If our side characterizes the other side in a violent dispute as "aggressors committed to conquest," we should not deceive ourselves into believing that the other side also regards itself in that light. We may perceive a cocaine trafficker as an international pariah. He, though, may well see himself as the employer of thousands of peasants who would otherwise starve because of neocolonial policies. The wise course in choosing how to influence another party is to operate on the assumption that they are sincere people who believe, all things considered, that they are pursuing a course of action that is morally right. The fact that they believe this does not, of course, make it true. But if the goal is to influence them, it is their state of mind that is critical.

A LEGITIMATE DEMAND EXERTS INFLUENCE

Governments need to justify their decisions within their own bureaucracy and to their own citizens. The range of international decisions they can make is circumscribed by their domestic opinion. Lyndon Johnson might well have believed that the cost of total military withdrawal from South Vietnam would be tolerable on the international level. But if he could not convince the American people it was the right course to follow, he would not want to do it. If Cuba wants the United States to end the embargo, it should be concerned with how that looks to the U.S.—for example, how it is consistent with American notions of democracy. It will be easier for a government to maintain support and morale at home if it can point out to its own people that making the decision we want that government to make is consistent with their own ideas about what is right and what is in their national interest.

A major concern of every government is with the precedent set by a given action or decision. If they give in now, they may open themselves up to giving in again and again. They will have yielded to pressure and done something they did not want to do. This fear of setting a harmful precedent can be overcome by legitimating our demand. If the decision appears consistent with their principles, no bad precedent will be set by going along with it. It will be easier for them to make the decision, and therefore they will be more likely to make it.

Playing to the Home Audience

Governments usually formulate demands in just the opposite way: they first try to make the desired decision appear legitimate in the eyes of their own people. They ask, "What is the domestic climate? How can we defend to our constituents what we are doing?" The United States justified its actions in Iraq by identifying its adversaries as evil aggressors acting in a grossly illegitimate way. "They are murderers and violators of international law. They are behaving outrageously." Such characterization helps rally support both domestically and, perhaps, among third parties. However, it makes it less likely that the other side will make the decision our side wants. It often makes more likely the failure of our international efforts, with its attendant domestic political costs.

According to official Soviet policy, the principles on which Soviet foreign policy rested are those of peaceful coexistence, respect for sovereign territory, and noninterference in the internal affairs of other states. The Soviet government was more likely to be influenced if the United States could have convinced them that a decision the U.S. wanted was consistent with those principles than if the U.S. convinced them that it was consistent with the Monroe Doctrine or with the principle of free enterprise. The North Vietnamese were less likely to stay north of the 17th parallel, not more likely, when the U.S. argued that to do so was consistent with the containment of communism.

An attempt to point out to the other side that they ought to make a decision where the "oughtness" is based on one side's ideas of fairness, history, principle, or morality is at best a diversion from the immediate task at hand; at worst it is destructive of the result that party wants. If changing their mind appears to further their own policy, it will be easier for the other side to do it.

If a party begins by making its objective legitimate to the home audience, it may also tie its own hands. The British justified their sanctions against Rhodesia by labeling Ian Smith a traitor. They subsequently found themselves under considerable criticism for agreeing to negotiate with traitors. Labeling the other side is likely to limit a party's ability to make concessions, to negotiate, or to change its position in any substantial way without appearing to be selling out its principles.

It is not hard to understand why the more consistent a request can be made with another government's notions of right and wrong, with their principles and values, the more reason they will have to grant it. In 1966 an American touring in Russia was apprehended and convicted for stealing an iron statue of a bear. The American lawyers who helped appeal the case did not attempt to argue that the Russian court should have sympathy for this young American, or that in his trial he had been denied due process. Instead they turned to the grounds for punishment authorized in the Soviet statute. The only relevant one was "rehabilitation to conform to Soviet standards of morality." They pointed out that for this particular crime the reasons for punishment did not apply, since the best way to prevent further violations of Soviet morality would be to expel the youth. The lawyers did not argue that the Russian rules were bad ones. They said, in effect, "Your rules say you should turn this man loose and send him out of the country." The argument was directed at making the request legitimate in the eyes of the Soviet court according to its own principles. For the first time, the conviction of an American tourist was reversed on appeal.[1]

A demand exerts more influence if it appears legitimate to third parties as well. They can exert independent influence, and even if they take no action, their views may make a difference. The other side will incur an increased political cost by refusing to go along with a decision that third parties regard as fair. And we reduce the political cost to ourselves of pressing the demand. Further, the fact that the demand seems fair to third parties will itself make it seem more legitimate to the adversary. But legitimating the demand in the eyes of the adversary is still more important than legitimating it in the eyes of others. To demonstrate that a demand is legitimate because it is con-

---

[1]Conversation with Professor Harold Berman. See also "Tourist Freed by Soviet Starts Trip Home," *The New York Times,* March 21, 1967, p. 3, col. 5.

sistent with precedent, or because it affects both sides equally, lets the other side make the decision without adverse effects on third parties or on our own public opinion.

SOME WAYS TO FORMULATE LEGITIMATE DEMANDS

Linking the Demand to Past Actions

One way to legitimate our demands is to have our objective—the decision we want another government to make—closely related to that government's past actions. Most international disputes are concerned with events that have already occurred. One side charges the other with having broken an agreement, violated rights, or committed an outrage of one kind or another. But what has happened is water over the dam. We usually overlook the fact that the sole reason for a government's communicating a judgment about the past is to affect the future—in our case to influence what another government will do. We may be interested in knowing privately the facts regarding the justification that Israel had for launching its military offensive in June of 1967 so that we will be better able to predict what the Israeli (and Arab) leaders are likely to do in other circumstances. Such knowledge may also help us to identify some realistic and attainable objectives. But the primary reason for our making public statements about Israel's conduct and for characterizing it in one way or another should be for the purpose of legitimation. Our rhetoric may help make more legitimate (in the eyes of those we are trying to influence, in our own eyes, or in the eyes of bystanders) what we are asking for, what we are offering, or what we are threatening.

One way to use the past for legitimation is to formulate decisions in such a way that they appear similar to, or at least consistent with, previous decisions made by the adversary or other governments under similar circumstances. Governments find it easier to do things that have been done before. Not all precedents are good; the other side may not even like the precedent we are invoking. But they will usually feel that the risk of serious criticism of action for which there is a precedent is less than the risk involved in doing something that has never been done before. Suppose a government discovers that a foreign diplomat is engaging in espionage. To ask that the diplomat apologize and give a formal promise not to do it again might be an extremely reasonable request—but one without precedent. Therefore his government would probably find it difficult to decide that he should give such a promise. On the other hand, a request that the diplomat's government withdraw him would almost certainly be granted. The latter would be effective not because one side was asking for less, but because there are many precedents for the recall of a diplomat upon the request of another government.

There are other ways in which the past can be used to lend legitimacy to our present demands. The fact that an adversary has in the past promised to do something makes it more legitimate to ask for it now. Or if an adversary has done something in the past, we may be able to relate our demands to that action on a tit-for-tat basis. A demand will also be more legitimate if it apparently seeks to restore the *status quo ante*. In the Cuban Missile Crisis, President Kennedy's demand that the missiles be removed from Cuba looked legitimate because Russia's action was identified as a radical change from the preexisting balance of force in the hemisphere.

Making the Demand Reciprocal

Another way to legitimate a demand is to use the form and language of reciprocity. A demand will be more legitimate if it appears to affect both sides in the same way. Ho Chi Minh's suggestion in 1965 that all troops except those native to South Vietnam be removed appeared more legitimate than President Johnson's suggestion that the United States stop its troop increases and that North Vietnam stop troop increases, troop replacements, and the sending in of supplies.

Changing the demand to ask for agreement on a procedural rather than a substantive step can make the demand more legitimate if the procedure has a built-in "fairness" to both sides. In Vietnam, the U.S. objective was sometimes identified as a non-Communist government for South Vietnam and sometimes as a government freely chosen by the people of South Vietnam. The second formulation was obviously more legitimate to adversaries of the United States.

Involving a Third Party

Another way of legitimating a request is to have it reflect the view of an impartial third party. This is most effective when the request comes initially from a third party who is obviously independent. If the first call for negotiations in Vietnam had come from the Soviet Union or the Organization of African Unity rather than from the government of the United States, North Vietnam might have found the request easier to accept. A demand for a cease-fire that comes from the secretary-general or the Security Council of the United Nations is usually more acceptable than one that comes from an adversary. The fact that the call for a cease-fire in the Middle East in June 1967 came from the United Nations probably made it more effective than it would have been had it come from Russia or the United States, or even from both of those countries together.

A good way to legitimate an objective is to defer in advance to the views or decision of a third party. A government may call on an adversary to submit the dispute to arbitration or to the views of some other impartial body. This method is useful not only for legitimating requests but also for legitimating action taken in furtherance of an objective. When Egypt refused to comply with a 1956 Security Council decision on the Suez Canal it greatly strengthened its case by saying that its action was subject to review by the International Court of Justice. If any signatory of the Constantinople Convention of 1888 wanted to contend that Egypt should take Israel-bound cargo, Egypt agreed to accept the jurisdiction of the International Court and be bound by its decision. This was a useful thing to do. The Egyptians were saying, "We think we are right. There is the Court. If you think we are wrong, take it to the Court."

When the United States gave military aid to Greece and Turkey in 1947, the Congress, at the instigation of Senator Arthur Vandenberg, provided that if at any time the Security Council should ask the U.S. to get out, all military personnel would be withdrawn and that for that purpose the United States renounced its right of veto in the Security Council. That clause greatly increased the legitimacy of U.S. intervention.

Similarly, U.S. military intervention in the Dominican Republic in 1965 could have been accomplished with far less political cost had the U.S. legitimated its action there by such an arrangement. The U.S. could have stated that it was going in as a neutral and not on one side or the other of the conflict; that its military forces were there only pending maintenance of law and order by the Organization of American States; and that as soon as the OAS or the United Nations felt that they had the capability to keep the peace and asked the U.S. to leave, it would do so. The OAS would have been extremely unlikely to ask the U.S., by the necessary two-thirds-majority vote, to leave. Even if it had, the U.S. might have taken some time to withdraw. The U.S. statement that it would get out under such circumstances would have made U.S. intervention more tolerable for others and less damaging for the U.S.

CONFRONTING MORAL CHOICE

In international relations, each government faces difficult choices when dealing with governments that may be dictatorial or communist, militant or repressive. What advice should we give, for example, to a European democracy or to a new African state, as to how to deal with governments like those of Franco's Spain, Stalin's Soviet Union, de Klerk's South Africa, or, in recent years, Albania, North Korea, Cambodia, Cuba, Nicaragua, Burma, Libya, Haiti, Panama and so forth? It is said that he who sups with the devil should have a long spoon. Just how is that accomplished in international affairs?[2]

Standard answers are to suggest that each person has his or her own morality; that moral standards cannot be taught; that on moral questions—as on political ones—there are partisan perceptions; and that everyone is entitled to his or her own view. An even more common approach is to avoid the question entirely. We have decided not to avoid the question in this book.

---

[2]Roger Fisher, Elizabeth Kopelman, and Andrea Kupfer Schneider, *Beyond Machiavelli* (Cambridge, MA: Harvard University Press, 1994), pp. 106–112.

While we are thinking rigorously about pragmatic questions, we must also try to think equally rigorously about moral questions.

To propose in a few pages how moral considerations can be integrated into the conduct of international relations is, in one sense, the height of arrogance or folly. It is to march in boldly where even those who are divinely inspired tread far more circumspectly. Yet to fail to suggest practical ways for bringing moral ideas to bear in governmental decision making is to make the powerful statement that moral considerations can safely be ignored. To ignore them here is to suggest that moral considerations need not be explicitly considered. We would be sending the wrong message by ignoring moral dilemmas, even if we accept that it is a complex and controversial subject not adequately addressed by a single section in a book. Rather than try to lay out all the different choices, and the pros and cons of each, we suggest a process goal.

A Workable Goal: Minimize Regrets

At every stage in the process that we have been going through, moral criteria are relevant and are brought to bear, consciously or unconsciously. A fair goal is to minimize the chance that we will regret what we do. If we make a decision today and later learn things that cause us to regret that decision, we have, in one sense, made a mistake. If we had known more we would not have acted as we did. A reasonable goal is to try to act so as to increase the likelihood that no matter how wise we later become, we will believe we have acted properly. But even this standard of minimizing regrets does not feel sufficient if we remember that our partisan perceptions help us to screen out nonconforming data. A better standard would be that we have no regrets even after questioning and testing our assumptions.

Sorting Out the Problem

Morality only regulates conduct where there is a choice. Having good intentions for our actions are important, but not enough on their own. It may be helpful to sort our moral concerns into four categories. First, there are the questions of *purpose*. Although good intentions will not be enough to justify all conduct taken in their behalf, bad intentions can morally contaminate actions that are otherwise acceptable. Our purposes will have to be held up for scrutiny against some standards.

Second, our proposed *conduct* will also have to bear close inspection. Sometimes we will justify or condemn conduct without regard to its consequences. In such circumstances we argue that our conduct is the right thing to do, whether or not it does any good. Some things, we insist, are wrong (such as turning on the gas in the Nazi gas chambers or participating in ethnic cleansing) even if we are convinced that by doing it ourselves we could do it more humanely or inflict less harm than would be the case if we should refuse and others were to act in our stead. Other things, according to this deontological approach, are simply right because of the nature of the acts themselves—like voting, and not littering—irrespective of whether others follow suit.

On other occasions we use a more utilitarian approach and judge the conduct by its calculated consequences. The morality of a military operation depends on the predictable consequences: What costs fall on whom for what benefit? We will thus need criteria for judging both when an act is thought to be inherently good or bad, and when the ends are said to justify the means.

The third issue in moral assessment relates to *criteria*. Where do we find the standards by which to judge purposes, conduct that is inherently good or bad, and conduct that is justified as doing more good than harm, or as being better than the available alternatives?

The fourth issue is that of *process*. By what process do we bring the proposed criteria to bear on the facts—on the ends we propose to pursue and the means we suggest for doing so?

On each of the four points mentioned above, some operational ideas will be advanced. We will take them up in reverse order.

Process: Think and feel.   The basic prescription is, think. If moral concerns are to have an impact on our actions they will have to be consciously addressed. Rational thought should not exclude gut feelings, but intuitive feelings are no substitute for careful sustained thinking about what we propose to recommend, what standards or principles make it the right thing to do, what may be wrong with it, and how we propose to resolve such questions. For example, the Bush administration did not apply moral criteria toward U.S. relations with China in a standard way. Bush condemned other countries over the issue of human rights and nuclear proliferation. However, he did not apply those standards and principles consistently to China, an inconsistency that undermined his moral stance in relations with other countries. Consistent consideration and articulation of moral standards will make us more persuasive.

Criteria: Civilization's best windows.   The fact that there is no single criterion by which acts can be judged right or wrong causes some to conclude that there are no criteria at all. The fact that people differ as to what is right and what is wrong causes some to conclude that there is no standard to which to adhere. Put another way, they conclude that since people differ we should not search for standards or adhere to those in which we believe. But the fact that there is no single legal standard does not mean that there is no law. The fact that lawyers and judges differ about law in no way suggests that we should not comply with law. Nor do such differences free a judge or a lawyer from searching for the best view of the law that he or she can find, and adhering to the law in which he or she believes.

Moral standards are not governmentally designed or enforced; they are not interpreted by judges. But moral standards, like legal ones, cannot be disproved or dismissed because of differences of opinion. In fact, it is those very differences that illuminate moral questions and help us resolve them. A simple statutory rule is nowhere near as illuminating as the combined opinions of a dozen judges dealing with different cases in which a problem covered by the rule has been raised.

To cope with moral choice, we will want to benefit from the best that our civilization and culture, or those of others with which we can make ourselves familiar, has to offer. Thus, one option is to turn for guidance to the humanities, which serve as the repositories of the wisdom of human society. To minimize the chance that we will later regret our decision because we have learned more, we will want to make as much use as possible of knowledge that has heretofore been accumulated. History, philosophy, law, religion, and literature each has a lot to say about good and bad standards. No one of them can provide a definitive answer, but each can ask questions that shed light. A list of possible questions appears in Chart 15–1. Such questions do not impose an external judgment upon the purpose or action we propose as much as they help us think about what we already know. They do not impose somebody else's moral judgment; they help us turn into a moral judgment values that we have already acquired.

Such criteria can be applied directly to judge the purpose of our proposed actions. The questions would be slightly rephrased when asking about purpose rather than conduct, but the same set of questions should help us examine the morality of our ends. Those purposes may look selfish and mean or noble and enlightened.

Conduct and Purpose: Examine the Consequences

We sometimes judge conduct to be right or wrong independent of a precise calculation of whether the net costs or benefits are expected to outweigh those of pursuing an alternative course of conduct. Feeding a starving man is good even if letting him starve to death may generate a needed public program to save more lives. The act of a pacifist or vegetarian is not to be assessed by a careful calculation of its ultimate consequences but rather by looking at the act itself and its direct consequences. The actor is asserting that he himself is doing good or avoiding harm, and that is what counts.

Can objective criteria be applied to actions so justified? It appears that in such cases the actors are behaving the way they would like us all to behave. If all others behaved similarly, these actors believe that that would be good. They are not arguing that others will follow their example, but that the act itself is inherently good. For a long time people have thought that it is moral to behave as one would like others to behave. In these cases people believe the act itself directly does good or avoids doing harm. However, if the goodness of an act depends upon indirect consequences, the act should properly be judged by those consequences.

In short, if one makes moral decisions based on the possible consequences, there is a moral requirement to be pragmatic—to calculate the re-

CHART 15–1
Questions That May Help Illuminate Our Own Moral Criteria[3]

History

How do I guess future historians are likely to judge conduct like this?
If, years hence, I myself look back at this conduct, am I more likely to be proud of it or ashamed of it?
Will it be cited to my credit or will I have to defend it?

Philosophy
What are guiding principles of which my proposed action is an application?
Are they principles that I would commend to all?

Law
Is the proposed conduct legal?
Would comparable conduct within most countries be legal?
Would the conduct be consistent with wise laws as they should be established and interpreted?

Religion
Is the proposed conduct consistent with the teachings of the world's religions?
Would the conduct be seen as an example of how a deeply religious person ought to behave?

Literature
How would I have to behave so that if a novelist or dramatist were basing a work on this incident I might be the hero of that work?
Is the proposed conduct more like that of literary heroes or literary villains?

Family and Friends
Would I be pleased to learn that a parent had behaved as I propose to behave?
Would I be proud to learn that my child had behaved this way?
Would I want my child to use this bit of conduct as a guide for his/her future actions?
If, through no doing of mine, a full account of my proposed conduct appeared on the front page of tomorrow's newspaper, is it more likely that l would be proud or embarrassed?

---

[3]Fisher, Koppelman, and Schneider, p. 113.

sults of one's action and to assess the good and the bad. Most of this book is devoted to this exercise. Before finishing an action program, we should review the coherence of our theory about what we are doing, run through our ends and our means, and check them against the moral criteria suggested by the humanities (as suggested in Chart 15–1).

To go through such a process does not guarantee that our judgment about what is moral will agree with that of others. Nor does it guarantee that two individuals, whom we would agree are equally moral, will come up with the same conclusions. It is not immoral to assign different probabilities to what is going to happen; it is not immoral to place relatively different values on short-term concerns as contrasted with long-term ones, or on social concerns as contrasted with economic or environmental concerns. To judge the morality of someone's conduct we need to have a good idea of the purpose of that action, and of the process by which the conduct was decided on. Conversely, if we know, first, that purposes were carefully selected; second, that the situation was analyzed; third, that the means were carefully designed to serve those purposes; and fourth, that both ends and means were consciously assessed in the light of the highest standards, that is about as much as we can ask.

USING INTERNATIONAL LAW MORE EFFECTIVELY

We can legitimate our demands by bringing international law to bear. The fact that there is often disagreement about points of international law has obscured the extent to which international law determines what governments want and what they are willing to do. International politics rests on foundations that are basically legal ones. Governments are legal institutions. They exercise authority over countries that are defined by legal boundaries.

Suppose a volcano erupted and created a new island off the Aleutians. If the Russians began landing troops there, the central question for the United States would be, "Is that island theirs or ours?" If it were theirs, the U.S. would expect them to put troops there. If it belonged to the U.S., the Russian action would be intolerable. Whether such an island belongs to the U.S. or to Russia is a legal question influenced by legal arguments based on maps, treaty clauses, prior discovery, occupation, and so forth. If we heard that Chinese troops had marched to within 300 miles of New Delhi, our political reaction would depend less on the physical fact than on a question of law. The first thing we would want to know is where the Indian–Chinese boundary was located.

It is worthwhile considering explicitly how international law and institutions fit into the process of causing another government to change its mind. A substantial number of people argue that law works because it is a command backed up by force, and that it takes force to influence another government. In other words, international law cannot restrain a government from doing what it wants. Each of these statements, however, is essentially false. Although there is an element of truth underlying the statements, the generalizations are wrong.

Domestic Law Restrains a Government's Behavior

There is a tendency to make a distinction between international law and "real" or domestic law, which is backed up by force. The argument then goes that since international law is not backed up by force, the kind of law that works domestically cannot be expected to work internationally. But the premise is wrong. For those in whose conduct we are interested—national governments—domestic law is backed up by less force than is international law. The process by which national governments are controlled by domestic law is more than an analogy; it demonstrates the susceptibilities of the very governments we are interested in.

The command theory of law, which was used to distinguish the law that *is* from the law that *ought to be*, was developed out of an examination of the typical private action for a tort or on a contract. If a court declared that a defendant must pay a plaintiff a stated amount, the sheriff and the marshal stood ready to enforce the judgment with the full power of the state.

That was the situation envisioned by the legal philosopher John Austin when he spoke of laws as commands. But his definition of law did not apply to rules restraining the behavior of a state. The power of the government, he said, "is incapable of *legal* limitation."[4] It followed that, in his view, a government had neither legal rights nor legal duties.

Such a definition of law, however, fails to take into account the actual behavior of governments. More than half the cases before the United States Supreme Court involve the rights or duties of the federal government, all of which are considered legal and are dealt with by legal institutions. The command theory of law—the notion that domestic law works because it is backed up by superior force—is plainly wrong when dealing with public law. Governments regularly comply with adverse court decisions. This is true not only for constitutional law, administrative law, and tax law, but even for criminal law. When a man charged with a crime is acquitted, and the court orders the government to release him, the government does so, and not because it is compelled to do so by a threat of force superior to that of the government. Legal limitations upon a government, whether they be those of constitutional law or international law, succeed or fail for reasons other than the existence of superior military force. By and large, law with respect to governments works because it affects political consequences, not military ones.

During the course of the Korean War, the steel industry of the United States was threatened with a strike. Considering the pros and cons as they

---

[4]John Austin, *Lectures on Jurisprudence or the Philosophy of Positive Law* (London: J. Murray, 1885), p. 263.

then looked, President Truman decided to seize the steel industry in order to keep it operating, and did so. The steel companies disputed the government's right to seize the industry and took the matter to court. After a few weeks of litigation the Supreme Court ordered the secretary of commerce, who had taken charge of the steel mills at the president's request, to return them to their private owners.

The Supreme Court had no regiments at its command. It had no greater force vis-à-vis the government than does the International Court of Justice sitting at The Hague. Yet the steel mills were returned. There can be little doubt that in a showdown between "the government" and the Supreme Court, the government would have won. If the president had wanted to continue to hold the steel mills, the army would have obeyed him.

The government had an initial choice when taking over the steel mills. It decided that the national interest made the action desirable. The subsequent legal process worked because it changed the question with which the government was confronted—in a number of respects. Before the Court spoke, the demand on the government was both vague and general. If articulated by the management of the steel companies, it would have been that the government must never seize private property without specific legal authority. So far as this demand was based on the Constitution, it was a general rule, coming from no one in particular and going to no one in particular. So far as the demand came from the steel companies, it came from biased persons with a personal interest in the outcome.

The consequences to the government of yielding to the demand may have looked serious. To allow steel production to stop because of a strike while American soldiers were dying in Korea would have produced a hostile political reaction within the United States. It also might have affected the conduct of the war. To accept the proposition that in time of emergency the government could do nothing to keep the most important industry operating would establish a disastrous precedent. The consequences of seizing the steel industry were more attractive. At the worst, somebody might take the case to court, and the government could face that problem when and if it arose.

The decision of the Court changed the demand to the government. It now came from a respected and disinterested body and was directed to a named individual, the secretary of commerce. The decision was not in the form of a general restriction against interfering with private property, but in the form of a narrow and explicit demand that he refrain from asserting further authority over the steel companies' property.

The fact and form of the demand also changed the consequences of the government's decision. So far as internal politics was concerned, it now made more sense to go along with the Supreme Court than to defy it. The precedent that would be established by going along with the Court's decision became a favorable one from the point of view of the government rather than an unfavorable one. On the other hand, to defy the Court's decision would establish a disastrous precedent that others might follow. Finally, the decision of the Court was narrowly directed at the particular way in which the government had acted. To accept the decision was merely to take one step back. The same end could be pursued by the government by other means.

Law enforcement against a government does not involve a command backed up by force. Rather it involves so changing the choice with which the government is confronted that its long-range interest in orderly settlement of disputes outweighs its short-run interest in winning this particular dispute.

Domestic courts may thus be taken as a model, not only for how international courts may be expected to exert influence on governments, but for other international institutions as well. Although we may not expect the statement of an international body to carry the same political impact on a government as does the legally binding decision of its own court, its impact will be greater the more its statement resembles that of a domestic court.

International Law Can Influence the Other Side

We tend to believe that, on international questions, it takes force to exert influence on other governments. But every decision of a government is a domestic one in the sense that it is made by a domestic government. Whatever the nominal subject, governmental officers are affected by the anticipated consequences of a decision both within and without the territorial limits of the country.[5] And underlying this entire book is the idea that no one ingredient of the influence process is either all-important or unimportant. Force is relevant but not all-important. In some cases it will be necessary, in others insufficient. A government will take into account the whole picture as they see it. In one situation the greatest hope of exerting influence may lie in changing one element; in another situation it will lie in changing another element, or in changing several at the same time.

To confirm the limited role that force plays—and to suggest opportunities for law and legal institutions—let us examine some ways we could exert influence on another government similar to that exerted by a court. You will note that these ways also reflect many of the concepts discussed in the previous chapter.

Make the desired decision explicit.   The more unambiguous the request the easier it is for a government to deal with.

Make the request one for inaction rather than action.   If the decision desired is not only reformulated but is reformulated in such a way that, rather than requiring a new decision, the request will be met if the other government fails to make a decision to act contrary to the request, the chance of success is further increased.

---

[5]See Peter B. Evans, Harold K. Jacobson, and Robert D. Putnam, eds., *Double Edged Diplomacy* (Berkeley, CA: University of California Press, 1993).

Have the request come from a neutral party.   If the revised request comes from an impartial source, there is a greater likelihood that the government will make the desired decision. The political cost of going along with a neutral request is far less than that of "giving in" to an adversary. In fact, under these circumstances, to decide as desired tends to establish a helpful procedural precedent, rather than a harmful one.

Have the request formed in terms of principles accepted by the other government.   If the proposed decision is formulated as one that is required by standards, policies, or rules accepted by the government we are trying to influence, it will be more readily acceptable to that government's officers. They may even regard it as their duty to go along with it.

Have the request narrowly limited to the next step.   The immediate cost of yielding to a request will be less if less is asked.

Change the decision desired.   To present a government with a different decision than the one they had previously declined to make both provides an occasion for decision and permits a decision we would like without requiring a reversal of position.

The above summary of important ways to exert influence on governments turns out also to be a summary of important ways in which international institutions can deal with an international dispute. When a dispute is referred to an international institution, whether it be the General Assembly, the Security Council, the International Court of Justice, or an *ad hoc* tribunal, commission, or committee of any kind, the foundation has been laid for changing the question facing each government. Each government is likely to be more influenced by what the international institution asks than by what an adversary asks.

A decision or recommendation of an international institution typically asks of a government something less than what was asked of them by their adversary. A neutral institution is freed from the temptation to include something extra in its demand to give it negotiating room. On the contrary, no further bargaining is usually anticipated, and the institution will recognize that the less it asks, the greater the chance of compliance with its request. Even where it asks no less, the institution can be extremely explicit about what it is asking for. The demand also comes from a neutral. Each of these facts tends to make it politically easier for a government to yield to the demand.

Law Acts As a Restraint

Although in a limited sense law cannot restrain a government from doing what it wants, law clearly affects *what* a government may want. In the absence of a legal rule to the contrary, the United States government might well conclude that it wanted to take over the oil fields of Kuwait. The existence of a rule of international law that makes it improper for the United States to seize the oil fields of Kuwait results in the United States government's not wanting to seize the fields. Even when Iraq invaded Kuwait, it tried to justify the invasion by relying on international law. Iraq argued that Kuwait was illegitimately stealing oil from Iraq's oil fields and that the border delineation between Iraq and Kuwait was illegitimate since it was carried out by colonial powers. Law, by affecting what governments want, does restrain them from doing things which they would otherwise want to do.

Example: The Cuban Missile Crisis

The variety of ways in which international law and legal institutions do and do not affect government decisions can be illustrated by looking at the predominantly nonlegal decisions of the United States government in October 1962, on what to do about the Soviet introduction of intermediate- and long-range missiles into Cuba. This example also illustrates the importance of the formulation of the demand. The following brief analysis is based on the accounts of the Cuban Missile Crisis by Elie Abel and Theodore Sorensen.[6]

The action that caused the United States government to have a problem on its hands was the secret placing in Cuba of intermediate- and long-range missiles and bomber aircraft by the Soviet Union after it had previously assured the United States that it was not doing so and was not going to do so. U.S. officials knew that they did not like what had happened and what was going on. The United States wanted the missiles not to become operable with nuclear warheads and wanted to be confident that this was the case.

International law had little to do with this objective. The United States wanted the missiles to become inoperable independent of its legal rights. But international law did play a crucial role in creating the problem. What made the U.S. response so difficult was the fact that the Soviet Union had apparently acted within its legal rights under international law. If the Soviet Union had installed the missiles on an island in the Caribbean belonging to the United States, or in an unoccupied corner of Alaska—in clear violation of international law—the U.S. would have been presented with a problem that looked totally different. The fact that the provocative act of the Soviet Union was not illegal and the fact that the objective desired by the U.S. was not one to which it was automatically entitled as a matter of international law were both central to the crisis.

International law affected what the United States tried to accomplish. It affected, implicitly if not explicitly, the selection of the three narrow objectives: having the weapons now in Cuba removed, having no further offensive weapons sent to Cuba, and having some form of international verification. No doubt U.S. military authorities would have liked to acquire the Soviet missiles and study them, for example, but the Soviet Union still had legal ownership of the missiles. There were essentially three substantive de-

---

[6]Elie Abel, *The Missile Crisis* (Philadelphia: J. B. Lippincott, 1966); Theodore Sorensen, *Kennedy* (New York: Harper & Row, 1965), p. 714.

mands: the stopping of shipment of offensive weapons to Cuba, the removal of offensive weapons that were already there, and verification. The law as such played little role in the formulation of these demands, except that the demands were limited to those on which the United States had the strongest ground. The requested relief was not to eliminate communism from the Western Hemisphere, to oust Castro, to stop all shipments to Cuba, or even to stop all shipments of arms to Cuba. It was narrowly limited to stopping shipments of offensive weapons at a designated point on the high seas and to remove forty-two missiles and other offensive weapons from Cuba.

International law provided a set of tools for the United States. International law helps one government communicate to another about the choice with which it is confronted and about the consequences of making or not making the desired decision. Law and legal institutions can help present a government with a new occasion for decision. They can also clarify and alter both the decision that is required and the consequences of making and of not making that decision.

The resolution adopted by the Organization of American States, the draft resolution submitted to the United Nations, and the proclamation of a naval quarantine issued by the president all presented the Soviet Union with new decisions.

A major way in which law operates as a tool to help one government influence another is in making more legitimate what is being asked. Legality is not simply window dressing; it can be crucial to success. The essential demand of the United States—that the Soviet Union not have nuclear missiles in Cuba—was converted by the OAS vote from the purely political demand of a nuclear adversary to the unanimous request of twenty countries of the Western Hemisphere, acting through formal procedures and pursuant to a pre-existing treaty. Countries such as Mexico and Brazil, which had demonstrated their independence of the United States, supported the resolution. The existence of the Rio Treaty and the Organization of American States made it possible to strengthen and legitimize the U.S. demand in this way. Robert Kennedy regarded this vote as crucial:

> It was the vote of the Organization of American States that gave a legal basis for the quarantine. Their willingness to follow the leadership of the United States was a heavy and unexpected blow to Khrushchev. It had a major psychological and practical effect on the Russians and changed our position from that of an outlaw acting in violation of international law into a country acting in accordance with twenty allies legally protecting their position.[7]

Taking the case to the Security Council of the United Nations also operated to strengthen the legitimacy of the United States position.

The particular demand with respect to the quarantine and the stopping of ships was undoubtedly strengthened by having it done with proper care to legalities. A formal proclamation was used, and it was issued only af-

---

[7]*McCall's,* November 1968, p. 172.

ter the vote of the Organization of American States. Abel reports that Ambassador Llewellyn Thompson "made the point that the Russians were impressed by legalities" and that "If, for example, the Organization of American States should pass a resolution endorsing the blockade, Moscow might be inclined to take it seriously."[8] Making the quarantine as legal and legitimate as possible was important not only for its direct effect on the Russians. The more legitimate the quarantine appeared to third states, the greater would be the indirect effect of their views on the Soviet Union.

On the other hand, the demand for international inspection of Cuba was never supported by a good—or even plausible—legal case. U.S. insistence on inspection was supported by a Soviet promise, but the Soviet Union clearly had no legal right to invite international inspectors to Cuba. The U.S. objective of verification had to be satisfied by air surveillance instead.

The effectiveness of an action often depends upon its legality. In discussing the quarantine, Sorensen reports:

> We could not even be certain that the blockade route was open to us. Without obtaining a two-thirds vote in the OAS—which appeared dubious at best—allies and neutrals as well as adversaries might well regard it as an illegal blockade, in violation of the UN Charter and international law. If so, they might feel free to defy it.[9]

It was on October 22 that President Kennedy announced that "All ships of any kind bound for Cuba from whatever nation or port will, if found to contain cargoes of offensive weapons, be turned back." Nevertheless, recognizing that the effectiveness of the quarantine might depend upon its legality, Kennedy held up the signing of the formal proclamation until after the Organization of American States had authorized it. Abel writes:

> The President was fully prepared to act alone if necessary. But he understood the importance of holding back the proclamation until the OAS had voted. It was, therefore, not until seven o'clock [October 23rd] that the President signed the proclamation, basing the blockade squarely on the unanimous OAS vote invoking Articles 6 and 8 of the Rio Treaty of Reciprocal Assistance.[10]

Sorensen has reported the fear that illegality might make the quarantine ineffective:

> Llewellyn Thompson . . . had emphasized the fundamental importance of obtaining OAS endorsement of the quarantine. . . . Thompson's interest was the added legal justification such endorsement would give to the quarantine under international and maritime law as well as the UN Charter. That was important, he said, not only to our maritime allies but to legalistic-minded decision-makers in the Kremlin.[11]

---

[8] Abel., p. 87.
[9] Ibid., p. 687.
[10] Ibid., p. 135.
[11] Ibid., p. 706.

Despite Khrushchev's assertion that for the U.S. Navy to stop Soviet ships on the high seas would be "piracy," it did not look like piracy to the Soviet Union or to anybody else. The formal proclamation, the designated zones, the limited list of what would be stopped—in short, the "legalistic" aspects of what was being done—were tools used by the United States better to accomplish its task.

International law may also operate as a restraint by raising the political cost that a country pays for engaging in certain conduct. There can be little doubt that one of the considerations that restrained the United States from an immediate air strike against the missile sites in Cuba was the gross illegality of such action. The attorney general is reported to have compared such a surprise attack with the attack led by Japanese Admiral Tojo on Pearl Harbor and stated, "My brother is not going to be the Tojo of the 1960's."[12]

By making offers and threats more legitimate, the law not only made them more acceptable it also made them more credible. The United States supported each of its three demands with a separate threat. The demand that Soviet ships stop was supported by the threat of shooting them (and the consequent risk of escalation) if they did not. The demand that the missiles be removed was supported by the threat of an air strike or an invasion (and the risk of escalation) if the missiles were not removed. The demand for international inspection was supported by the threat of continued unilateral aerial reconnaissance (and perhaps more) if such inspection were not established. The stronger the U.S. legal case, the more credible each of these threats, and the less costly it would have been to the U.S. to carry them out. The international procedures followed and the legal rhetoric advanced in support of the U.S. position thus operated to make the threats more influential.

TESTING THE USE OF LEGITIMACY, MORALITY, AND THE LAW

As is true for a decision made by a judge, wisdom is likely to be enhanced if a decision both makes sense in the particular case and can be justified on broad grounds. The traditional requirement that a judge write an opinion explaining her decision in terms of reason and principle helps assure that a judicial decision is a wise one. If an opinion "won't write," a judge is wise to reconsider her proposed decision.

A good check on the wisdom of any decision we propose to have somebody make is to write out the principle of which that decision is an application. This process can be used both to assure that the decision is consistent with some general policy, and that that policy appears to be a wise one.

Chart 15–2, a Tool on Policy, suggests one way of relating individual decisions to broader policies, and of checking those policies for their wisdom.

---

[12]Ibid., p. 64.

CHART 15–2
TOOL ON POLICY

Case: _____

Proposed decision-maker _____

As of: ___*(date)*_____

Proposed decision:_____

Policy: What is the policy of which the proposed decision is an application?

Step one: Draft several alternative policy statements (of, say, two or three sentences each) that a decision-maker might approve or announce at the time of his decision if he approves our proposed action program.

Step two: Review each possible policy statement against criteria that you think wise for policies, such as the following:

1. The statement is not only a sound justification of this action, but is also a wise guide for future action.

2. The statement focuses on the purpose of the action (future) rather than its cause (past).

3. It directs attention to our interests rather than to our position.

4. It provides flexibility within which we will be able to respond easily to unexpected future circumstances.

5. It reflects an objective principle, rather than an *ad hoc* judgment.

6. The principle is one we would recommend to other countries to follow.

7. The principle builds on the best of past principles.

8. The statement of principle is one that we want other countries to follow.

9. The statement tends to invite a constructive response from the other side.

To the extent that we can exploit the advantages of making a demand more legitimate in the other side's eyes, consider and articulate our moral standards, and make better use of international law, we will be more persuasive. Legitimacy becomes of practical value to our attempts to influence another party.

CHAPTER
—16—

Selecting a Point of Choice

Throughout this book, we have suggested that one of the continuing questions we ought to ask ourselves in trying to produce a decision is: Whose decision is it we are trying to affect? Within any government those making a decision must take some things as given and some as subject to their own choice. The more precisely we can focus attention on those we are trying to influence, the more accurately we will be able to make a judgment about what it is possible for them to do and what is beyond their capacity. Thus a critical decision will be to determine whom we want to influence.

We may need to rethink our assumption about the person whose choice we have been considering. So far, it has been the person whom we have presumably been trying to influence. It may be that we need to shift to some more promising target. The tools and charts offered in this book are most useful if we are flexible about how we use them. For example, if, after analysis, the prime minister of France does not appear likely to make a constructive decision that we want made, perhaps we should shift our focus onto some other French citizen in business, professional, or political life. One of the key aspects of converting a troublesome situation into an operational choice is to focus on somebody who can do something about it. Disliked symptoms are simply problems until we start to think in terms of individuals or institutions that are in a position to make a difference. Our original working assumptions about "the other side" may need to be reexamined so that we are directing our efforts in the direction that we conclude is most promising. Who is it that we ought to consider the target? The person who is "their prince" may change as we evaluate who shows the most promise for being open to influence and being in a position to change the situation.

ASK THE PERSON WITH THE POWER TO DECIDE

One of the reasons one side often makes unreasonable demands is that it is, in effect, asking the wrong group within a country, the wrong country, or perhaps the wrong group of countries, and those it is asking to decide are unable or unwilling to make the decision it wants. A party's estimate of how much those it is presently asking take as given and not subject to change is approximate at best, since what it is possible for them to decide is partly a function of how hard they try. Having this in mind, one side may want to let its reach exceed its grasp—but not by too much. One side's chance of success will be enhanced if it can change its demand so that those it is asking to decide are capable of doing so.

In the Cuban Missile Crisis, for example, it was usually quite clear when the United States was talking to Cuba and when to Moscow. The U.S. failed only when it asked Moscow to agree to on-the-ground inspection in Cuba, a demand on which the Russians could not, and therefore predictably did not, deliver. The U.S. had made a demand of a party that was not able to make the decision, and it wisely accepted the substitute of air surveillance.

In selecting the party on whom we try to exert influence, we should look ahead to the decision we want instead of looking back at those who may have caused the situation we do not like. The government of North Vietnam, for example, may have trained and supplied the Vietcong, organized, financed, and established the National Liberation Front, and directed the entire effort to overthrow the South Vietnamese government. But these military and political forces having been set in motion, it did not follow that the leadership in North Vietnam could have been able by itself to call off the entire war of liberation.

Outsiders almost invariably oversimplify the unity of the political body they are trying to influence. Many people in the United States talked of trying to influence "the Communist world" to abandon its aggressive ways or to reach some other decision, when it was abundantly clear that the numerous governments and revolutionary leaders who were thus lumped together rarely, if ever, reached a collective decision on anything.

The lumping of U.S. adversaries in Vietnam, for example, into one personified "enemy" confused what the U.S. was trying to obtain. The coalition against which the United States fought in Vietnam included China, Russia, and North Vietnam under a strained political alliance with people from the South, including hard-core Communists, nationalists, anticolonialists, loyalists, and local politicians interested in their own positions. It is difficult to think of any position which that group, acting together, could have made in negotiations. If the U.S. required a collective decision in response to its bombing program, there was probably no decision that particular conglomeration of political interests could have made except to continue what they had been doing—fighting, resistance, terror. Even supposing that the U.S. had been able to draft and present a proposition for a cease-fire or mutual program of de-escalation that would have been attractive to some of these groups, others would have demurred and continued fighting.

If the U.S. had asked itself more accurately whom it was trying to influence, it might have attempted to pursue a policy of influencing individual groups that were more inclined to be influenced by the U.S. and that were sufficiently cohesive to split off and make a favorable decision. Perhaps district leaders in the South had sufficient command in their villages or districts to be able to decide to opt out of the war and to accept some kind of local cease-fire agreement. If the only decision we can imagine our adversaries conceivably making collectively is one that we do not want, we should pursue policies that attempt to influence them separately. Analogous to the military policy of divide and conquer, we should divide so they can decide.

BE SURE THE DECISION ACTUALLY BENEFITS THE DECISION-MAKER

One way to improve the impact of an offer is to focus on the beneficiary of the offer and his relationship to those we are asking to make the decision. We may be able to improve the effectiveness of the offer by changing those on whom it has its primary impact. It may be possible, for example, to have the beneficial consequences of a decision fall on those who are more closely involved in the decision. The offer for many years to all South Africans of "free participation in a political democracy" if they would agree to constitutional government was not much of an offer to those who had the power to make a decision. They were not going to be better off in terms of power. An offer addressed to the white South African government needed to deal with ways of lessening their fear of a takeover in the near future by the black majority. When we have identified those to whom the offer is being made, we want to be sure that it appeals to them.

Typically a government making a gesture of friendship looks first to its domestic constituency. Does what we are promising our adversary sound good at home? We also test the offer by the reactions of spectators—international third parties. Does this offer sound generous to others? Only occasionally does it seem important that the consequences of a desired decision be attractive to those we are trying to influence. The normal tendency is to treat the offer part of a decision as window dressing for domestic consumption. We measure our offer in terms of our own values or those of neutrals rather than by the values of our adversary. But the offer will not exert influence unless it appeals to those we are asking to make a decision. They are the ones whose reaction counts most. It is just as important to identify clearly those we are attempting to reward as it is to identify those we are trying to threaten.

CHOOSE A FEASIBLE DECISION-MAKER

Among those capable of making the decision we should select the most promising target. A domestic lobbyist knows that any congressperson might introduce some proposed legislation, but he concentrates on the most promising one. Depending on the character of the decision, we may wish to focus on a group or on an individual. Groups are prone not to reach certain kinds of decisions. Taiwan, for example, may be best able to influence the United States to reverse its policy of nonrecognition of Taiwan by having the matter raised in Congress. Although the nominal power of recognition resides with the president, a congressional debate could have a substantial and accelerating effect. On the other hand, if China wishes the U.S. to continue its policy, it might concentrate on having the matter raised privately for presidential decision.

Since the very concept of decision involves some finality, we may be unable to influence those on whom we have been working to change their collective mind. One attempt at influence having failed, we may wish to identify a different person to influence simply to try somebody different. Having failed to persuade the Soviet Union to reconvene the Geneva Conference to deal with Vietnam, the United States might have tried to select some other influential neutrals, such as the pope or the Organization of African Unity, and to develop a comparable decision that they might be expected to make.

NOMINATE POTENTIAL "PRINCES" ON THEIR SIDE

A standard approach to sound decisionmaking is first to generate a range of options and then to select from among them. Generating such a list here will free us from any fixed view about who it is that we should be trying to influence. A checklist of categories of people and organizations may be helpful. The tool in Chart 16–1 suggests a simple form that may be useful. Chart 16–2 is an example filled in, dealing with the violence in Northern Ireland; "we" are seen as a would-be peacemaker looking for points of choice where decisions might be made that could result in reducing the violence. In these circumstances we have the broadest range of princes—they might be on one or the other side of the conflict or they might be potential third parties. The concept of "our prince" is clearest when we are on one side of a conflict or when we have a fixed and certain advisee. In Northern Ireland we might, for example, assume that we are advising the head of an American group that wants to end the violence in Northern Ireland. If we have no fixed advisee, we may be looking for one. In these circumstances, any person on our list of significant decision-makers is not only a potential "their prince" but, if we might find access to him, a candidate to be "our prince" as well.

The important feature of such a list is that each item on it should be a decisional unit—someone or some entity that is capable of making a decision by itself. "All American companies investing in Northern Ireland" would not be a point of choice since no choice is made by that group acting jointly. Companies investing in Northern Ireland do not sit down together and reach a decision. We often speak of large groups as though they could solve the problem if only "they" would behave in a certain way. "If Americans would stop being so ethnocentric, the world would be a better place." "If international news media devoted less attention to political violence, there would be less incentive to commit it." But Americans do not jointly decide how self-centered to be. Nor do the international news media reach a collective decision on how much time and space to devote to the reporting of political violence.[1]

---

[1]Roger Fisher, Elizabeth Kopelman, and Andrea Kupfer Schneider, *Beyond Machiavelli* (Cambridge, MA: Harvard University Press, 1994), pp. 99–100.

CHART 16–1
POINT-OF-CHOICE TOOL
Selecting a Point of Choice

(Names of persons—or small groups that decide as a unit—
who could make an important decision that we would
like made, on whom we might focus our efforts)

Case: _Violence in Northern Ireland_
Our role: _Peacemaker_
"Their side": _IRA provisionals_
Other Party: _Protestant extremists_
As of: _1996_

Some Kinds of People	Particular Persons Whose Decisions Might Be Worth Seeking
Governmental _governmental decision-_ _makers as such_ _top leader_ _minister / cabinet officer_ _diplomat_ _other government_ _official_ _legislator_	
Other political leader	
Military person	
Business corporation or _business leader_	
Religious leader	
Person with money	
Writer / journalist	
Media executive	
Academic	
Nongovernmental _organization_	
International organization	
Musician / Artist	
Athlete	

CHART 16–2
POINT-OF-CHOICE TOOL
Selecting a Point of Choice

(Names of persons—or small groups that decide as a unit—
who could make an important decision that we would
like made, on whom we might focus our efforts)

Case: _Violence in Northern Ireland_
Our role: _Peacemaker_
Their side: _IRA provisionals_
Other party: _Protestant extremists_
As of: _1996_

Some Kinds of People	**Particular Persons Whose Decisions Might Be Worth Seeking**

Governmental
   governmental decision-
     makers as such
   top leader
   minister/cabinet
     officer
   diplomat
   other government
     official
   legislator
	British government
	Republic of Ireland
	
	Senator Edward Kennedy
	
	Ulster Protestant politician

Other political leader	_Northern Irish Catholic politician_
Military person	_Paramilitary leadership on_ _Protestant side_ _Leadership of IRA paramilitary_

Business corporation or
  business leader
	Corporation investing in Northern
	  Ireland

Religious leader	_The pope; Archbishop of Canterbury_
Person with money	
Writer/journalist	_An editor at the_ Christian Science Monitor

[Others may include media executive, academic, nongovernmental and international organizations.]

SELECT THE TARGET POINT OF CHOICE[2]

From among the names on our list we should tentatively select the most promising candidate—the one our future efforts will be intended to influence. This will be the person who, taking into account all of the analysis about purpose and strategy, is best situated for making the decision we want. In the light of further work we may change our mind and decide to work on somebody else, but at all times as we go about the task of designing a target choice it is helpful to have in mind, at least provisionally, some specific point where that choice could be made.

If we are seeking to influence a group, such as a committee, a cabinet, or a board of directors that does not act as a decisional unit, it may still help to think of our efforts as being directed toward one person within that group—somebody who is going to take the initiative and then be able to carry that group along with him or her. We will want to think of what will be needed to convince that person, and then of the arguments that he or she will need in order to convince others. As we look over our list of potential points of choice we may want to note special features that make one candidate or another more attractive from our point of view.

The great virtue of this list lies in the extent to which a muddy problem is clarified by looking at it in terms of the possible actions of first one person and then another. Issues of group dynamics and organizational behavior are seen as they impinge on the single decision-maker that we have selected. We are not trying to predict what that person is in fact going to do. We have rather picked this person as someone who could make a difference if he or she could be persuaded to do so.

If this process of selecting a point of choice has resulted in our focusing on a person other than the one whom we were treating as our presumptive adversary, we should now construct a Currently Perceived Choice for this new person. For example, if we have decided to give up on the prime minister of France and to work on someone else instead, then we should prepare a list of estimated consequences that we use to outline the currently perceived choice of the person we have selected, using the tools first introduced in Chapters 4 and 5.

---

[2]Fisher, Kopelman, and Schneider, pp. 100–101.

CHAPTER
—17—

Finding a "Yesable" Proposition

❖ ❖ ❖

As we seek to influence someone to take some action, we need some way to estimate whether what we propose to do is likely to produce the results we desire. If we are to undertake various actions in order to be effective in exerting influence, we need a way of looking at the new choice we are trying to create for the other side to say "yes" to. This will help us organize their perceptions and interests, as well as our new thinking on the problem, into a way that we can understand and that will make it easier to construct such a new choice.

Before trying to change a party's choice, we will want to design the new situation, one in which they will face a choice to which a decision-maker might reasonably say "yes." In doing so we will take into account the things we may be able to change and those we may not be able to change. For example, if the Currently Perceived Choice of a decision-maker is "Shall I give in to the rebels?" we might want the new choice to look more like "Shall I take a chance on the new five-point program proposed by a third party?" Whatever the "five-point program" is, the very structure of the new choice already looks more attractive to our decision-maker.

RETURN TO THEIR CURRENTLY PERCEIVED CHOICE

The suggested approach is again to focus on the consequences of a choice. This time, rather than making an intelligence analysis of the currently perceived choice of the person we are going to try to influence, as we did in Chapter 5, we look ahead a few weeks or a few months and design a future choice that we may be able to present to the decision-maker. How would that future choice have to look in order for this person to decide as we would like him or her to decide?

In building a Target Future Choice chart we will look back at the CPC (Chart 5–5)—the chart that reflects our estimate of the decision-maker's currently perceived choice. The present situation reflects the existing problem: the decision-maker is not saying "yes" to the choice that he sees. In the Target Future Choice, the decision-maker should see his choice so that in our judgment the consequences he will anticipate from saying "yes" have a good chance of looking more attractive to him than the consequences he will anticipate from saying "no."

We consider the specific consequences that will be most important to a specific person on the other side, such as "I look good" or "I keep power." Other important elements for him may be the support of his colleagues, legitimacy in his own eyes, or keeping his options open.[1]

Each Target Future Choice (TFC) is an attempt to construct consequences that one side might realistically be expected to foresee if it should say "yes" or "no" to the same question. Such questions might be: "In view of the terms of reference, should we attend the conference to which we have been invited?" or "Should we comply with the cease-fire as ordered by the Security Council?" or our earlier example, "Shall I accept the five-point plan proposed by a third party?" Having developed an understanding of how the consequences should strike each side, we are better equipped to try to draft the terms of the proposed decision. We basically work backwards in constructing the choice. First we look at what type of choice, any choice, might be acceptable to the other side and then we determine the specifics of that choice.

DRAFTING A TARGET FUTURE CHOICE

The following four pages illustrate the process of drafting a Target Future Choice chart. At this point, we do not know the specifics of Plan X. We are rather analyzing the factors that any plan would have to take into account in order to be accepted. The following charts illustrate an analysis of the issue of East Jerusalem. Charts 17–1 and 17–2 show the Currently Perceived Choice with respect to Jerusalem, first as it appears to the government of Israel and then as it looks to Palestinian leadership. Charts 17–3 and 17–4 show Target Future Choices, as they should perhaps appear if each side is going to respond affirmatively to the question: "Should we agree to Plan X for East Jerusalem?"

---

[1]Roger Fisher, Elizabeth Kopelman, and Andrea Kupfer Schneider, *Beyond Machiavelli* (Cambridge, MA: Harvard University Press, 1994), pp. 56–66.

CHART 17–1
CURRENTLY PERCEIVED CHOICE TOOL

Case: *The Sovereignty of East Jerusalem*
As of: *1995*

The Currently Perceived Choice of *The prime minister of Israel* .
Question faced: *" Shall we agree to return East Jerusalem to Arab Sovereignty* ?"

Consequences If We Say "Yes"	Consequences If We Say "No"
– We will be fiercely criticized by our constituency and condemned as traitors by many. Perhaps we will be thrown out of office.	+ We have the strong backing of our constituency.
– We weaken our bargaining position as the Arabs ask for more.	+ We maintain a strong bargaining position.
– We don't know what we'll get in return.	+ We won't have given up anything.
– Walls and barbed wired divide Jerusalem again.	+ Jerusalem remains united.
– We will lose access to the Wailing Wall, the Old City, the Jewish Quarter, the Mount of Olives, and the rest of East Jerusalem.	+ We continue to have free and secure access to the Old City, and to all of Jerusalem.
– The security of West Jerusalem will be threatened by saboteurs and hostile soldiers.	+ We maintain our security.
– Tens of thousands of Israelis will be expelled from their homes in Ramot, Ranot Eshkol, etc.	+ The residents of the new quarters in East Jerusalem continue to live there and the building continues.

But:	**But:**
+ We might increase the chances for peace with the Arab states.	– We may delay peace with the Arab states. (However, we won't get peace with the Syrians anyway.)
+ The world, including our ally the U.S., is pleasantly surprised.	– Foreigners may criticize us.

CHART 17–2
CURRENTLY PERCEIVED CHOICE TOOL

Case: *The Sovereignty of East Jerusalem*

As of: *1995*

The Currently Perceived Choice of *Yasser Arafat*   .

Question faced: *" Shall we agree to the Israeli claim of sovereignty over East Jerusalem   ?"*

Consequences If We Say "Yes"	Consequences If We Say "No"
– *We will be fiercely condemned as traitors by our people, and will lose our positions, prestige, and perhaps even our lives.*	+ *Our people strongly back us.*
– *We destroy our unity—our chief strength.*	+ *We maintain our unity.*
– *We give up our claim to rule ourselves.*	+ *We stick to our goal of self-determination, which we will probably achieve sooner or later.*
– *We give up our claim to patronship over the Al-Asqa Mosque, the Dome of the Rock, and Jerusalem, the third holiest city in Islam.*	+ *We maintain our claim to occupied Jerusalem which we may get back.*
– *We resign ourselves to confiscation of our lands, Israeli police control, humiliating security checks, Israeli taxes, and interference in the education of our children.*	+ *We continue to protest Israeli occupation and repression.*
– *Our Arab brothers condemn us as traitors.*	+ *We have the strong backing of the whole Arab world.*
– *The whole world, including the U.S., is stunned.*	+ *The whole world, including the U.S., supports our legitimate demands.*
– *The Israelis will still want more and may raise their demands seeing our concessions and weaknesses.*	+ *We maintain a strong bargaining position.*

But:	But:
+ *The Israelis will be pleasantly surprised.*	– *The confrontation continues.*
+ *We may get some local autonomy in East Jerusalem.*	– *We may get some local autonomy anyway.*

CHART 17–3
TARGET FUTURE CHOICE TOOL

Case: *The Sovereignty of East Jerusalem*
As of: _1995_

The Possible Future Choice of *The prime minister of Israel* .
Question faced: "*Should we agree to Plan X for East Jerusalem* ?"

Consequences If We Say "Yes"	Consequences If We Say "No"
+ *We enter peace negotiations with the Arab states and the Palestinians.*	– *We forgo what may be the <u>last</u> chance of peace.*
+ *The whole world, including the U.S., praises us.*	– *We are criticized by the whole world.*
+ *We are supported on the whole by most of our constituency.*	– *We are strongly criticized at home.*
+ *Terrorism might abate.*	– *Terrorism will probably be stepped up. There will probably be a war sometime in the near future.*
+ *Jerusalem will prosper with an increase in tourism and trade with the Arab countries.*	– *Jerusalem will continue to be in financial trouble.*
+ *Jerusalem will remain an open, undivided city.*	
+ *We will continue to control the Wailing Wall and the Jewish Quarter.*	
+ *We will continue to enjoy free and secure access to the whole of Jerusalem.*	
+ *Israelis can continue to live in any part of the city. Israelis in the new quarters in East Jerusalem will remain in their current living conditions.*	

But:	But:
– *There is still considerable opposition, including many in our own party who call us traitors.*	+ *We will have some domestic support.*
– *There is a chance that the arrangements will break down and Jerusalem will be divided again.*	+ *We safeguard with our own forces a united Jerusalem.*

CHART 17–4
TARGET FUTURE CHOICE TOOL

Case: _The Sovereignty of East Jerusalem_
As of: _1995_

The Possible Future Choice of _Yasser Arafat_   .
Question faced: _" Should we agree to Plan X for East Jerusalem   ?"_

Consequences If We Say "Yes"	**Consequences If We Say "No"**
+ We rule ourselves in East Jerusalem for the first time in history.	– We lose what will be the last chance for a long time to rule ourselves in East Jerusalem.
+ We are supported on the whole by our people.	– New leaders, ready to accept Plan X, are emerging with popular support.
+ We regain patronship over the Haram-al-Sharaf.	– Israel retains control over Haram-al-Sharaf.
+ There is no more confiscation of lands. Lands confiscated since 1967 are compensated at fair rates.	– Our lands continue to be confiscated as we increasingly become an Arab island in a Jewish ocean.
+ We police and tax ourselves. We control our own schools.	– We continue under Israeli occupation; Israel controls taxes and education with no end in sight.
+ Our security is guaranteed.	– There will probably be a war in the near future in which our people will suffer greatly.
+ We are supported by most Arab countries, including Saudi Arabia and Egypt.	

But:	**But:**
– There is still some opposition among our people.	+ We still have much support among our people.
– Some Arab states may criticize us.	+ We still have the support of many Arab states.

We finally reach the question: What shall we do? Rather than starting with that question, as is so frequently done, we have first analyzed the situation, acquired an understanding of the Currently Perceived Choice of the other side (in the case of Jerusalem, two "other sides"), and have developed a general idea of the choice we would like to see them face in the near future in the furtherance of our purposes. Now we have to decide what specific question to ask of what party in order to put our ideas into action. We now implement the concepts which we have discussed in the book in order to decide what our specific question should be.

In moving from broad approach to detailed application, we are going to have to proceed by cutting and fitting, by trial and error, and by modifying variables over and over again until what we propose to do makes sense as tested in different ways. Intuition, common sense, experience, and judgment will all save time in inventing a program of action that we are prepared to recommend; but that program should stand up to a series of objective tests of a fairly rigorous kind. The key task of devising an action program is to figure out what one party should do in order to change the choice of a decision-maker on the other side from the one he currently perceives to the choice that we would like him to perceive in the near future. We should craft our action program to produce circumstances paralleling the Target Future Choice charts of the parties. These charts, which elucidate the possible choice of the decision-makers, are designed so that the choice is both one that our action program will be able to produce and one that is likely to cause the decision-makers to make affirmative decisions. This is to be accomplished by going back and forth, adjusting one then the other. We need not seek 100 percent confidence that they will decide as we want; all we want is a sufficient chance of success to justify our effort.

CONSTRUCTING A "YESABLE" PROPOSITION

As suggested in the discussion of formulating a Target Future Choice, it is often best to start by looking at the way some important consequences will have to be seen by their prince in order for us to expect a favorable decision. How will the pros and cons of "the X Plan" have to appear in order for their prince to find it acceptable? Now we have to turn to the precise content of that plan. What are some specific decisions that we might want and might expect the parties to make? Instead of simply confronting parties with a problem, we should identify one or more specific solutions to that problem that we would like them to accept.

Putting our objective in the form of a decision to which a party could say "yes" makes us think through our position and the ways in which we will want to go about exerting influence. As we pointed out in Chapter 14, too often our demand—the decision we desire—is vague simply because our own thinking is vague. Events have not forced us to be specific, and we have failed to recognize the impact that a specific offer or requested decision might have. We will almost always have a better chance of getting something we want if we know some specific things we would like to have.

There are strong advantages in communicating a simple and decidable question to the government we are trying to influence. Essentially, these advantages flow from the fact that the more work we do the less work there is for them to do, and the more likely they are to do it. It is not enough to present a government with alternative consequences: "If you do nothing about your population problem, you will be ruined; if you solve it, you can have economic growth and prosperity." The government will clearly prefer the second set of consequences to the first, but no decision will result. There is nothing to which they can say "yes" that will get them there. A memorandum to a government official that makes a particular proposal and ends

Yes   _____
No   _____

is far more likely to produce a decision than one that points out a problem and suggests that something ought to be done about it.

What is likely in the case of a decision by an individual is even more likely in the case of a decision by a group of individuals such as those who constitute a government. Here the difficulties of group decision are superimposed on the difficulties which each member of the group would face in reaching a decision by himself or herself. Within a bureaucracy, those who have worked out a specific plan and come forward with a "yesable" proposition are likely to carry the day.

The deliberations leading up to the Bay of Pigs disaster provide a good example of the importance of developing "yesable" propositions. President Kennedy's decision to go ahead with that operation against Cuba was no doubt affected by the fact that on one side he was presented with a well-staffed proposal in a "yesable" form. If the president accepted the recommendation of the Central Intelligence Agency, things would happen. He would not immediately be presented with a host of additional problems to work out. His alternative recommendation was to "do something else." Apparently there were no specific suggestions as to what should be done with the Cuban refugees training in Guatemala, how the government should deal with the disclosure problem, and what public position the president should take to minimize the domestic and international political costs. If there had been equally well prepared plans in equally "yesable" form for this alternative, the president's decision might well have been different.

Much international communication is like smoke signals in a high wind. The more ambiguous the message the greater the chance for distortion and misunderstanding. The more strained the relationship the more likely that an adversary will interpret an ambiguous proposal or demand in the worst possible light. By presenting another party with a specific draft—a "yesable" proposition—we can cut through some of the suspicion about our intentions and encourage them to evaluate the real costs and benefits of making the decision we want them to make.

Operationally, it is good to write out drafts of the very words that we might like another party to accept. It often helps to write out several alternative versions in varying degrees of detail. One can think of it as writing out the brief statement that their decision-maker might sign, or might send as instructions to some subordinate official.

Time and again those involved in an international conflict fail to convert their objective into the decision that they would like an adversary to make. Although they often think of themselves as doing what they are doing in an effort to influence their adversaries, they do not go so far as to think out just what kind of decision they might reasonably expect of their adversary. For example, those who organized political violence on behalf of the Palestinian cause failed for years to formulate a plausible decision that the Israeli government might make in response to that violence. From the Israeli point of view such violence killed fewer Israelis than were killed by the taxi drivers of Israel on the highway from Jerusalem to Tel Aviv; it was terrible but there was no realistic decision that could bring it to an end. The Palestinians offered them a problem, not a solution.

Similarly, those in authority who were trying to reduce the political violence committed by Catholic extremists in Northern Ireland proceeded for years without offering the IRA a "yesable" proposition. Presumably the decision desired was for the IRA to issue an order to stop all violence—in exchange for nothing. Such a choice was unlikely to appear realistic to those who at great risk had been fighting for years for a cause they considered just. The formulation of a "yesable" proposition is a useful way of converting our general objective into a specific one. It can be performed internally by those on one side. Whether to communicate a proposed "yesable" proposition to the other party, and if so, how, are questions that are separable from the construction of the proposition. It may be that direct communication from us will look like an ultimatum in which they have had no input. Perhaps the suggestion should come from a third party. Even so, we should work on it. We should know some decisions that would satisfy us, either to transmit them ourselves or to suggest to a third party.

We can return to the example of Vietnam to illustrate the difference between the demand made by the United States and the "yesable" proposition that could have been made. Perhaps the clearest statement of the U.S. position in Vietnam was in the president's speech of September 29, 1967, the so-called San Antonio formula:

> The United States is willing to stop all aerial and naval bombardment of North Vietnam when this will lead promptly to productive discussion. We, of course, assume that while discussions proceed, North Vietnam would not take advantage of the bombing cessation or limitation.

This was not a casually drafted statement. Walt Rostow, special assistant to the president, later explained that every word had a purpose and a meaning: discussions must be held "promptly," they must be "productive," and so forth.

The president's statement was, however, a carefully drafted answer to the wrong question. It was an answer to the question, "What should our policy be?" If the U.S. really wanted productive discussions to be held promptly, the U.S. should have said something that would have made that event more likely. As it was, it was not enough for North Vietnam to respond that talks would be held promptly after attacks on North Vietnam stopped. The United States then engaged in extensive "probes" in an effort to determine what North Vietnam "intended" when it agreed that talks would be promptly held. Rather than having confronted North Vietnam with a statement of U.S. "policy," the U.S. could have made sure that the North Vietnamese were confronted with a choice that both was mechanically simple and stood a good chance of being politically acceptable.

An illustration of the kind of "yesable" proposition that might have shortened the war in Vietnam would have been, for example, an invitation from some legitimate source to a specific conference to be held at a given time and place. For example, India, as chairman of the International Control Commission, might have sent a note along the following lines:

> The following parties are hereby invited to send representatives to attend a meeting of the International Control Commission in New Delhi at the Ministry of External Affairs Building to be held for three weeks beginning at 10 A.M. local time on Monday, the 4th of next month:
>
> > The government of the Democratic Republic of Vietnam, Hanoi
> > The government of the Republic of Vietnam, Saigon
> > The National Liberation Front of Vietnam
> > The United States
>
> The governments of Poland and of Canada, being the other members of the Control Commission, have each already indicated their willingness to have a representative attend the meeting. The purpose of the meeting is to advise the Commission as to measures that might be undertaken (1) to establish and maintain a cease-fire throughout Vietnam, and (2) to implement the Geneva Accords of 1954.
>
> To facilitate the work of the Commission and to improve the prospects for peace in Vietnam, all parties are hereby requested to implement effective at 2:00 A.M. local time on Sunday, the 3rd of next month, a general reduce-fire throughout all Vietnam, such reduce-fire to include a cessation of all major offensive military action, including a cessation of the bombing and other armed attacks against North Vietnam, it being understood that no party should take military advantage of the reduced military activities on the part of an adversary.
>
> Any party not wishing to send a formal representative to the meeting may send an unofficial observer or may designate any person, including the representative of some other party, to convey their views officially or unofficially to the Commission, to others attending the meeting, or to both. The meeting will

take place as scheduled whether or not all invited parties decide to attend the opening sessions, provided only that the Commission finds that the general reduce-fire is in effect in Vietnam.

The above example is not intended to prove that North Vietnam would in fact have accepted such an invitation or to prove that discussions if held would have been productive. It is intended to illustrate what is meant by a "yesable" proposition.

CHECKING OUR CHOICE

You may have been so concerned with constructing an action program that would influence those on the other side that you may have neglected to look at that action program from our side's point of view. If you have been careful in your work, the action program should be one that has a good chance of successfully exerting influence on the other side. But is the result worth the effort?

We may now construct a simple balance sheet looking at the choice for our prince. Our prince is the decision-maker we are asking to make a proposal to the other side. The question facing our prince is, "Should I accept the recommended action program?" We have given him a "yesable" proposition, but is it one to which he ought to say "yes"? If he does say "yes" the primary advantage, presumably, is that there is a good chance that the other side will make a decision that we would like them to make. But what are the negative aspects of implementing the action program? Presumably there are costs in terms of time and effort. There may also be some expectable negative reactions from others, or costs in terms of precedent, reputation, or some other purpose of ours on which we were not, for the moment, concentrating our attention. A rigorous look at our prince's balance sheet is essential before we convert our bright idea into a recommended decision. Chart 17–5 is an example of our prince's Target Future Choice.

CHART 17–5
TARGET FUTURE CHOICE TOOL[2]

Case: _Proposal of the X Plan_
As of: _____

The Target Future Choice of _Our prince_ _____ .
Question faced: " _Should I agree to propose Plan X to their prince_ _____ ?"

Consequences If We Say "Yes"	Consequences If We Say "No"
+ _Plan X meets my interests._	
+ _I need not abandon any prior positions._	
+ _If Plan X succeeds, I get the credit and my influence grows._	– _I have little chance for recognition._
+ _If plan X fails, I can avoid the blame._	
+ _I keep my options open, and can propose, or not propose, other solutions in the future._	– _I miss a fading opportunity, and there will be more obstacles in the future._
+ _It is easy. All I have to do is sign a document / make a statement._	
+ _There is a chance of success._	
+ _The issue is (at least partially) resolved._	– _Nothing is resolved._
But:	**But:**
	+ _I have not abandoned my position._

> _If we are to propose to a decision-maker that he or she take some action—for example, to propose a course of action to another party in the conflict—our proposal to the decision-maker must be formulated in such a way that the proposal is in the decision-maker's interest as well._

---

[2]Fisher, Kopelman, and Schneider, p. 104.

The choice will have more chance of being accepted if we look at the parties' restraints on making a choice. This is not to say that even understanding their restraints will lead to a favorable decision, but if there is a possibility of acceptance, making it more likely to be accepted will only help.

As one formulates a "yesable" proposition and tries to make it potentially acceptable, the proposed decision often becomes smaller and smaller. We find ourselves wanting to propose a course of conduct involving many decisions over a period of time, yet coming to recognize that decisions are made one at a time. To some extent this can be met by pointing out that one of the advantages of making decision A is that it can be followed up with decisions B, C, and D. Another technique is to propose as the first decision a public statement, which includes commitments to a course of conduct (this method is usually more appropriate when trying to influence our prince than when trying to influence someone in a more adversarial role).

TESTING OUR ADVICE

One of the most difficult tasks is that of assessing the political viability of new ideas. The reality of the world imposes serious constraints on the decisions that political leaders and others are in fact willing to make. Faced with the statistical probability that small proposals of a routine nature are more likely to be approved than fresh and unusual suggestions—and working in an environment where success is often measured by appearing to be "sound"—bureaucrats tend to overemphasize the restraints on a leader's choice. One can rest assured that it was no bureaucratic underling who suggested that Sadat fly to Jerusalem, or that President Carter commit himself to two solid weeks of a Camp David meeting. Staff tend to assume that political constraints are greater than they are.

Yet serious political restraints on choice do exist. How to estimate them is difficult. In countries with a parliamentary democracy, one might in theory try to count votes. Or where public opinion polls exist, one might look to them. But in all countries, leaders are not wholly confined by public opinion; they have some power to lead. How can we best assess the political constraints on new ideas?

Any leader who makes a new decision will want to be able to justify it to his or her constituents (whether colleagues or the public) and will be concerned with the criticisms that others may advance. One way to get a feel for the plausibility of a proposed decision is to write out two or three strong points that the decision-maker might make in support of his or her decision. Then one can write out two or three strong attacks on the decision that might be publicly made by critics at home or abroad. Looking at the extent to which the proposed decision is vulnerable to criticism may help us reformulate it to make it less vulnerable. Writing out the strongest statement that we think could made in support of the decision may also suggest possible improvements. The two sets of statements should help us assess the possibility that the decision-maker might be persuaded to go ahead.

Another useful way to think about the affirmative case for a decision is to draft the text of a possible radio or television broadcast announcing it. A few sentences or a couple of paragraphs will often be enough to suggest either that an idea is wholly unrealistic or that it might, in fact, be possible.

In the course of suggesting to Iran and the United States that they accept Algerian mediation of the 1980 hostage case, and that the basis of these discussions be that neither side should get more than that to which it was entitled, each government was shown drafts illustrating how each could explain such a mediated outcome to its constituents. These drafts are set forth in Charts 17–6 and 17–7.[3]

CHART 17–6
POSSIBLE IRANIAN STATEMENT

During the past year, Iran has asked from the United States nothing more than that to which in our view Iran is entitled under international law, morality, custom, and the right of self-determination.

1. We wanted the world to be aware of the grievances which Iran suffered from more than 25 years under Mohammed Reza, who was actively supported by the United States Government;

2. We insisted that the Shah not be free to live abroad in luxury while the Iranian people suffered from the results of his reign;

3. We demanded that the United States Government fully accept the Iranian revolution;

4. We demanded a firm commitment from the United States Government never again to intervene in our internal affairs;

5. We demanded an end to economic warfare against the Iranian people;

6. We demanded assurance that no more punitive action would be taken against Iran by the United States;

7. We insisted that the United States cooperate in helping locate public funds wrongfully removed from Iran by the ex-Shah;

8. We demanded that the "nest-of-spies"—the U.S. Embassy compound from which the CIA aided the Shah—be closed and that future diplomatic facilities be established only by agreement with the Islamic Republic of Iran.

On all these points we have now succeeded. The ex-Shah has gone to face a judgment far more severe than any we could impose upon him. The United States has now accepted the above demands. The U.S. hostages no longer serve any useful purpose here, and they are accordingly being returned to their families.

---

[3]Fisher, Kopelman, and Schneider, pp. 116–17.

CHART 17–7
POSSIBLE U.S. STATEMENT

I am pleased to announce that all American hostages held in Iran since last November have now left Iran on their way home to the United States.

The release of the hostages constitutes a great success for the principled steadfastness of the American people and of the hostages themselves. In connection with their release I would like to make three major points:

1. We paid no blackmail. The American people have shown that they will not be coerced. We refused to turn over the Shah; we refused to pay ransom of any kind. Iran is receiving no more than that to which they would have been entitled under our own interpretation of international law if they had never taken the hostages.

2. Iran has been punished. As the result of measures taken by the United States and other countries, Iran's economy is in a disastrous state. Its international prestige has never been lower. Domestically the government is beset by infighting and disarray. Thus, Iran has paid a high price for its outrageous action. In return, they have gotten nothing that they could not otherwise have obtained much sooner.

3. The stability of the region is more important than further punishment of Iran. Although Iran may deserve still more punishment, we must give higher priority to the United States' long-term security interests in that part of the world. Ending our dispute with Iran will strengthen the independence and security of all the peoples of the Gulf region and reduce the risk of Soviet intervention. While we must not forget the past—the courageous steadfastness of the hostages and the bravery of those who gave their lives trying to rescue them—we need now to look to the future.

Accordingly, the Government of Iran has been informed that the official policy of the United States toward Iran shall be as follows, effective immediately:

To assess the vulnerability of the idea to criticism, we might identify two or three key individuals who would not like it and who might say so publicly. If we were drafting a press release for one of them, and wanted to generate a quotable quote for tomorrow's press, what is the worst thing about the decision that the critic could honestly say? What might other critics say?

Drafting a public announcement of a decision is not only a way to assess existing restraints on choice. It is also a good way to prepare a document useful in selling the idea. The decision-maker is likely to be reluctant to buy an idea unless he sees how it could be sold to others. In writing such a statement, we will want to look for precedents and prior statements that suggest this is the right thing to do. It will also help to be able to articulate the principle that the proposed decision implements. This is basically what lobbyists do to convince representatives that voting for a specific proposal, for example, will sound good to their constituents.

Chart 17–8 suggests one way of assessing the political restraints that may impede the other side's prince from deciding as we would like. This approach is illustrated in Chart 17–9, which analyses the restraints on the choice of the Israeli government in 1979 were it to have considered opening direct talks with the PLO.

CHART 17–8
POLITICAL RESTRAINTS ON THEIR CHOICE

Substance of the decision: _____

Case: _____

Our side: _____

Their side: _____

Date: _____

How They Could Present the Decision Most Favorably	**The Vulnerability of the Proposed Decision to Political Criticism**
	Some potential critics (from right and left)
Possible announcements	
Prior statements	Attacks on the decision that they could possibly make
Precedents	
Principle	

CHART 17–9
POLITICAL RESTRAINTS ON THEIR CHOICE
Substance of the decision: *Agree to talk with the PLO*

Case: *Israel vs. PLO: no talks*
Our side: *3rd party peacemaker*
Their side: *Government of Israel*
Date: *1979*

How They Could Present the Decision Most Favorably	**The Vulnerability of the Proposed Decision to Political Criticism**

<table>
<tr><td></td><td><u>Some potential critics</u>
(from right and left)</td></tr>
</table>

Possible announcements

"PLO officials who are willing to meet with officials of the Israeli Government in their capacity as such will be meeting with Israeli officials and others at the UN in New York."

Hard-line generals (like Ariel Sharon)

"These talks are without prejudice to the position of Israel or any other party."

Hard-line religious leaders (settlers on the West Bank)

"Although there is as yet no formal PLO commitment to accept Israel's rights, that is one subject which they have agreed to discuss."

Opposition Labor Party leaders

Doves

"No one in the government has the slightest fear that a representative of Israel will negotiate away Israel's right to exist, or that the PLO will accomplish by words what it has proved unable to accomplish in more than 30 years by deeds."

Attacks on the decision that
they could possibly make

"The prime minister has given up the one position on which 90% of Israelis agree: never talk with terrorists; never talk with the PLO."

Prior statements

In the UN Charter, Israel agreed that "All members shall settle their disputes by peaceful means . . ."

Prime Minister Meir long ago said that Israel would sit down and talk with any Arab willing to seek peace with us. We are fulfilling that pledge.

"The prime minister has broken commitments made to the Knesset and the people."

"Talks with the PLO are the entering wedge for a terrorist-dominated Palestinian state."

"To reward murderers of our children with a seat at the table is to invite more murders and terror."

How They Could Present the Decision Most Favorably	**The Vulnerability of the Proposed Decision to Political Criticism**

Precedents

The PLO, Syria, Iraq and others with whom Israel does not yet have peace have for years participated with representatives of Israel in meetings of the Security Council and the General Assembly.

"Israel has given the PLO what it wants in exchange for nothing; not even an acceptance of our right to exist."

"If Israel is to make peace with the Palestinians, it must grant genuine mutual acceptance, not just token participation at a UN meeting."

Principle

Israel will use every weapon in the fight for its rights. In a just cause, words are powerful weapons; we shall not deprive ourselves of them.

Another lens through which we can test the plausibility of what we intend to do and how it will look to the other side is to formulate the new "message" that we hope to communicate to them. Here we concern ourselves with the communication problem—what we should be saying and what they should be hearing.

We can look at our analysis of the old message and then try to write out the message we want them to be hearing in the near future. The "long form" of a complete message in Chapter 5 (Chart 5–1) provides a useful checklist of what we would want them to be hearing with respect to each element. On some elements we may conclude that there should be silence or ambiguity, but if so, that should be the result of a conscious and clear decision, not of muddy thinking. We should have for ourselves explicit reasons for being silent; clear and cogent reasons for being ambiguous. For example, leaving the resolution of the West Bank ambiguous in any invitation for talks makes it more likely that Israel and the Palestinians will be willing to talk. Explicitly resolving the West Bank issue with a statement like "We invite you to a meeting to discuss the complete independence of the West Bank" would almost ensure that one crucial party to the dispute would not show up.

Having tentatively drafted what we think we would like them to be hearing, we can draft, equally tentatively, the message that we should be transmitting. The process requires both imagination and judgment. Our thinking should be stimulated by the reservoir of fresh ideas that we should by now have on hand, but our provisional selection among those ideas should be tempered by a realistic appraisal of what may be possible. And given the next step we have taken in coming up with a proposal, we may want to research and choose a new prince who may be more likely to agree.

To conclude, it is in our interest to have them see themselves as confronted with a "yesable" proposition—a choice to which the answer "yes" meets certain tests:[4]

1. "Yes" is a sufficient answer.   We have not simply asked them to "do something" about a problem. Rather, they see themselves as having a specific option before them—something to which a simple affirmative is an adequate response.

2. "Yes" is a realistic answer.   There is a good chance that they might in fact find the proposition acceptable. There may be a greater chance that they will say "no" but it is plausible that they might say "yes." We are not looking for a guarantee of success, but rather for a realistic objective that is worth trying for. Depending on the effort required on our part, an estimated one-in-five chance of success will often be enough.

3. "Yes" is an operational answer.   If there is an affirmative response to our proposal, some specific thing happens. A cease-fire will take place, a meeting will be held, a representative will be appointed, or some other action in the real world will occur. Rarely, if ever, is it worth focusing our efforts simply to produce a statement of principle: "Yes, we agree that peace is important." Once such a decision is reached, everything again stops dead as we try to figure out what to do next. It is better to have any such statement of principle accompanied by an operational decision about what is to happen next, such as ". . . and we will meet next Tuesday at 10 A.M. to consider what to do about it."

Whenever we are trying to exert influence we are seeking to produce a decision. The more clearly we know a specific decision that we want and might expect, the more likely we are to obtain it. As suggested, formulating a "yesable" proposition is no guarantee that the other party will in fact say "yes" to it. "No" is an equally probable or more probable answer. But formulating a "yesable" proposition makes certain that we at least know some particular decision that we are trying for—we know some decision that we would like and might reasonably expect.

PUTTING IT ALL TOGETHER: DISPUTE RESOLUTION AS PROBLEM-SOLVING

Yesable propositions are the most action-oriented of the tools this book has to offer. When carefully designed, yesable propositions are the culmination of the two main ideas behind successful conflict management in international disputes: looking at a decision-maker's choice, and focusing on the development of good advice regarding who should do what tomorrow morning.

---

[4]Fisher, Kopelman, and Schneider, pp. 96–98.

Analyzing a Choice

Attention to points of choice means systematic planning and attention to process. What picture are they seeing now? How can we learn about the history and context that led them to see it that way? What message are they hearing from us, and how does that message compare to the one we intended to send? What incentives do the other side's decision-makers face in terms of likely reactions from constituents and critics?

Developing Advice

Developing good advice means going beyond what the other party sees now to thinking about what we want them to see in the future. This part of the process starts with making our own interests and objectives explicit, confronting constraints, and, where appropriate, designing an internal process to help us generate and evaluate fresh ideas. The hard work involved in each of these activities should be complete, or at least substantially underway, before we even engage the other side. A great deal of what we call dispute resolution is actually the difficult spadework of research or the intricate internal negotiations around objectives. Ideally, we would then repeat this process of reviewing interests, constraints, and new options jointly with the other side.

Focusing on Process Design

Traditionally, what interests many students and scholars about international negotiations is their substance—with process issues relegated to anecdotal accounts of endless dickering over the shape of the negotiating table. But planning the process—by taking it apart and examining each facet, then diagnosing barriers to progress, and then designing each phase with careful attention to the choices faced by each player—can often improve substantive outcomes. Attention to process does not denigrate the importance of substance, nor does it make process advice generic. A serious student of international relations develops an area specialty (South Asia, Latin America, the Balkans), a field of expertise (arms control, water rights, foreign investment), as well as language and research abilities. This student can then integrate her background knowledge and information-gathering skills with an ability to analyze, discriminate, and persuade. This book fills a gap in the traditional equation by emphasizing the often-unrealized potential of process design.

Revisiting the "Activist Stance"

At its best, international dispute resolution is about problem-solving. And the problems involved are the most complex, compelling, and urgent of our times. The archaic, chivalric realm of diplomacy now encompasses the transborder problems of drug trafficking, terrorism, and environmental degradation. We are all depending on the best minds of the younger generation to adapt what we have called an "activist stance" in the face of these complex and vexing issues. Such activism will mean thinking about each dispute as part of a systemic whole as well as on a case-by case basis. The same problem-solving skills that go into designing a small-scale yesable proposition—"Shall we have a meeting at 8 A.M. tomorrow to consider the X proposal?"—can also aid in redesigning larger systems—"What forum should decide about international toxic waste?" "Can third parties effectively exert influence in conflicts designated as civil wars?" "What verification measures will insure the integrity of an international chemical weapons ban?"

Looking at the big picture is sometimes best done from the outside. Do not assume that because no one may have asked you, that your fresh insight or new approach is irrelevant or doomed to obscurity. Write an editorial, enlist a decision-maker's aide, draft a proposal with a cover letter from a supportive local politician, academic, or business professional. Keep a clippings file and telephone roster for each situation that interests you. Put yourself in the shoes of a decision-maker—you may find the shoes fit more comfortably than you ever could have imagined.

Index

A

Abel, Elie, 246, 248
Acceptance, in working relationship, 120, 124, 126
ACDA. *See* Arms Control and Disarmament Agency
Acheson, Dean, 153
Action memorandum, 18–26
Adversary process, 89–90
Adversary's decision, influencing, 68–86, 175
  consequences for decision maker, 70–71, 80–86, 253–54, 259–65
  message analysis, 72–79
  policy objectives in, 68–69
  targets for, 70, 79–80, 252–53, 254–58
  timing in, 71, 74
  "yesable" proposition and, 265–79
  See also Demands; Sanctions; Threats
Alliance for Progress, 215
Allison, Graham, 79
Antiballistic Missile Treaty (ABM) of 1972, 96–112, 130
  chronology of, 111
  climate of mistrust, 97–99
  domestic politics and, 103–7, 134
  executive leadership in, 107–8
  levels of negotiation, 96
  negotiating proposal, 99–101
  SALT I negotiations, 101–3, 118–19, 132, 152
  Strategic Defense Initiative (SDI) and, 108–10
Arab–Israeli conflict, 27–44
  ambiguous offers in, 222–23
  chronology of, 41–43
  historical claims in, 27–29
  Israeli War of Independence, 31–33
  Jerusalem sovereignty and, 260–65
  legitimate demands in, 234
  during Palestine mandate, 29–31, 32
  Palestinian state and, 39, 156
  Palestinian violence and, 267
  partisan perceptions of, 48, 51–53
  peace negotiations in, 2, 12, 40, 42, 141, 275–76
  reconcilable interests in, 66
  refugee problem in, 33–36
  Six-Day War, 36–37, 41
  third party in, 235–36
  tit-for-tat approach in, 159–60
  unilateral action in, 6
  and West Bank withdrawal, 1, 85, 86
  Yom Kippur War, 37–39
Arafat, Yasir, 43
Argentine, in Falkland Islands crisis, 2, 58, 59, 80
Argov, Shlomo, 42–43
Arms control. *See* Antiballistic Missile Treaty

Arms Control and Disarmament Agency (ACDA), 101, 104, 108
Assumptions:
  alternative, 48–51
  implicit, 148
  questioning, 128–30, 144–46
Assumptions/Data Tool, 48–51
Austin, John, 3, 242

B

Balfour Declaration, 29, 32
Bangladesh, purposes of, 166–67
Bao Dai, 178
Barshefsky, Charlene, 114
Basque separatists, 212–13
BATNA (Best Alternative To a Negotiated Agreement), 207–8
Bay of Pigs invasion, 10, 266
Begin, Menachem, 2, 30, 40, 42, 43, 48, 141
Ben-Gurion, David, 31, 41
Brainstorming, 152–53
Brazil, 215
Britain:
  in Falkland Islands crisis, 2, 58, 59, 80
  Palestine mandate of, 29–31
  sanctions on Rhodesia, 70, 198, 220, 233
  in Vietnam, 178
  See also Northern Ireland conflict
Brooke, Edward, 97, 104
Brown v. Board of Education, 5
Bunn, George, 101, 102, 103, 108, 118–19
Bureaucracy:
  constraint on creative thinking, 148
  decisionmaking of, 87–95
Bush, George, 43, 116, 238

C

Camp David accords, 40, 42, 141
Caradon, Lord, 133
Carter, Jimmy, 2, 40, 42
Central Intelligence Agency, 266
Chamberlain, Neville, 2
China:
  and Hong Kong, 214
  human rights issues in, 238
  Nixon in, 106
  in Vietnam, 178
  working relationship with, 114, 116
Churchill, Winston, 2, 31
Circle Chart, 153–56
Clinton, Bill, 114
Communication, in working relationship, 120, 124, 126

Compliance:
  first-order, 226–27
  second-order, 228–30
Congruent problem-solving, 138–43
Consent principal of international system, 4–5
Consequences for decision maker, 80–86
Corson, Bill, 189–90
Costs & Benefits Circle, 203–6
Creative thinking:
  constraints on, 147–50
  generating new approaches, 151–57
Cuba:
  Bay of Pigs invasion of, 10, 266
  U.S. embargo against, 94, 198, 200, 215–16, 232
Cuban missile crisis:
  decision-making in, 91
  international law and, 246–49
  legitimate demands in, 235
  partisan perceptions of, 54–55
  purposes in, 165
  target of demands, 252
Currently Perceived Choice Tool, 81–86, 260, 261–62
Cyprus, negotiations over, 2, 128–30, 207–8

D

Decision-maker perspective, 8–10, 16–18
Decision-making:
  of adversaries. See Adversary's decision, influencing
  bureaucratic, 87–95
Defense Department, 87–89, 90, 168
De Gaulle, Charles, 182, 210
Demands, 68, 69, 70, 74, 209–30
  credibility of, 217–20, 224–26
  dividing up, 214–16
  elements of, 73
  legitimate, 71–72, 232–36
  padding, 219–20
  pros and cons of changing, 210–11
  reframing, 211–14
  specificity of, 220–24
  timing of, 216–17
Diem, Ngo Dinh, 180, 181
Diembienphu, siege of, 178
Dobrynin, Anatoly, 101, 105
Dominican Republic, U.S. intervention in, 236

E

Educational strategy, 171–75
Egypt:
  in Arab–Israeli conflict, 31, 36, 38, 41
  and international law, 235–36
  in peace negotiations, 40, 42, 141

Eichmann, Adolf, 170
El Quneitra, 38
Emotions and Motives Tool, 57–61
Eshkol, Levi, 36
Essence of Decision (Allison), 79
European Community:
    compliance mechanisms in, 228
    conflicting purposes in, 161
Eye for an eye policy, 124–25

F

Falkland Islands crisis, 2, 58, 59, 80
First-order compliance, 226–27
First Position, 47, 48–51
Force, use of, 6, 7, 168, 170, 244
Foreign Service Institute, 45
France:
    and Greenpeace bombing, 205–6
    in Vietnam, 177–80
French-Indochina War, 178–80
Friendly bargaining, 136, 137–38, 139

G

Garthoff, Raymond, 105
Gaza Strip, 36, 43
Gemayel, Bashir, 43
Geneva Conference of 1954, 178, 180, 184, 213
Germany:
    immigrant relations in, 171–74
    World War II strategy against, 170
Gervasi, Frank, 27–28, 31
Glassboro summit, 98
Goals, *vs* purposes, 166
Golan Heights, 12, 36, 38, 41, 46, 52, 66
Golden Rule, 123–24
Gorbachev, Mikhail, 43
Greece:
    in Cyprus negotiations, 2, 128–30, 207–8
    U.S. military aid to, 236
Greenpeace bombing, 205–6
Gulf of Tonkin Resolution, 181
Gulf War, 208

H

Haganah, 33
Haggling model, 135
Haj Amin el-Husseini, 30, 31
Hard bargaining, 136, 137, 139, 142, 143
Harvard Negotiation Project, 14
Haycraft Commission, 30

Heritage Foundation, 110
Hersh, Seymour, 106–7
Herzog, Chaim, 39
Hiroshima bombing, 170
Hitler, Adolf, 30
Ho Chi Minh, 178, 184, 187, 188, 218, 219, 223, 235
Ho Chi Minh trail, 181
Hong Kong, 214
Human rights issues, 238
Humphrey, Hubert, 99, 188
Hussein, Saddam, 79

I

ICBM (intercontinental ballistic missiles), 99, 104
India, in water agreement, 134
Interests:
    in congruent problem-solving, 140
    enlightened self-interest, 160
    long-term *vs* short-term, 167
    opposing, 64
    reconcilable, 61–62, 64–66
    vs positions, 132–33
Interim Agreement, 105, 106
International Court of Justice, 236
International law:
    compliance mechanisms and, 3, 226–30
    consent in, 4, 5–6
    Cuban missile crisis and, 246–49
    effective use of, 241–42, 244–50
    legitimate demands and, 232–36
    moral criteria and, 236–42
International negotiation:
    basic premises of, 2–3
    case studies. *See* Antiballistic Missile
        Treaty; Arab–Israeli conflict; Viet-
        nam War
    congruent problem-solving in, 138–43
    constraints on creative thinking, 147–50
    cross-cutting cleavage in, 134–35
    explicit and implicit, 7
    friendly bargaining, 136, 137–38, 139
    hard bargaining, 136, 137, 139, 142, 143
    improving process of, 12–14
    new approaches to, 151–57
    objectives in, 130–31
    personal relationships in, 132–33
    pivotal role of, 1–2
    political restraints in, 271–77
    positions vs interests in, 131–32
    reciprocity in, 118–19
    requirement of, 3–7
    standard moves in, 135, 136, 138, 139
    third parties in, 134, 151, 152–53, 235–36
    working assumptions in, 128–30, 144–46
    working relationships in, 114

International relations:
  action memorandum on, 18–26
  bureaucratic decisionmaking and, 87–95
  decision-maker perspective on, 8–10, 16–18
  influencing adversary government in. *See*
      Adversary's decision, influencing
  military force in, 6, 7, 168, 170
  points of choice in, 10–12, 251–55
  purpose in. *See* Purposes
  viewpoints in. *See* Partisan perceptions
  working relationships in, 113–27
Intifada, 43
Iran:
  hostage crisis, 222, 272–73
  U.S. condemnation of, 158–59
Iraq:
  in Israeli War of Independence, 31
  military sales to, 170
  and Syria, 42
Iraq, King of, 29
Irgun, 33
Irish Republican Army (IRA), 7, 48, 267
Israel:
  creation of, 31
  self-help strategy of, 170
  See also Arab–Israeli conflict;
      Palestine

J

Jackson, Henry, 97
Japan:
  atomic bombing of, 170, 175
  surrender of, 1, 170, 211, 213–14
  in Vietnam, 177–78
  working relationship with, 123
Jarjoura, Rayek, 39
Jason report, 190
Jerusalem, sovereignty over, 260–65
Jewish Chronicle, 30
Johnson, Lyndon B.:
  and arms control, 97–98, 104
  Vietnam policy of, 181, 183–84, 185, 219,
      223, 232, 235, 267–68
Joint Chiefs of Staff, 98, 113
Jordan, 31, 39, 42, 43
Justice Department, 5

K

Kahn, Herman, 69
Kennedy, John F., 2, 10, 132, 215, 235, 248,
      266
Kennedy, Robert, 188, 247
Khalidy, Rashid, 39

Khomeini, Ayatollah Ruhollah, 2, 158
Khrushchev, Nikita, 2, 185, 187, 249
Kissinger, Henry:
  in Arab–Israeli conflict, 38, 41
  in arms control negotiations, 99–108, 132
  on foreign policy establishment, 8–9
Kosygin, Andrei, 97, 98, 182

L

Law:
  adversary process in, 89–90
  command theory of, 242
  implied consent in, 4–5
  public, 242–44
  See also International law
Law of the Sea Conference, 63, 142
League of Nations, 29
Lebanon:
  in Arab–Israeli conflict, 31
  Israeli invasion of, 42, 43
Legitimate demands, 232–36
Levinger, Moshe, 28
Lind, Michael, 110

M

Machiavelli, 11, 17, 87
Maddox, 181
Marshall, Thurgood, 5
Massachusetts Institute of Technology (MIT),
      deep-seabed mining model of, 142
McCarthy, Joseph, 122
McFarlane, Robert, 108
McNamara, Robert, 97, 98, 104
Mead, Margaret, 231
Meir, Golda, 31, 33, 38
Message analysis, 72–79
Mexico–U.S. natural gas negotiations, 60, 62
Middle East. *See* Arab–Israeli conflict
Military force, 6, 7, 168, 170, 244
MIRV's (multiple independently targeted
      reentry vehicles), 98, 103, 104
Moral choice, 236–42
MX missiles, 207

N

Nagasaki bombing, 170, 175
Nasser, Gamal Abdel, 36, 41
National Liberation Front (NLF), 181, 182,
      184, 188–89
National Liberation Front for South Vietnam
      (NFLSV). *See* Vietcong

National Security Council (NSC), 100, 113
Needs, purpose and, 161
Negotiation. *See* International negotiation
New Republic, 110
New Yorker, 114
New Zealand, and Greenpeace bombing, 205–6
Nicaragua, 116
Nixon, Richard:
   in arms control agreement, 98–108, 130
   in China, 106
NLF. *See* National Liberation Front
NLFSV. *See* Vietcong
Nonproliferation Talks, 102
Noriega, Manuel Antonio, 78, 79, 167
North Atlantic Treaty Organization (NATO), partisan perception of, 50
Northern Ireland conflict:
   diagnostic statement on, 155–56
   IRA violence in, 7, 267
   message to adversary government, 75, 77
   new approaches to, 155
   partisan perceptions of, 48
   targets for influence, 254–58
North Vietnam, bombing of, 181–83
   cost/benefit analysis of, 190, 203–5
   costs to U.S., 198, 199
   effectiveness of, 195, 196, 202
   negotiation attempts and, 74–75, 185, 187, 221, 222, 225, 267–68
   See also Vietnam War
Nuclear Nonproliferation Treaty (NPT), 99
Nuclear test ban, 132
Nuclear weapons, use of, 170, 175

O

Objectives of negotiation, 130–31
O'Brian, John Lord, 122
Offers, 68, 69, 70–71, 73
   ambiguous, 220–23
On Escalation (Kahn), 69
Operation Flaming Dart, 181
Operation Rolling Thunder, 181–82, 190
Options:
   brainstorming, 152–53
   listing, 151–52, 254–58
   multiplying, 153–56
Organization of American States (OAS), 3–4, 236, 247, 248
Organization on Security and Cooperation in Europe, 3–4

P

Pact of Paris (1928), 93
Padded position, 219–20

Pakistan, 134
Palestine:
   Arab state of, 39, 156
   Mandate, 28–33
   partition of, 31, 32
Palestine Liberation Organization (PLO), 39, 43
Palestinian refugees, 29, 33–36
Panama, U.S. invasion of, 75, 78, 167
Paris Peace Conference, 29
Partisan perceptions, 45–67, 231
   in Arab–Israeli conflict, 48, 51–53
   in Cuban missile crisis, 54–55
   of emotions and motivations, 57–61
   in Falkland Islands crisis, 58, 59, 80
   First Position, 47, 48–51
   obstacle to working relationship, 118, 123, 124, 125
   of positions and interests, 61–66
   role-playing, 56
   Second Position, 47, 51–66
   in U.S.–Mexico natural gas negotiations, 60, 62
Peace, as purpose, 161–65
Peace-through-strength lobby, 97, 99, 104, 106, 134
Perceptions. *See* Partisan perceptions
Perle, Richard N., 109
Persuasion, in working relationship, 120, 124, 126
Pham Van Dong, 187
Point-of-Choice Tool, 256–57
Positional bargaining, 137
Positions, *vs* interests, 132–33
Positions and interests tool, 63, 65–66
Potsdam Conference, 178
Power, as purpose, 161–65
Prince, The (Machiavelli), 11
Problem-solving:
   constraints on, 147–49
   dispute resolution as, 277–78
   four steps to, 153–55
   framing problem, 151
   reducing constraints, 151–54, 155–56
   specialist viewpoint in, 156
Provisional agreements, 131
Purposes, 158–68
   one at a time, 166–68
   prioritizing, 160–61
   strategy design and, 168–76
   victory, power, and peace as, 161–65
   vs goals, 166
Purpose Tool, 163–65

R

Rabin, Itzhak, 2, 43
Rainbow Warrior, 205

Rapporteur of brainstorming session, 153
Rationality, in working relationship, 124, 126
Reagan, Ronald:
    and Arab–Israeli conflict, 43
    Strategic Defense Initiative (SDI) of, 108–10
Reciprocity principle, 118–19, 123–26, 235
Reliability, in working relationship, 120, 124
Rhodesia, British sanctions on, 70, 198, 220, 233
Rio Treaty, 247
Rogers, William, 100
Role-playing, 56
Rostow, Walt, 268
Rusk, Dean, 183, 185, 187

S

Sadat, Anwar, 2, 40, 42, 48, 141
Salah el Din Bin Bey, Mohammed, 34
SALT I Agreements, 105, 106, 107, 108
SALT I negotiations, 97, 100, 101–3, 118–19, 132, 152
San Antonio formula, 267
Sanctions:
    cost/benefit analysis of, 203–6
    costs to imposing country, 198
    effectiveness of, 100–202, 194–97
    targets of, 70
Saturday Evening Post, 91
Saudi Arabia, 42
Second-order compliance, 228–30
Second Position, 47, 51–67
Self-fulfilling prophecy, 79
Self-help strategy, 169–71, 175
Semenov, Vladimir, 102
Shamir, Yitzhak, 84, 85, 86
Sinai Desert, 8, 36, 141
Sinn Fein, 48
Six-Day War, 36–37, 41
SLBM (submarine-launched ballistic missiles), 98–99
Smith, Gerard, 102, 103, 105, 109
Smith, Ian, 233
Sorensen, Theodore, 246, 248
South Africa, 225
Soviet Union:
    in civil aviation agreement, 215
    collapse of, 110, 161
    foreign policy principles of, 232
    at Glassboro summit, 97–98
    in nuclear test ban negotiations, 132
    personal relationships and, 133, 134
    in SALT I negotiations, 101–3, 105
    and Vietnam War, 182, 185, 187
    working relationship with, 118, 120
    See also Cuban missile crisis
Spain, Basque separatists in, 212–13

Sri Lanka, economic sanctions in, 70
Standing Consultative Commission (SCC), 106
State Department, 90, 113, 168, 185
Stevenson, Adlai, 91
Stimson, Henry, 93
Strategic Arms Limitation Talks. *See* SALT I negotiations
Strategic Defense Initiative (SDI), 108–10
Strategic design, educational, 171–75
Strategy design, 168–76
    military *vs* political, 168–69
    self-help, 169–71, 175
    tit-for-tat approach, 159–60
Suez Canal, 38, 41
Supreme Court, U.S., 5, 242, 243–44
Syria:
    in Arab–Israeli conflict, 12, 31, 36, 38, 41
    interests of, 66
    and Iraq, 42
    perceptions of, 52

T

Target Future Choice Tool, 260, 263, 264, 269–71
Taylor, Maxwell D., 183
Technology transfer, 63
Thatcher, Margaret, 80
Third parties, 134, 151, 152–53, 235–36
Third Position, 47
Thompson, Llewellyn, 248
Threats, 68, 69, 71
    cost/benefit analysis of, 203–6
    costs to imposing country, 197–99
    effectiveness of, 194–97, 200–202
    elements of, 73, 74
    implementation of, 199–200
    vs warnings, 207–8
Tool on Policy, 249–50
Treaty of Rome, 228
Truman, Harry S., 10, 243
Trust, in working relationship, 120, 124
Turkey:
    in Cyprus negotiations, 2, 128–30, 207–8
    U.S. military aid to, 236
Turki, Fawaz, 33

U

Understanding, in working relationship, 124, 126
Unilateral action. *See* Military force
United Kingdom. *See* Britain
United Nations, 3–4
    Arab–Israeli conflict and, 36, 39, 41, 42, 222–23

Cuban missile crisis and, 247
Palestine partition and, 31
personal relationships in, 133
Vietnam War and, 185
United States:
    in Bay of Pigs invasion, 10, 266
    bureaucratic decisionmaking in, 87–95
    in civil aviation agreement, 215
    Cuban embargo of, 94, 198, 200, 215–16,
        232
    economic sanctions of, 70
    educational strategy of, 171
    in Gulf War, 208
    in Iran hostage crisis, 222, 272–73
    Iran policy objectives, 158–59
    at Law of the Sea Conference, 142
    legal system in, 4–6, 242–44
    –Mexico natural gas negotiations, 60, 62
    military intervention and, 236
    MX missile deployment and, 207
    in nuclear test ban negotiations, 132
    in Panama invasion, 75, 78, 167
    peace-through-strength lobby in, 97, 99,
        104, 106, 134
    self-help strategy of, 175
    working relationships of, 114, 116, 117, 123
    World War II strategy of, 170
    See also Antiballistic Missile Treaty;
        Cuban missile crisis; North Viet-
        nam, bombing of; Vietnam War
U Thant, 182, 185

V

Values, shared, 122–23
Vance, Cyrus, 42
Vandenberg, Arthur, 236
Vassiliou, President of Cyprus, 207–8
Verfication Panel, 100
Victory, as purpose, 161–65
Vietcong (NLFSV), 181, 183, 184, 187, 188,
    189–90
Vietminh, 178
Vietnam War:
    chronology of U.S. involvement, 191–93

historical background to, 177–80
Johnson's statements on, 183–84, 223, 232,
    267–68
lack of communication in, 79, 185
peace negotiations in, 185, 187, 188, 210,
    212, 218, 219, 224, 235
rebel activities in, 180–81, 189–90
target of demands, 252–53
U.S. military aid in, 181
U.S. purposes in, 168–69, 213, 235
U.S. withdrawal from, 190–91
See also North Vietnam, bombing of

W

Warnings, vs threats, 207–8
Warnke, Paul, 183
West Bank, 36, 39, 43, 85, 156
Wilson, Woodrow, 178
Working relationships, 113–27
World Bank, 134
World War II:
    atomic bomb in, 170, 175
    Japanese surrender in, 170, 211, 213–14
    and Jewish refugees in Palestine, 30–31
    self-help strategy in, 170
    Vietnam in, 177–78
Wu Yi, 114

Y

Yates v. United States, 5–6
"Yesable" proposition, 265–79
Yom Kippur War, 37–39
York, Herbert, 99

Z

Zero-sum assumptions, 129–30
Zionism, 29, 30, 39